"*A Soulful Marriage* is transformative   their connection. With clear and pract̲   s down the essential pillars of a fulfilling partnership: responsibility, growth, priority, and purpose. Her insights into self-awareness, 'friction' resolution, and spiritual intimacy offer invaluable tools for couples to navigate challenges and nurture their love. This book is for anyone seeking to cultivate a more meaningful and joyful partnership."

—Monica Berg, cohost of *Spiritually Hungry* podcast and author of *Rethink Love*

"Follow the sage advice in *A Soulful Marriage* and it will strengthen all of your relationships, including the one with yourself. Dr. Rachel Glik provides a unique and positive guide that thoroughly illustrates how your growth process, through education, meditations, exercises, and case examples, will lift you and your partner's connection to the highest level."

—Jennifer L. Abel, PhD, author of *The Anxiety, Worry, and Depression Workbook*

"Dr. Rachel Glik masterfully weaves together the powerful psychological principles of couples therapy with rich insights drawn from diverse religious and spiritual traditions, including Kabbalah and Judaism. The result is a beautifully integrated compendium of theoretical and practical tools that she has used to turn around hundreds of marriages, including her own. The book encourages us to understand that our happiness in relationships is in our own hands. I highly recommend this book to anyone looking to deepen their capacity for love and create a thriving partnership."

—Anna Yusim, cofounder of the Yale Mental Health and Spirituality Center and author of *Fulfilled: How the Science of Spirituality Can Help You Live a Happier, More Meaningful Life*

"Through her book, Dr. Glik offers an exceptionally honest, practical, and thoughtful road map for a joyful, fulfilling, and spiritual way of life to couples. I recommend her book to anyone seeking to start a meaningful and stable relationship."

—Saaid Khojasteh, MD, professor of psychiatry at the
Washington University School of Medicine in St. Louis

"Dr. Glik writes with energy and insight about the joy you can achieve if you spend time reflectively with *A Soulful Marriage*. Understanding the four pillars will change the depth and intimacy of your relationship."

—Dr. Deborah Miller, author of *More Than Sorry:*
Five Steps to Deepen Your Apology After
You Have Committed Infidelity

"Beautifully written with an invisible but distinct mixture of spirituality, psychology, and humanness. The book is filled with stories, including her own, and relatable examples that bring Rachel's wisdom to life. I can't wait to share this book with my clients."

—Evonne Weinhaus, LPC, LCSW,
certified Imago couples therapist and
coauthor of *Stop Struggling with Your Teen*
and author of *Stop Struggling with Your Child*

A Soulful
Marriage

A Soulful Marriage

Healing Your
Relationship with
Responsibility, Growth,
Priority, and Purpose

Rachel Glik, EdD, LPC

morehouse PUBLISHING

Morehouse Publishing, 19 East 34th Street, New York, NY 10016

Morehouse Publishing is an imprint of Church Publishing Incorporated.

Cover design by David Baldeosingh Rotstein
Typeset by Andrew Berry

Library of Congress Control Number: 2024946879

ISBN 978-1-64065-768-7 (pbk)
ISBN 978-1-64065-769-4 (ebook)

Printed in Canada

To Jeff, my number one

Contents

PILLAR 3

Priority

PILLAR 4

Purpose

Preface

How the Journey Began

Let me fall if I must fall. The one I will become will catch me.

—The Baal Shem Tov

I have started writing this relationship book too many times to count. Session after intimate session, for over thirty years as a marriage counselor, and married even longer, the hunger to share my experience with more people has become my constant companion. I often tell my clients that if I could influence the school curriculum for youth, I would mandate two essential life skills: (1) starting as early as preschool, to learn deep listening skills, and (2) from middle through college, to receive incremental training in what it takes to build a lasting, loving relationship, starting with the most important person—yourself.

Most everyone is winging it. I know I was. Two years into my marriage, my fantasy of a relationship making everything good in my life became shattered. "My greatest awakening and gift," I say now. But oh, was it excruciating! In the depth of my confusion, I remember pulling out a blank sheet of paper and drawing a pie chart to try to map out what makes a life happy and fulfilled. This was the beginning of my soul searching, which led to a sharp turn for a doctorate in counseling, leaving my almost completed PhD in organizational psychology behind. I devoured every opportunity to gain answers to the pie chart of love and life, using myself and my marriage as the laboratory—with an eye toward helping others with the same. Next came a dive into spiritual wisdom, along with my husband, which culminated in our joint discovery of the universal teachings of Kabbalah. In fact, much of what you'll find in this book, and what helped turn our marriage into what it is today, is a result of delving into the universal knowledge contained in Kabbalah.

Because of the profound shift, within me and in the quality of our marriage, I wagered a serious, experimental pivot in my private practice to see how I could weave universal spiritual ideas into traditional marriage therapy. I remember the first time I took this risk with a couple as if it were yesterday. I had no idea what this would mean, to integrate the two, but as the process naturally unfolded, couple after couple, I marveled at the healing I witnessed. I knew I was on to something.

Many of the clients I meet with have no idea that the guidance in our interactions has anything to do with spirituality. This is because what I love most is when spirituality meets human psychology and practicality. Regardless of your worldview, the principles I will be sharing in this book can be found relevant and transformative. Whether you are religious, spiritual but not religious, humanitarian, new age, atheist, agnostic, scientific, you name it—I have found that these principles can speak to anyone with a desire for a better relationship and a willingness to learn and grow.

My deepest desire is to help you harness the kind of pain that held my husband and I hostage in the earlier years. The goal isn't to eliminate pain—something that is not possible—but to help you learn ways to prevent unnecessary suffering and losses and to offer you a path to embrace and understand your problems so they can be *used purposefully* to help you awaken desire for growth, elevate your relationship, and create your best life experience.

This book is a life's work and a thank-you note to the Universe for guiding my husband and me to the secrets of lasting love, and for guiding me to find real tools to help other couples. I may not be able to sit face-to-face with you privately, but please know that I will be sharing my experience from doing just that—sitting face-to-face, up close with literally thousands of clients struggling to some degree or another in their relationship. My hope is that through sharing with you my approach, you will shift your thinking much the way my husband and I did, and take one step at a time to heal and build a happy married life.

Introduction

T he troubles that push couples over the edge to seek my help run in consistent themes, and I have a hunch you might be opening this book for some of these same reasons. Common issues center around communication, sex, kids, betrayal, money, in-laws, attachment style, and division of household labor. Running beneath these is what matters most—how you *feel* in your relationship. We all want to be in a relationship that feels good inside. Below are some of the emotional struggles I see day after day (some of which I faced myself). I share these to give you a sense of trust and hope, because solutions to these painful feelings in your relationship will be addressed in the coming pages. See if any of these reflect how you feel, regularly or from time to time:

- Angry and sad because my needs are not being met
- Overwhelmed by the fighting—going from 0 to 10 in an instant, aggressively or in silence
- Unheard because no matter how I try, my partner won't listen or change
- Unjustly blamed for the problems in the relationship
- Unappreciated and never good enough, regardless of all I do and who I am
- Crushed from a revealed or suspected secret relationship or other betrayal of trust

- Missing the connection and spark we once shared, or maybe never shared
- Stuck and hopeless from our differences in personalities, values, or goals
- Lonely and insecure because my partner is emotionally unavailable or aggressive
- Depleted and anxious with life's responsibilities leaving little room for myself or time as a couple
- Afraid staying means settling and a life unfulfilled

By the time most couples sit on my couch, they have been postponing getting help for many years, even though they have been unhappy for some time. Maybe that's the case for you as well, but please know that wherever you are is a good place to start. The tendency to avoid is natural, but not recommended. Like I do with my clients, I encourage you to *approach* versus avoid your weak spots. That you've decided to take this step is already a good sign.

The belief that things won't change also prevents couples from seeking help sooner. If you feel a sense of hopelessness, know this is common. I see it with my clients and I've been there too. The bottom line is that change is the law of the universe. Every moment is a new beginning and we have such limited vision of what's possible. Wherever you find yourself in your relationship, whatever mistakes you've made or challenges you face, keep this thought handy: *I can change and my relationship can change.*

Recently, one of my happy-to-be-divorced clients asked me, "How do I learn what healthy couples do in a successful relationship?" That's exactly what this book is about. I do not promise or suggest that every relationship will be turned around or saved, or that each should be. I *can* say that the ideas in this book are top to bottom what I have come to know as the solution for building, and healing, your relationship into one that not only lasts but that grows in joy and love.

THE FOUR PILLARS

After decades of counseling hundreds of couples, and experiencing tremendous transformation within my own marriage, I asked myself what are the core components of a relationship that is deeply fulfilling, and lasting—not trading one for the other. Even more, what does it take for the depth of love and bond to be ever growing. Everything I had learned and experienced personally kept bringing me back to four truths, which have proven unshakeable over time. Here are *the four pillars* that I will be guiding you through to heal and strengthen your relationship, one pillar at a time.

Pillar 1: Responsibility
We are each responsible for our own happiness and well-being.
Pillar 2: Growth
We use our friction to help us grow, individually and together.
Pillar 3: Priority
We make our mate the most important other person in our lives.
Pillar 4: Purpose
We make the world better through our bond.

I invite you into a beginner's mindset, normalizing the idea that lasting love is a trainable skill, something you learn and mature into. Yes, bring what you know and have learned. However, let yourself be a student, to fall and get up, and fall again. I love this folk saying, "You never understand wisdom until you fail at it."

When you work through the four pillars in this book, the goal is to get to a *soulful marriage*. I describe a soulful marriage as an environment you create together where each of you feel cherished and admired as you are, and yet challenged to be your best—all the while growing ever closer as one. You feel a sacred "just the two of us" bond and, at the same time, a sense that you're together for a reason, something bigger.

Within the four pillars you are creating a sanctuary—a structure and an environment. You are building this together and it's up to each of you to make it a space that is conducive for love to enter and grow, and to help you become who you are meant to become.

Each of the four pillars start with a consciousness, that is, a foundational attitude toward your relationship that is a lay-up for positive action. This will, at times, feel new and uncomfortable. I tell my clients during our first session, "You can have a better relationship, but this will mean preparing yourself to be uncomfortable." To make the most of the four pillars, I promise you the same. Don't worry, the process should also have fun and laughter. Nonetheless, change will require personal growth and new habits. So be ready to make friends with going out of your comfort zone.

Throughout this book, you and your mate will have a chance to assess where you stand with each of your four pillars, individually and as a couple. While it's important to build on all four pillars, you'll want to especially identify and work on the most neglected ones. Investing in your frailest pillars will likely be the most uncomfortable work but yield the greatest transformation in your relationship. Rest assured, growth will be ongoing with fruits along the way and don't hesitate to use all of your resources to support you. Good luck on your journey and do your best to inject joy and kindness along the way. We all grow better when it's light and we are having some fun.

Responsibility

Responsibility

*We Are Each Responsible for Our
Own Happiness and Well-Being.*

Asoulful marriage begins when partners understand that their
happiness and fulfillment belong in their own hands, not their
partner's. Nothing is going to work if we cannot take responsibility
for ourselves, to create our own flow of energy in our lives—and we
must appreciate the degree that this is instrumental. This is precisely
why *relationship with self* is placed as the first pillar: It's the foundation
upon which we can earn a true bond with another. To take this kind
of personal responsibility includes knowing yourself, loving yourself,
taking care of yourself, and working on yourself.

I remember learning this foundational secret within my own marriage. Early on, my husband and I were both under a shared delusion.
I thought he was responsible for my happiness, and he also thought he
was responsible for my happiness. This was the root of our early crash
and, ultimately, our greatest breakthrough. No one can hold and carry
your north star. They will drop it eventually. We need to hold our own;
only we can handle the weight of our own happiness and well-being.
What a relief we both felt when we discovered the delusion and woke
up to the truth.

This delusion is connected to a teaching I learned early on in my
Kabbalah studies. What we often call "love" is actually "need." While

it's human, need is reactive or selfish love, based on seeking energy from someone else. Need-based love, if you can even call it love, is being in love with the feeling someone is giving you. This is finite, that good feeling will come to an end one way or another. Either your partner will stop fulfilling that need, or it won't taste sweet anymore. It's important to be sensitive to each other's needs and express them to one another. However, the idea is to continually grow more proactive in your relationship by seeing it as a place to infuse love and not just for the fulfillment of your needs.

Proactive love is where the good stuff happens. This is what building a soulful marriage and this book is about, learning how to distinguish between the delusion of love and the reality, how to add more proactive love into the relationship and how to diminish the selfish reactive love—step by step.

I'm thinking of a married couple I worked with, not unlike many I have seen who couldn't keep from focusing on what the other was lacking, not doing, not being what they needed. One partner finally said, "They need to change before I'll change."

I explained that while it's natural and understandable to respond to your husband based on his actions, this tit-for-tat impetus for how you show up in the relationship will keep you both in an endless cycle of frustration. You're both doing the same thing, hovering in an "I'll-be-my-best-when-you _____" mindset. This makes your behavior an effect of each other, not a conscious choice from the power of your true self. To turn your relationship around, you need to move into what feels illogical. Make your focus on your relationship with yourself first. Meaning, make being the best version of yourself your primary goal.

The chapters in Pillar 1 address the importance of taking personal responsibility first, which include knowing yourself, loving yourself, taking care of yourself, and working on yourself. You will see this in chapter 1 on self-awareness, chapter 2 on self-love, chapter 3 on self-care, and chapter 4 on self-development.

CHAPTER ONE

The Practice of Self-Awareness

Who looks inside, awakes.

—Carl Jung

WHAT IS SELF-AWARENESS?

Self-awareness is an ongoing process of living consciously, listening to your inner world as you relate to your outer world. Your inherent ability to observe yourself and be honest with yourself about your experience is one of your greatest gifts—it's your first power tool to create your own happiness and well-being. Directing your consciousness toward your inner world is an act of choice, a choice to live responsibly and to strive toward your human potential. I try to inspire my clients to never lose appreciation for their self-awareness when I see it unfolding. Insight gives you the power to decide who you want to be and grants you the most important relationship you will ever have, with yourself.

So many of the answers you seek, the guidance and growth, can be found in the center of your own being. Only by turning inward can you hear the endless wisdom of your unique soul. Otherwise, you risk living by your learned behaviors and survival responses, driven by the desire for approval or to assuage your fears and pain through distraction and avoidance. Self-awareness is the essential first step for creating and recreating a better life experience, for developing as a person, for living true to yourself, for feeling a sense of oneness and peace with your existence. Ultimately, self-awareness is the launchpad for taking responsibility for your own happiness and well-being and for building a soulful relationship.

BRAVE CURIOSITY

Self-awareness is a brave way of life, a self-curious one. Brave and curious means radical honesty and being willing to dig deeper. A foundation for creating a life you enjoy, self-awareness directly impacts your ability to connect with your mate, including handling conflict effectively and reaching your potential as a loving partner. This is why self-awareness must also include an understanding of how others think and feel, particularly how your words or actions might be impacting them.

Knowing yourself well involves basically everything that makes you, you. *Such as* your:

- Self-talk
- Body sensations
- Character, attachment style, neurology, and core beliefs
- Hopes, desires, expectations, and motives
- Values, gifts, fears, and insecurities
- Emotional sensitivities and growth areas
- And how each of these change depending on who's around you or your circumstances

Your self-insight puts you in the driver's seat of your own consciousness. It's vulnerable to get quiet enough inside to hear some of the more uncomfortable thoughts and feelings you might have. Remember this well: *You are worth knowing.*

None of us "arrive" at a final destination of self-awareness. Consider it like an onion: You have layers upon layers to who you are and who you can grow to become. Like an onion, the closer to the center you touch, the sweeter life becomes. A crucial facet of self-awareness comes with a healthy dose of humility. We must all appreciate how limited our perceptions can be, especially of ourselves. Just when I think I know myself well, I get another hit of self-knowledge that sometimes takes my breath away—something about me that I couldn't see before. As Nobel Laureate Daniel Kahneman explains in his book *Thinking, Fast and Slow,* "[W]e can be blind to the obvious, and we are also blind to our blindness."* Self-awareness is the practice of unpeeling the layers of your awareness to discover as many surprises about yourself as possible—the becoming and not-so-becoming parts. The more blind spots you reveal, the better able you are to reveal the true you, your soul, which lights your path toward real and lasting happiness.

SELF-ACCEPTANCE

Many of us who value self-awareness are unfortunately more self-critical than aware. While keen self-examination has great value, the overall practice of self-awareness is best approached through the lens of self-acceptance. According to self-esteem expert Nathaniel Branden, "self-acceptance, in the ultimate sense, refers to an attitude of self-value and self-commitment that derives fundamentally from the fact that I am alive and conscious, that I *exist*. It is an experience deeper than self-esteem."†

True self-acceptance comes with a respect for your own experience, an unwillingness to be at war with yourself as you become conscious of your thoughts, feelings, and tendencies. Self-awareness is how you begin the practice of self-acceptance. *You cannot accept that which you don't even take the time to know.* And you cannot make changes in the right spirit without first embracing and accepting whatever you discover

---

* Daniel Kahneman, *Thinking, Fast and Slow* (Farrar, Straus and Giroux, 2011), 24.
† Nathaniel Branden, *How to Raise Your Self-Esteem* (Random House Publishing, 1988), 65.

about yourself. It's important to maintain the part of you that likes yourself, faults or no faults.

I cannot emphasize this point enough: Accepting and embracing yourself right where you are builds the strongest foundation for making significant personal growth and change. Self-acceptance primes you to grow because you love yourself and your life, not because you feel shame and disdain.

AUTHENTICITY

To live authentically is to live with honesty and courage, bravely choosing for yourself and celebrating your uniqueness as an individual. This will likely mean going against the crowd at some point or another, overriding the relentless pull toward seeking approval or living who you think you're "supposed" to be. There is nothing more joyful than being true to yourself, and nothing more unpleasant than self-betrayal.

Authenticity is a favorite topic for my husband and me because of its importance in bringing us to where we are today. The more we have learned to be ourselves, the more we have resisted our people-pleasing tendencies and the closer and better our relationship has grown—in equal measure. Those who are drawn together as lifetime partners tend to share similar issues they're here to work on.

In her book *Rethink Love*, Monica Berg emphasizes the importance of releasing the shame of wanting in order to live authentically—and building a muscle for not always being accepted or valued by others in the process. Unfortunately, too many of us can feel guilty or embarrassed to go after what we really hope for and fear the change or rejection that might come if we try. About finding yourself, Monica says it straight up, "If you're nobody on your own, then you are nobody in a group and if the group is gone, then so are you."*

---

* Monica Berg, *Rethink Love: 3 Steps to Being the One, Attracting the One, and Becoming One* (Kabbalah Centre Publishing, 2020), 33.

THOUGHTFULLY AUTHENTIC

While finding yourself might mean swimming against the current, this doesn't mean forgetting about others' feelings or becoming uncaring or unkind. Self-awareness should also include some degree of being sensitive to how you impact others. Like many instances in life, finding the balance between self and others requires finesse and knowing that you can be both: true to yourself and open-hearted to those you impact as you travel along your authentic path. In fact, when you are your own person, you might make others uncomfortable, but you are less likely to cause real harm. Sometimes, even if you do your best to be thoughtful of others, they can still feel hurt or disappointed by your decisions or change in course. This doesn't make you selfish or cold. You are simply taking proper responsibility for your own happiness and well-being and making sure you don't betray yourself.

REGRET

Authenticity in jeopardy is an underlying theme that runs through so many of the reasons clients initially reach out to me. Even for those coming solo to counseling, an issue in their relationship can quickly surface, and they can come to find that it's a consequence of not trusting and honoring themselves. This subjugation brings up a unique and bitter kind of pain—regret. Here are a few recent scenarios from clients dealing with regret that come to mind:

- Mary: An effervescent woman in her early fifties, who reached out for counseling ripe and ready to admit how lonely she felt in her thirty-year marriage. With time she broke her pattern of making everyone else's happiness more important than her own. She overcame her shame of wanting and finally confessed to her husband how his late nights working and focus on his friends made her feel isolated. She hadn't until now felt permission to tell him how unhappy she was. Eventually, her husband joined our sessions. I watched them grow closer beyond measure because Mary found the courage to be true to herself and ask for more.

- Maya: A professional woman in her late twenties was about to marry a man that she kept trying to convince herself checked all the boxes. Through sharing her innermost in counseling, she realized the outside approval would be the only substance that would fill her cup with this lovely but not-right-for-her man. With the wedding just two weeks away, guess who found the courage to face her fears and break off a grand wedding? She did and just the right match came into her life soon after.

- Tom: After twenty-eight years of a long-suffering marriage, he couldn't keep people pleasing his way forward with his wife any longer. Chronically squelching how he really felt and what he needed, the pain of the status quo overcame the risk of rejection if he was honest with his wife about how unhappy he was. In this case, Tom determined that leaving the marriage, in spite of all those committed years, was the right thing to do. He regretted taking so long to be true to himself, and yet he is in awe of all that he's discovered now that he is learning to honor himself.

What's in common for all of these clients? Deep regret, or the urgency to prevent further regret, as a result of not being genuine. No one wants to reach their dying days looking back wishing they had found the courage to speak up sooner or to risk upsetting the status quo for the sake of honoring one's uniqueness. Many clients lament to me about the years they feel they wasted. While I try to discourage judging past decisions made at a time when they didn't know what they now do, I also encourage everyone to use the potential for regret as a motivator to live life in line with who they really are.

Wherever you are in your life, anytime is the right time to get the support, to find the strength and courage, to choose you. Rather than giving sway to everybody else around you, take the steps to live honestly with yourself, to trust and express your uniqueness. Each of these stories above show the inspired life you can live, no matter your age or circumstance, when you listen to and follow your truth.

A Mini Visualization

I'd like to invite you to try this. Allow yourself to get comfortable wherever you are. Pause, breathe, and relax (PBR). Repeat that a few times. Now imagine the feeling of allowing yourself and having the strength to accept and express the true you. Create a silo around you so it's only you and your true self. Try saying out loud, "I accept and trust myself and my choices. I give myself permission to be real and honest with my thoughts and feelings, desires and decisions. I can choose the life that's right for me." Now, notice your body sensations, your breath. How do you feel inside, and around your heart?

AUTHENTICITY AND HAPPINESS

Self-awareness is a first step in taking responsibility for your own happiness because it ultimately allows you to live more authentically, and in turn, more happily. We all need to know what fills us up and build the courage to act on it. Countless studies[*] have found that authentic people are happier, with themselves and their lives. Those who report living authentically tend to have greater self-esteem, stronger mental well-being (i.e., less anxiety and depression), and also report greater satisfaction in their relationships. People living true to themselves feel more grounded in who they are and make life choices that align with what will make

---

[*] Elizabeth Hopper, "The Study of Authenticity (Positive Psychology Series #3)," *HealthPsych* (blog), February 12, 2018, https://healthypsych.com/the-study-of-authenticity/.

them truly fulfilled. When we are self-aware and living authentically, we pursue things that are more enjoyable and fulfilling, go places we feel drawn to, and connect with the type of people we love and enjoy.

HOW SELF-AWARENESS IMPACTS OUR RELATIONSHIP

Self-awareness is the first ingredient for emotional intelligence (EQ). The elements of EQ include self-awareness, self-regulation, motivation, empathy, and social skills. EQ has been found to be a major predictor of relationship success because with higher EQ you can identify what you're feeling, what those feelings mean, and how your behavior impacts others. Self-awareness is a stepping stone to all of the elements of EQ, particularly to regulating your emotions and having productive conversations to address conflict in the relationship.

Not only does knowing and living from your true self fulfill you with an incomparable level of personal joy and freedom, but the practice of authenticity also provides the very foundation for a true connection with your partner. *Happier and healthier people are more likely to create happier and healthier relationships.* Unconditional love, deep connection, safety, acceptance, friendship, support, excitement, validation, passion—for all that you seek in a relationship, you must start with an ongoing practice of knowing, accepting, and being true to yourself. Otherwise, you are at risk to live as a stranger inside your own existence, and this empty feeling perpetuates a constant chasing for something external to try to make you feel whole, secure, and enough.

Self-awareness → Self-acceptance → Authenticity

Case: Meet Lynn: The Benefits of Self-Awareness and Authenticity

One of my clients, Lynn, was heavy as a child and fell prey to terrible bullying, even in her own family. Though she grew up to be an average size, the narrative about herself as unacceptable and inferior never left. She compensated by doing everything she could to be likable. We all struggle with the fear of rejection, with the isolation that comes from a sense of not belonging. We are tribal by nature and survive by the acceptance of the clan. Nonetheless, for Lynn, her degree of outward approval-seeking—especially within her own family—became debilitating and contributed to her anxiety, depression, and escape-seeking behaviors. Caring so much about what other people thought, Lynn was having trouble even knowing, much less trusting, what she wanted in her life. She would dress the way others thought she should, pursue jobs that she perceived would be acceptable, and only said what she thought others would like to hear.

Through the process of therapy, of working on her self-understanding, Lynn began taking responsibility for her own happiness by first getting to know herself better, accepting what she found, and bravely making choices in line with her real self. Recently she announced an epiphany, "I care more about what *I* think now. And I don't want to live anyone else's life. I want to live my own." With every brave step, Lynn freed herself to be her own person, walking into my office taller, brighter, and with a more positive outlook. This came with upsetting the applecart in her family, which caused her great pain. This is why authenticity takes such courage. It often requires us to individuate and find our strength from within. Through Lynn's transformation, she not only forged a stronger relationship with herself. You might have guessed where this is going, her relationship with her husband also reached new levels of strength and joy.

Case: Meet Mark and Jessica: The Perils of Lacking Self-Awareness

Mark and Jessica slouched onto my couch days after his affair became known. Visibly destroyed and lost, they had no idea how their young relationship fell so hard. What did Jessica want most?

Answers! Mark, however, so out of touch with his feelings, couldn't even begin to explain. With Jessica beside him in therapy, Mark began dipping his toe into self-awareness. Tears running down his face, he quickly got in touch with how invisible and insecure he truly feels, though he keeps this hidden, even from himself. He came to realize that he was grabbing for the distraction of another woman because he didn't know how to cope now that he was not the center of her attention all the time.

Like Mark, Jessica came from a troubled household and was terrified that Mark would leave her if she expressed the problems she was sensing. Instead of being open and honest about her feelings, she did what she was used to growing up, ignoring what she felt and pretending *I'm fine, we're fine*. Until the bomb exploded, slamming them into the kind of people they never expected to become: *soul searchers*. And with urgent necessity.

SELF-AWARENESS BY CRISIS OR CONSCIOUS CHOICE

Many, like Mark and Jessica, seek counseling when some sort of crisis erupts, like the reveal of a secret relationship, an intolerable conflict, or a level of disconnection that has them frightened about their future together. Some rare partners, however, come in wanting to enrich their relationships or when the alarm bell is only ringing on low. Truth be told, we tend to become more self-aware in life from being pushed "from the back,"* that is, from some kind of pain or suffering that opens the gates to self-reflection and change. This is human nature, say both the scientists and the spiritualists.

Growing "from the front" requires a motivation from the inside and an appreciation for how important your relationship with yourself is. This is what I hope for this chapter, and all of Pillar 1: that it gives

---

*Michael Berg, ed., *The Wisdom of Truth: Twelve Essays by the Holy Kabbalist Rav Yehuda Ashlag*, (Kabbalah Publishing, 2008).

you the inspiration to choose learning about and transforming yourself "from the front" as much as possible. Whether you're reading this in a time of crisis or because you want to enrich your relationship, you've come to the right place. Becoming more emotionally intelligent about yourself, and ultimately about each other, is the first essential step in making your relationship strong.

SOUL SEARCHING: SPIRITUAL SELF-AWARENESS

Spiritual self-awareness means getting to know your soul. Consider this spiritual view: Each of us have two natures, body and soul. Your body nature includes the desire to receive pleasure and fulfillment—and all the thoughts, feelings, habits, urges, and needs that come with this basal drive for comfort and pleasure. It's the engine that keeps you seeking and striving for more. At least on a physical level. From the body's perspective, your experience is the effect of what happens to you or around you. When you feel vulnerable physically or emotionally, this can activate fears, traumas, limited thoughts, jealousies, insecurities, and all of the reactive, short-sighted, and selfish tendencies that come with being human.

On another level, you have a soul nature, which is calm and pure and filled with limitless energy. This is what it means when you hear people talk about the power of within, that you have everything you need inside of you. Spiritual self-awareness means to understand and grow progressively more in touch with your essence, which is already whole and complete. This is who you really are. From a spiritual perspective, your deepest yearning is to express the godly DNA of your soul, which is an extension of the Source of Life, that is, an all-encompassing creative force of goodness. True and lasting fulfillment is found through connecting with and expressing your soul nature.

CREATING A SOULFUL MARRIAGE: SOUL-TO-SOUL CONNECTION

The beauty and power of prioritizing your self-awareness, combined with soul-awareness, is that you gain more self-control by the opportunity to differentiate between the desires of your body and the desires of your soul. The deeper and more consistent your self-awareness practice becomes, the better able you are to hear the voice and messages from your soul, which not only allow you to feel more deeply fulfilled but also have significant implications for uplifting your relationship. Spiritual self-awareness helps you discern whether something you are struggling with in your relationship is coming from your body nature or soul nature, which gives you the free will to use the mind and voice of your soul to approach a solution. Through knowing and connecting more with your true self, you develop your ability to create a limitless soul-to-soul connection with your beloved versus a finite, need-based ego-to-ego connection.

What you will find in the coming chapters may not seem like a spiritual journey. Many of my clients don't view themselves as coming for this objective. They just want to be happier in their relationships. Rest assured, building a more soulful relationship is actually simple and practical (though not effort-free), and the process overlaps with building an overall healthy, close partnership. So, everything you do to improve your relationship builds the foundation for growing more spiritually connected.

TRUE SELF: WHO WE ARE FROM A SPIRITUAL VIEW

Self-awareness, and by extension inner peace and happiness, can expand further when you tap into a heightened awareness of who you are from a spiritual lens. Spiritual self-awareness means understanding the god spark within you, that who you are goes beyond the desires of your physical body or the masks you have learned to wear in society. Connecting with who you are at the core means seeing yourself (1) beyond your accomplishments, talents, or habits, (2) more powerful than your limitations, self-doubts, or fears make you think you are, and (3) as a valuable spark of holiness regardless of the approval you receive.

Turning inward allows you to connect with your inherent true self and celebrate the power of within. Some refer to this inner power as the soul, the holy spirit, the Creator within, the wise mind, the god spark, the actualized self. Please use whatever resonates best with you. You will see me use terms like these interchangeably. This inner part of us is connected to the endless Source of Life and goodness, and transcends our identity, personality, and our methods for trying to feel good enough. We all have an essence that is already whole, perfect, and infinite.

EXISTENTIAL EXPLORATION

The process of soul searching can also include digging for one's deeper often unconscious concerns. Contemporary psychiatrist Irv Yalom named four basic issues that all people struggle with that deal with existence. They include fear of death, the drive toward freedom, the desire to avoid isolation, and the need for meaning in life.[*] Some people are more in touch than others, yet these deep and fundamental needs run beneath the surface of whatever we face in life. There is no single solution, no mastery over these existential problems. *The idea is to embrace them, and ultimately use our awareness as motivation to live more fully and rise above.* Unexplored, these ultimate concerns can impact your mental well-being and your capacity for a true connection.

IDEA INTO ACTION: LET'S BEGIN A JOURNAL

A simple way to gain self-awareness is through the power of the written word. Some people have an aversion to journaling. You can consider this as jotting down notes or making lists. I encourage you to try even if you feel resistance popping up. The act of writing can help us let go and brings up truths that typically stay underground. Here are some tips to use your journal:

---

[*] Irvin D. Yalom, *Existential Psychotherapy* (Basic Books, 1980).

Break your journal into 4 parts, one for each pillar: Responsibility, Growth, Priority, Purpose

- **Pillar 1 will be your longest section.** You can allocate a third or half of your journal to this first pillar.
- **Protect your privacy.** Find places unlikely for family to look or create a couple or family agreement of privacy. You can also lock up your journal or use code words and metaphors.
- **Be honest and real,** uncensored. Your journal as a sacred outlet is important. As long as you protect your privacy, allow yourself to be authentic.

Optional: Invite **your partner to do the same exercise below and share with each other.**

Sentence Completion

Sentence completion is a tool to access your unfiltered inner thoughts, to circumvent the masks and "shoulds" that can hide your honest voice. Try to finish the sentence stems below as freely and rapidly as you can with your first thoughts uncensored. List six to ten spontaneous responses for each incomplete sentence. Don't worry if your answers are not logical or profound. The wisdom of your body and soul comes through when we allow ourselves to let go.

In Pillar 1 of your journal, answer the following prompts:

Your Core: What I know about myself

- I am happiest when . . .
- Ten things I know about myself without question are . . .
- I have always believed that . . .
- I am very passionate about . . .
- Five best and worst thoughts about myself are . . .
- The most impactful messages from my childhood about myself are . . .

- What I feel most proud of about myself is . . .
- I feel most safe and secure when . . .
- I feel about myself . . . I feel about my body . . .
- My five best and worst habits are . . .

Dreams and Inspirations

- I have always dreamed of . . .
- If I weren't afraid or embarrassed to go after it, I would love . . .
- I feel moved and inspired when . . .
- The kind of work that fulfills me . . .
- To be who I want to be, I would like to become more . . .

Fears and Concerns

- I am afraid of . . .
- I get anxious when . . .
- I have let fear stop me from . . .
- I am afraid of what people think of me when . . .
- What soothes and grounds me when I'm distressed is . . .

Relationships

- I feel most loved and supported when . . .
- Five important elements for me in a relationship are . . .
- What blocks *me* from being a loving partner is . . .
- I am most comfortable with people who . . .
- I receive feedback best when . . .

CHAPTER TWO

The Practice of Self-Love

*Love yourself first, and everything else falls in line. You really
have to love yourself to get anything done in this world.*

—Lucille Ball

SELF-LOVE IS ESSENTIAL

To create your own happiness and well-being, *self-love is essential.* When
you feel unconditionally caring toward yourself, and treat yourself with
the same compassion that you would treat someone you truly love, you
walk through life with an inner happiness—regardless of your triumphs
or failings. A positive self-regard brings a sense of lightness, a resilient
baseline of well-being that can include a sense of humor along the
natural ups and downs of life. Those who practice self-love think, feel,
and act gently and generously toward themselves and have greater capacity to reframe situations into opportunities. When you believe you
are worthy, and have a warm internal dialogue, you are more likely to
carry good feelings inside yourself and less likely to externalize your
needs and bad feelings onto others.

Self-love also comes with a hefty and refreshing dose of desire.

STEPPING STONES

Creating your own happiness and well-being is like walking along a
path of stepping stones. You start with the practice of nonjudgmental

self-awareness, which paves the way to reach self-love. When you care to know more about yourself, you are essentially saying, *I am worth knowing and I accept myself for who I am, authentically.*

Self-awareness → Self-acceptance →
Authenticity → Self-love

An interest in your inner world is the foundation for a loving relationship with yourself in part because you can catch it when you're being self-critical and need more self-love.

SELF-LOVE: SELF-INDULGENCE OR SELFISHNESS?

Self-love can be misunderstood as self-indulgence. True self-love actually prevents self-indulgence because you are aware of the perils of overdoing and falling into instant gratification.

Self-love could be confused with selfishness, or even narcissistic types of tendencies. Yet, when you understand self-love in its truest meaning, there could be nothing farther from the truth. Selfishness comes with the intention to take from others, even using or manipulating others without empathy or considerations for their well-being. Self-love inspires you to care for your needs in a balanced way and not at the expense of others. You allow yourself to fill your cup and have empathy and compassion for your own humanity. From this place of fullness, you can grow your capacity to care for others and have greater access to your pure essence of giving. *Our soul is filled with self-love, the desire to bestow goodness, and appreciation for the Source of Life to which we are connected.*

Case: Meet David and Sonya

David walked into my office with his stunned wife, as he was preparing to move out to an apartment. A last-ditch effort, he sought counseling. David's chief complaint? He was starving for more intimacy and overall attention from Sonya. The action to move out wasn't from a lack of feeling connected to his wife. The opposite. He couldn't bear the pain anymore from feeling consistently overlooked. A surgeon in a large research hospital, Sonya learned early on that to survive, she had to make work her number one priority. She learned to create distance in her relationships growing up, as her family emphasized measurable success over warm and loving relationships. She had no idea that David's unhappiness reached this desperate level. Throughout the process of therapy, it became clear that a lack of self-love within both spouses emerged as the root cause of their broken marriage.

Sonya came to realize that she never felt good enough. This suppressed feeling had been her constant companion, driving a need to bury herself with work and do whatever it took to please her bosses. While David's yearning for a closer connection with his wife was totally valid, he quickly realized that he also did not know how to create a deep connection with Sonya. As a boy, he grew up in a home where love was scarce and complicated. Though he sought love, he didn't see himself as lovable. He quickly began to recognize how familiar it was for him to be chasing connection, yearning to feel being a priority. Chasing Sonya for validation felt familiar, as he never had a feeling of worth and love inside himself.

THE PERILS OF A SELF-LOVE DEFICIT

Like David and Sonya, I find that many of us feel inadequate and lack self-love. Honestly, I can hardly think of anyone who sits on my couch for counseling, who after some digging, doesn't discover they struggle with their self-esteem, self-worth, self-love. It's human and normal, to one degree or another. It can come by way of feeling like an imposter or never feeling good enough. Maybe it's not giving yourself the same grace when making a mistake as you might offer others. A lack of self-love often dwells at the epicenter of anxiety, depression, anger, feeling overwhelmed, and most definitely our relationship problems. While low self-love varies in degree, each and every one of us can benefit from growing the worth and compassion we feel within ourselves.

Without self-love, we are more vulnerable to perfectionism, addictions, and to base our worth on the validation we receive from people, accomplishments, looks, money, or attention. Therefore, a lack of self-love makes us vulnerable to need-based love. We become more dependent on the external in order to compensate for what we do not possess internally. This dependency, showing up most especially with our mates, is not a friend to a soulful relationship. No one, and nothing outside of us, can truly make us feel enough, loveable, and worthy. Yes, our environment can make a significant difference and help us to feel safe and valued. However, another person cannot replace the essential love and appreciation we must feel toward ourselves.

THE BEST NEWS OF ALL

Self-love is a practice, a learnable skill at which you can grow better and better—any time, no matter the state of your current relationship, regardless of anything that has happened to you or by you. Like every human being, you have an inherent core that is filled with self-love and that draws you toward this positive change.

SELF-COMPASSION AND SELF-ESTEEM

The term "self-love" is often used interchangeably with "self-esteem," "self-worth," "self-respect," "self-confidence," "self-compassion." They are cousins, if you will, not identical twins. Gaining steam in the 1960s, the self-esteem movement has been driven by the premise that bolstering one's self-esteem leads to greater social acceptance, mental and physical health, and motivation. And in certain ways, self-esteem enhancement has been shown to promote all of the above. However, the focus on higher self-esteem has its limits and can backfire because *self-esteem is essentially a form of evaluation.*

A pioneer in the self-compassion movement, Dr. Kristin Neff[*] explains, "Self-esteem is a measuring stick that we use to sum up our worthiness as 'good' or 'bad.'" With self-esteem, our thoughts and feelings of worth depend upon how we and others evaluate our performance and behavior. This standard sets up a dependency, a false and fleeting sense of self-worth waiting for a crash.

Unlike the evaluation focus of self-esteem, self-compassion allows us to adopt an accepting feeling of care toward ourselves—regardless of whether we are living up to our ideals or making horrible mistakes. We replace self-criticism—and the false identity that we are what we accomplish—with self-kindness, care, and concern. Showing ourselves compassion is about opening our hearts in a way that can transform our experience of life, and of ourselves.

Just as we should not confuse self-love with self-indulgence, self-compassion is not the same as being too permissive with ourselves. Self-compassion has actually been linked[†] to greater motivation to better oneself, not less, and to less procrastination. Further, self-compassionate partners have been shown to have better relationships. Turning our compassion inward awakens greater desire for true happiness and well-being from a genuine sense of care and loving-kindness. Becoming generous-hearted with yourself leads the way to being the same with your partner. I suggest this self-talk tool I personally use and share with my clients, "I love you, I care about you, I want what's best for you." My hope is that this inner message will remind and encourage you to feel true care for the quality of your life experience. Care and compassion from within can also motivate you to (1) embrace your challenges, (2) go out of your comfort zone for the sake of what's best

---

[*] Kristin Neff, *Self-Compassion: Stop Beating Yourself Up and Leave Insecurity Behind* (William Morrow, 2011).
[†] Juliana G. Breines, and Serena Chen, "Self-Compassion Increases Self-Improvement Motivation," *Personality and Social Psychology Review* 38, no. 9 (2012): https://doi.org/10.1177/0146167212445599.

long term, and (3) learn from your mistakes—all in service of feeling worthy of a happier life experience.

KNOW YOUR ENEMY: IDENTIFY YOUR SELF-LOVE DESTROYERS

A powerful strategy for building self-love is to become skilled in identifying its enemies. The more you can catch these pesky mindsets or bad habits in the act, the faster you can switch the channel and upgrade the way you are thinking, talking, and acting toward yourself.

Here are six key self-love destroyers (SLD):

1. Perfectionism
2. Destination addiction (I'll be happy or good enough when . . .)
3. Critical self-talk (internalized messages/lies from childhood or society)
4. Suppressing emotions
5. Overly concerned with pleasing others (Sociotropy)
6. Comparing

Here are some overall tips for turning each of your self-love destroyers into self-love builders. Below you will find some hands-on exercises to bring your self-love into practice.

- **Strive Toward Betterment, Not Perfection!** Perfectionism is a refusal to accept any standard for yourself short of perfection—which is an unattainable, nonreality. Born from insecurity, and oftentimes trauma, expecting perfection is a protective mechanism to escape from inner shame. Perfection as a goal is lethal to self-love, happiness, and peace of mind. Research findings[*] suggest that somewhat paradoxically,

---

[*] Karen Pace, "Research Shows That Practicing Self-Compassion Increases Motivation," Michigan State University, October 28, 2016, https://www.canr.msu

taking a nonjudgmental, accepting approach to your personal failures makes you more motivated, not less, to improve yourself. I often say to my clients, "No mistakes, only learning." I invite you to let go of seeking mastery and shift into *embracing and enjoying the growth process itself.*

- **Catch Your Destination Addictions and Embrace Yourself NOW.** Shift into the consciousness that where you are and who you are, right now, is more than enough, even with the inner growth you still want to manifest. There is no "*later*" or "*only when I . . .*" attached to your worthiness. We all need to beware of destination addiction,[*] a term coined by British psychologist Robert Holden that addresses the human tendency to perceive that our happiness will be found in what's "next." This future-seeking mindset prevents us from being happy where we are. We can fall into the same trap of believing that our self-worth is conditional too based on some future accomplishment, body size, relationship, or recognition. If you listen closely and hear yourself thinking, "I'll be loveable or enough when . . . ," this is a clue. Developing a good relationship with oneself means that we demote our false identities. For example, the false identity of "I am my accomplishments," turns into "I am worthy already, and I enjoy doing good work."
- **Talk to Yourself Like a Dear Friend.** One way to adopt an accepting attitude of loving kindness toward yourself is to talk to yourself like you would a dear friend. Some find it helpful to journal or speak self-kindnesses out loud. You can even write compassionate letters to yourself. Look out for the traps of self-doubt, guilt, shame, and self-criticism. Replace these

---

.edu/news/research_shows_that_practicing_self_compassion_increases _motivation.
[*] Robert Holden, *Authentic Success: Essential Lessons and Practices from the World's Leading Coaching Program on Success Intelligence* (Hay House Inc., 2011).

sharp blades with kindness, compassion, understanding, and permission to choose what makes you happy. We internalize messages, sometimes from growing up. *We need to create our own loving messages.* Self-kindness heals guilt and shame. This inner friendship flows into all your relationships.

- **Embrace Your Emotions.** Rather than running away, turn toward your feelings, accept and embrace them. This way, you can provide yourself with empathy and soothing. Be mindful and present when going through difficulty. You deserve your own concern. Move from your head to your heart and listen to your body sensations, to the emotions inside. They are trying to guide you, awaken you to something that needs attention and care, or perhaps that needs changing, within or around you. We create an internal environment suitable for growth, when we are *present and self-soothing with whatever we feel.*

- **Advocate for Yourself and Set Good Boundaries.** While kindness and sharing with others are qualities for which we are here to strive, going too far to please others diminishes our own value and leaves us depleted and anxious. Giving yourself permission to advocate for yourself, and live according to your own priorities, breaks the cycle of basing your worth on how others respond to you. Your value and usefulness are not based on the extent to which others are happy, or are happy with you. Your value is inherent and it's up to you to *set limits that help you thrive.*

- **Replace Comparing with Appreciating Your Gifts.** Whenever we catch ourselves comparing and feeling like "I'm not doing enough, not good enough, or don't have enough"—we know we have sunk into a place of lack and away from appreciation. This is emotionally dangerous and lethal to self-love. Losing appreciation for the gifts and opportunities we are given, within and around us, is something we all should fear. The minute you notice that you are comparing yourself and feeling less than or less fortunate, bubble yourself off from the outside world. Switch immediately into taking stock of what you appreciate, what you're proud of, what you feel so humbly blessed to be and receive in your life.

SUMMARY FOR TURNING SELF-LOVE DESTROYERS INTO SELF-LOVE BUILDERS (SLD → SLB)

Instead of:

- Perfectionism → Lovingly Enjoy the Process of Betterment
- Destination Addiction → Know That You Are More than Enough Now
- Critical Self-Talk → Talk to Yourself Like a Dear Friend
- Suppressing Emotions → Be Present, Curious, and Self-Soothing with Whatever You Feel
- People Pleasing → Identify Your Own Goals and Priorities; Set Boundaries Accordingly
- Comparing Yourself → Practice Self-Appreciation and Authenticity

SELF-LOVE IS A TONIC FOR YOUR RELATIONSHIP

The more you align with your whole and self-loving essence, the better equipped you are to give and receive love. When your partner says or does something that threatens your sense of value, which certainly happens living closely with another human being, self-love helps you respond more calmly. Filling yourself first with your own love strengthens your muscle for postponing reactive tendencies that escalate into defensiveness, resentment, and disconnection. When you feel good inside, you naturally have more to give. You are also in a better state to receive love—because you aren't afraid to ask for what you want and you feel worthy of receiving it.

IDEA INTO ACTION: LET'S CONTINUE WITH YOUR JOURNAL

Exercise 1: Getting Started

Identify your Self-Love Destroyers (SLD)

Now is a good time to open your journal to the Pillar 1 section. Look at the list of Self-Love Destroyers again and on a fresh page in your journal, write about which ones you see in yourself.

- Perfectionism
- Destination Addiction (I'll be good enough when . . .)
- Critical Self-Talk
- Suppressing Emotions.
- Overly Concerned with Pleasing Others
- Comparing Yourself

Becoming a Self-Love Builder (SLB)

Next, write down which areas you want to commit to becoming a Self-Love Builder (SLB).

Tip: Brainstorm ways you will take this idea into action. Then share these ideas with someone else in your life, ideally your partner. Often called an Accountabili-Buddy, teaming up with someone will give you more strength to make the changes you desire.

An example: If you identify with people pleasing, then commit to considering your own needs more and pausing before you say "yes" to someone. When appropriate, practice saying "no." Be on the lookout for hyper-apologizing and simply refrain.

Exercise 2: Practicing Self-Loving Thoughts

In the Pillar I section of your journal, designate a page for the following self-loving practice called "Turnarounds."

Turning Around Your Unhelpful Thoughts into Helpful Ones

This turnaround chart below is one of the most popular activities I do with my clients. Here you will go digging for the worst things you tend to think about yourself: the irrational, the unhelpful, the repetitive. Then write them down in the left column. Getting these infectious thoughts on paper gives clarity and motivation to transform these cruelties into loving messages. We typically don't even realize how harsh our inner voicer can sound until we see the ink on paper. The negative thoughts will fall under the Unhelpful Thought column. The turnaround thoughts, about yourself and your life, will be the Helpful Thoughts coming from the loving and affirming lens of your essence. As Louise Hay says in her book *Heal Your Body A-Z*,[*] "Be willing to change your words and thoughts and watch your life change."

On the "Self-Loving Thoughts" page, make a two-column table that looks like this:

Unhelpful Thought	Helpful Thought

In the left column, write down some of the worst things you say to yourself. This will be uncomfortable, but seeing these ugly thoughts on

---

[*] Louise L. Hay, *Heal Your Body A–Z: The Mental Causes for Physical Illness and the Way to Overcome Them* (Hay House Inc., 1998), x.

paper can give you perspective and motivation to choose kinder thoughts toward yourself. In the right column, create the most self-loving thought you can think of. Imagine what you would say to someone you care about dearly.

Here are some examples:

Unhelpful Thought	Helpful Thought
I'll be happy and good enough when . . .	I have value now, not as a result of anything else.
I can't believe I'm not farther along.	I am exactly where I need to be; the path I'm on is made for me.
I'm not good enough.	I'm enough and worthy.
If I don't do well, I'm a failure.	I might fail but this doesn't make me a failure.
What if they get mad or reject me?	I am okay, even if they aren't okay with me. I care most about what I think of me. I validate myself.
I'll be happy when . . .	I have everything I need inside of me to be happy now.
If I say no, they won't love me.	I honor myself by honoring my boundaries.
I am small and unimportant.	When I walk into a room, I fill it with Light—and I know it. I have a lot to give. I love and approve of myself as I am.
I'm afraid of being judged.	Living according to my values is what really matters. I care most about what I think of me.

Note: In addition to your thoughts and words, it's important to be mindful of building self-loving actions. You can do this by simply asking yourself, "What's the most loving thing I can do for myself?"

CHAPTER THREE

The Practice of Self-Care

*When you say "yes" to others make sure you are not saying "no"
to yourself.*

—Paulo Coelho

Self-care requires valuing yourself, and caring about having a good life experience. You must matter to you to take care of you. For those who value themselves, self-care is an easy bridge to cross. While self-love emphasizes a warm feeling toward yourself, self-care involves putting your love into action: taking care of your body, mind, heart, and soul. When you appreciate your value, and feel care toward yourself, you inherently desire to do what will benefit you and reject that which harms you. You are attuned within and appreciate how self-care impacts your happiness and well-being. While self-care and self-love influence one another bidirectionally, generally the flow looks like this.

Self-awareness → Self-acceptance → Authenticity →
Self-love → Self-care

The practice of self-care has great benefits. While research* supports the connection between self-care and well-being, let's be honest,

---

* Sneha Chatterjee and Jaya Jethwani, "A Study of the Relationship between Mindful Self-Care and Subjective Well-Being among College Students and

who hasn't experienced for themselves the remarkable difference when we are taking good care of ourselves. Yet, for so many, it's difficult to make ourselves a priority in this essential way.

REFRAMING SELF-CARE

Similar to the misconceptions about self-love, many people perceive self-care as self-indulgent, self-absorbed, or even selfish. Approached in the right way and with the right intention, the practice of self-care is the very opposite—it's the most responsible, generous thing we can do. The positive impact of our self-care directly benefits those who depend on us, who want to be closer to us, who care about our happiness. When we feel more solid and balanced, we show up more fully in our relationships. We are more likely to feel generous and share, to be present with ourselves and our partner, and to approach conflict without flying off the handle.

Self-care requires making friends with responsibility—adopting the idea "I, myself, am responsible for proactively taking care of myself." A part of us resists this ownership, but another part craves taking charge. In a soulful marriage, we owe each other, and the relationship, the investment of energy to do all we can to show up with the best version of ourselves. When we form a union with someone, we have to be more than ourselves individually walking side by side. We create an entity together—a dwelling place for love to flow. I call that dwelling place a sanctuary. Self-care strengthens your relationship sanctuary.

SELF-CARE PYRAMID: BODY, MIND, AND SOUL

The practice of self-care is just that, a practice. This means continuously investing in habits that nourish your whole being—body, mind, and soul. To practice self-care, you must first identify what that looks like for you. Consider this incomplete sentence: Something doesn't feel

right about my life unless I'm _____." Fill in the blank.
I ask my clients this question on a regular basis, and myself. How you
answer is a quick look into what lights you up and keeps you balanced.
As you read the body, mind, and soul sections below, take note of what
resonates with you. Look for activities and habits that when you're not
doing them, something in your life is not quite right. Perhaps some
are practices you already know work well for you and maybe some will
spark a new idea. While I have separated these self-care practices into
sections, they certainly overlap and work in harmony with one another.

BODY CARE

When my clients are really struggling, we always start with the body.
It's the foundation. When we feel good in our bodies, this aids in the
elevation of our mind and soul. This is why you see body care at the
base of the self-care pyramid in Figure 3.1. Body care includes:

Sleep—Who doesn't notice the difference of getting adequate sleep
on a regular basis? Good sleep benefits us even more than we often
realize. We experience less emotional and physical distress, think
and focus better, feel lighter, and attune to others' better. Good sleep
strengthens our immune system, helps control food cravings, and reduces inflammation.

Nutrition and Mindful Eating—Many people confess that their eating
habits and relationships with food are not something to brag about.
Overall, we fare best when we prioritize regular healthy meals, distinguish between stomach hunger and mouth hunger, drink more water,
and eat mindfully (versus reactively). Developing a good relationship
with food means paying attention to foods that make you feel good.
It's important to build a healthy joy of eating, while at the same time
getting support if you notice yourself binging or emotional eating or
operating from deprivation.

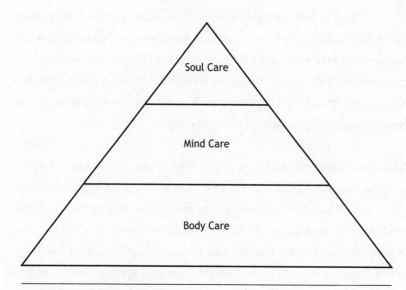

Figure 3.1   Self-Care Pyramid

Body Positivity—Our relationship with food is typically tied with our body image, both a large byproduct of the messages we received from our family and society during childhood. How we feel about our bodies directly affects how we feel about and treat ourselves, and how we interact with our partner. It's important to invest in feeling fit and strong and at home with your body with whatever size feels best to you. Taking care of your body means working hard to accept the beauty of your body, flaws and all. For many, this means grieving the body you have spent a chunk of your life striving toward and resisting the judgement society instills.

Find Your Favorite Movement—We are designed to move our bodies. It's vital to find something that you will look forward to, or dread the least in some cases. Maybe it's dancing, running, or walking outside. It doesn't have to be the gym and you might want to "move" with a friend. Move in your way! The gains are tremendous for your mind, body, and spirit—and your relationship. A client told me about a cognitive therapist she had seen to help her get unstuck from grief. At the first session, the therapist said, "For three weeks, I want you to elevate your heart rate in some way every day for thirty minutes. Then come back and we can start working on shifting your thoughts." Moving our bodies has been shown to improve physical health, satisfaction with life, cognitive functioning, and psychological well-being.*

Managing Stressors and Emotions—Stress can wreak havoc on our nervous systems, which ripples into how we react to everything and everyone. When our nervous system rises above our optimal arousal level, we move into a state of emotional distress beyond what our nervous system can effectively navigate. This makes us hyper-aroused (too hot), which induces feelings of overwhelm, anxiety, feeling unsafe, anger, and sometimes panic. Our nervous systems can then swing to the opposite extreme and become hypo-aroused (too cold), which causes a shut down, low or no energy, numbness, disconnection, ashamed feelings, and depression. Everything good happens, for us and our relationship, when we are in our regulation zone.

I refer to what you see in Figure 3.2 more than any other visual with my clients because of how empowering it is to understand what's happening in our bodies. We can work with it once we are aware. For couples, only when they are in their regulation zone can a true connection occur. It quickly becomes clear for partners that their unproductive times of conflict stem from one or both of them trying to engage when dysregulated, that is, out of their regulation zone.

Learning how to keep your emotions and thereby your nervous system regulated is not easy, but it is doable and important. A specialist in complex trauma, Deb Dana, LCSW, coined one of my favorite terms,

---

* Matheus Santos de Sousa Fernandes et al., "Effects of Physical Exercise on Neuroplasticity and Brain Function: A Systematic Review in Human and Animal Studies," *Neural Plasticity*, December 14, 2020, https://onlinelibrary.wiley.com /doi/10.1155/2020/8856621.

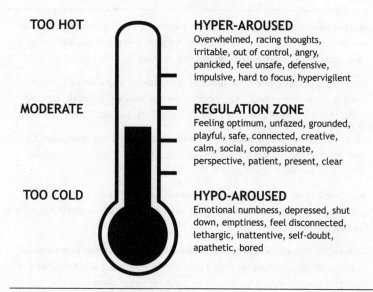

Figure 3.2 Emotional Regulation Zones

"Glimmers."* Glimmers are the experiences, people, spaces, and interactions that make us feel emotionally safe, warm, and connected. Body care must include getting to know what calms your nervous system. This is when true connection with your partner can happen, when you are grounded with yourself. Then, when need be, you can navigate conflict more calmly. When you feel centered and calm, you are more likely to feel light, playful, creative, and optimistic. In Figure 3.3, you'll see a sampling I put together from my clients' and my own favorite ways to get grounded. You can use these as thought starters for creating your own inventory of glimmers.

Physical and Mental Health—Each partner deserves to be with someone who is proactively taking care of their health, both physically and mentally. Not perfect by any means, it's about the effort of investing

---

* Deb Dana, *Anchored: How to Befriend Your Nervous System Using Polyvagal Theory* (Sounds True Adult, 2021).

Body—relaxed breathing, mindfulness, rocking or shaking, stretching, water immersion, dancing, yoga, power poses, wrapping in a soft blanket, hugging, hand on heart and belly, running, walking, moving.

Mind—mental tasks, podcasts, practice acceptance, organize/sort, make the bed, study lofty ideas, read fiction, think of recipes, do work, positive mantras, clean, meditate on the words "love," "gratitude," and "peace."

Heart—do random kindnesses, belly laugh, watch something heart-opening, read about kindness, get a good cry, look at pictures of positive memories, open up to someone you trust.

Soul/Spirit—play your favorite song, journal, sing out loud, attend spiritual services, read what inspires you, speak and do kindness to yourself and others, learn something new.

Connection to people and animals—spend time with familiar safe people, send loving/appreciative texts as a touchstone, reach out when you need strength, snuggle with pets, show care, and listen to others.

Nature and Outside—feel the warmth of the sun, go for a walk, stare up at the sky, hug and smell a tree, go into the woods, inhale fresh air, feel your feet in the grass or earth, garden, yardwork, adventure or hang out in nature.

Art/Creativity—create art, sing, color, bake, rearrange space, craft, improv, garden, listen to or play music, look at art, knit.

Figure 3.3   Grounding and Regulating Your Emotions

and taking responsibility. When we take care of our physical health, we are essentially saying to our partner, "I am doing my best to show up as an active participant in our relationship and life together." Probably more than any other aspect of our bodies, I see the influence that one's mental health has on the quality of a relationship.

Case: Meet Polly and Mike

Polly and Mike came to see me for counseling because Mike had finally admitted that Polly's anger was more than he was willing to accept anymore. The love between them was strong and unconditional, but the environment of anger and irritability was not healthy, nor conducive to intimacy. Mike also realized that he had a fear of confrontation, which exacerbated their problems. Through the process of therapy, Polly came to own responsibility for her mental well-being and discovered that anxiety issues were driving her anger. Her self-care practice included individual therapy to heal the root of her anxiety and develop tools to keep her in the window of tolerance. In Polly's case, she found that a low dose of medication took the edge off and gave her a stronger base to make the changes she needed to make.

Polly took responsibility for her inner healing and anger management. Mike's self-care practice got the ball rolling in the first place by expressing what was okay for him and what was not. He faced his fear of Polly's response and chose his own well-being over keeping the (illusion of) peace. They saved the quality of their marriage, and the marriage itself, through their practice of self-care. For many years to come, this happy couple would check in with me and acknowledge the pivotol turnaround these changes had made.

MIND CARE

Doing that which benefits your mind is a must when practicing self-care. Many don't realize the extent to which you can and must learn to create a positive environment within your mind. Think of your mind like the head of a river. When the head of your river is filled with positive, inspiring thoughts, you send joy, creativity, abundance, and inner peace downstream—to yourself and your partner. To turn your mind into a generous environment, here are some key elements to consider:

Your Thoughts Create Your Reality

You possess greater control over your life than you can ever imagine by the power you have to choose your thoughts. You can't always control the thoughts that enter, but you can decide which thoughts you believe in and use as a basis for the way you live your life. As I have heard my spiritual teacher Michael Berg say, again and again, "Where our consciousness is, that is where we are." The practice of self-care must include building a stronger muscle for directing your thoughts in ways that serve you.

Your thoughts about yourself and your partner determine what you bring to every encounter with your partner and how you perceive every interaction. If you believe the thought that you are unimportant and unworthy, you will be more likely to feel slighted or undervalued by your partner when an interaction doesn't go the way you'd like. If you hold onto angry thoughts about your partner, allowing their flaws to occupy your mind, you will send that out and attract the same.

You Can Control Your Thoughts—Once you appreciate that every thought you think is creating your future,[*] the next step is to practice choosing better thoughts—about yourself, your circumstances, and about the people around you. And especially your partner. Finding the demons of your limiting thoughts takes some digging.

It takes effort to identify your negative thoughts and an even greater force to consistently redirect your thoughts to a higher plane. At the core, most negative thoughts fall into 3 categories. Thoughts that we are: (1) unworthy and less than; (2) alone, unprotected, and unsafe and (3) less fortunate, a victim, not getting our fair share. Remember the turnaround chart you crafted in chapter 2, this is where you can transform these negative thoughts that hold you back. For example, "I am gentle with myself as I learn and grow." Regardless of what happens to you or around you, the truth is that you are born from wholeness and connecting to this within yourself becomes the foundation of the self-care for your mind, and ultimately for your relationship.

Your Self-Talk—An outcropping of your thoughts is how you actually talk to yourself. Yes, we all talk to ourselves all day long. Experiment

---

[*] Louise Hay, *You Can Heal Your Life* (Hay House, 2008).

with talking out loud and see how the words come out as you go about your day. What do you say to yourself when you wake up, when you drop something, get rejected, make a mistake, run late, do something well, change your mind? What do you say to yourself when your partner disappoints you, hurts your feelings, criticizes you, or gets angry? Some of these voices might be harder to identify, but to take care of your mind, I encourage you to really listen for the actual words you use.

To transform your harsh self-talk, try speaking to yourself like you would a close friend. This can instantly awaken the mercy and encouragement that you show others and help you direct that toward yourself. Make a conscious effort to appreciate all that you are, all you are trying to be, and all you have been given. Speak to yourself using kind words and compassion. Your mind will be a lighter, gentler place—and your relationship will follow suit.

We Become What We Consume—What kinds of books do you read? Which podcasts do you like to follow? What do you listen to or watch on the news or streaming? Our mind is porous, elastic. We want to be careful not to pollute it with angry, judgmental, or victim messages. This will impact your state of mind and branch out to your words and actions. Try and listen to more positive messages that show empowering ways to make your life, relationship, and the world better—messages that exude kindness and compassion.

Be careful who you have around you as well. As best you can, choose people who help create an environment of positivity, growth, and caring, and that guards against the human temptation to gossip, judge, and fall into a victim mindset.

Mindfulness and Radical Acceptance—Remember destination addiction that we talked about in chapter 2? It's the syndrome of: I'll be happy when, I'll be enough when, I'll be kinder to my partner when . . . Self-care for your mind must include building your capacity for accepting yourself and your present reality, with love—right here and right now. When you continually work to accept yourself and the present moment, you begin to feel increasingly more alive, fulfilled, and open hearted— and less anxious, empty, or critical.

PBR: Pause, breathe, relax. I suggest practicing what I like to call *micro-mindfulness.* That is, at any moment and as frequently as possible, say and then do these three steps: (1) *pause,* (2) *breathe,* and (3) *relax.* Then bring yourself into the center of this very moment to remember whatever mindful thought best serves you at this time. You can meditate on your highest spiritual intention, such as to feel and trust the light of your soul. After PBR, you can remind yourself, "Everything is okay." You can awaken gratitude or radical acceptance of this moment. You can remember the good heart of your partner or that you really want to be a patient spouse. The key with PBR is to become mindful and this will put you in the driver's seat of choosing where you want your thoughts to go.

Appreciation—A mindset of gratitude can help us climb out of a difficult mental state. We all know it's good for us, yet we completely underutilize this tool and higher state of mind. Grateful thoughts put the mind of our heart in charge. Try going beyond a list of what you're grateful for (which is good) and really spend time taking stock of every detail of your blessings, connect them to the Source of Life, and let the feeling of gratitude expand into your heart until it's overwhelming. Make appreciation a habit and a visceral experience.

SOUL CARE*

Connect with Your Soul

We nourish our soul when we connect with our soul and allow its expression. The soul voice is quieter than the body voice, with fewer

---

* From the Teachings of Rav Berg, *The Power of Kabbalah: Thirteen Principles to Overcome Challenges and Achieve Fulfillment* (Kabbalah Centre Publishing, 2018).

words, so we can more easily neglect this essential part of who we are more than any other. The soul part of us is connected to the infinite, to the endless force of goodness that is our Source. Anything we do or experience that brings us to feel expansive, open-hearted, in awe, fully present, inspired, calm, connected, empowered, joyful, uplifted—why do we love these feelings? Because we are touching the magic of our soul. We are unifying with the endless in these moments.

This may sound lofty and unattainable, but quite the contrary. Most often, the opportunities to nourish our soul come in the micro-moments of life, especially when we are present to them. In chapter 1 on self-awareness, we began to explore what it means to know your soul. The more we know about our soul, the better equipped we are to choose alignment with this expansive part of who we are. This alignment is the essence of soul care and the secret to reaching ever-expanding levels of happiness and well-being.

A Soulful Marriage Is Soul Care

When you put your energy into the growth and learning required to develop as a soulful partner, you are nourishing your soul, along with your partner's soul, and the sanctuary you are creating together. Love and oneness are the most fundamental ingredients of your soul, though being unconditionally loving can prove quite difficult in this physical world. Growing closer in your relationship, opening the endless chambers of love that exist within you, means you are walking a spiritual path. That is, living more as a soul housed in a body, versus a body who also has a soul.

Three Steps for Taking Care of Your Soul

Step 1: Get to Know Your Soul

Take a look at the chart on the next page, which shows what the soul loves and desires, and the qualities your soul is filled with. Remember, your soul is the essence of who you really are. The most precious

The soul desires to:	The soul is filled with the energy of (qualities):	
Give	Self-love	Appreciation
Grow	Trust	Compassion
Create goodness	Calm	Connection
Take initiative	Confidence	Patience
See the good	Clarity	Kindness
Love unconditionally	Perspective	Inspiration
Fulfill your purpose	Playfulness	Courage
Help others grow	Awe	Abundance
Unify with the Source of Life	Security	Joy
Commune with people, animals and nature	Wholeness	Well-being

Table 3.1   The Nature of Your Soul

things are the most concealed. So even if you feel far from living these attributes today, know that these desires and qualities dwell within you—and are patiently awaiting you to reveal them.

Step 2: Assess Where You Are

You can use the soul chart above as a guide map, at any given moment, to see if you're connecting with, and thereby nourishing, your soul. We will go further into exploring how you can develop these desires and qualities in the next chapter on self-development. For now, PBR—pause, breathe, relax—and assess which desire or quality you feel you're strong in and which needs some developing.

Step 3: Align with Your Soul

You probably already do things in your life now that align you with your soul. Let's start there. Think about when you feel playful, secure, kind, trusting, or compassionate. What are you doing or experiencing that brings you to this state? What do you notice helps you feel loving, grateful, uplifted, connected, or simply happy to be alive? This might happen when you're taking good care of your body, making time for your hobbies and passions, enjoying a good talk with a friend, or when you're volunteering. Maybe you feel at your best being in nature, after being intimate, giving for its own sake, learning something new, or creating. Does music move you? What about attending a house of prayer? How about watching kindness or going out of your way to be kind? Does journaling, meditating, or working with your hands make you feel connected?

We must make it a priority to do what puts us in touch with the magic of life, with the endless light of our essence. Having a soulful experience can be simple and right under our noses, like spending time with people we love; building something; being with animals; creating with words, paint, food, design, and more; studying awe-inspiring or spiritual ideas; running; yoga; dancing; learning a new skill; being in nature; volunteering; singing in unison; reading a poem; volunteering; traveling; holding a baby. Often a soulful experience enters when we are *in the present moment* in a state of calm and appreciation, regardless of what we are doing.

IDEA INTO ACTION: PICK A SIMPLE ACTION STEP FOR BODY, MIND, AND SOUL

Our body, mind, and soul are completely interconnected. Anything you do with one of these aspects will support the other two. Pick one action you can commit to for each of the areas of your well-being pyramid. Keep it simple—you'll be more likely to follow through consistently.

For example:

- For my body . . . I am going to commit to six weeks of going lights out at the best time for me.
- For my mind . . . I am going to repeat this mantra every day: I have so much good in my life, and I appreciate what I have been given.
- For my soul . . . I am going to focus on being kind no matter what is going on around me, because I know this aligns me with my soul.

The Practice of Self-Development

*Yesterday I was clever, so I wanted to change the world. Today
I am wise, so I am changing myself.*

—Rumi

Self-development is a natural extension of self-love and care. Not only will you receive better responses from people and the world, but the change process itself gives you the taste of self-mastery. Personal growth empowers you like nothing else can—think of it as a gift you give yourself. Stretching beyond the limits of what you thought you could achieve or become, even just a small shift, can make you feel full and powerful inside.

Personal growth doesn't mean something is wrong with you by the way. It's a paradox. You are meant to be wholly you, and yet to reveal all that you are, you need to move and change. If there were no striving, no overcoming, then life would feel empty and unfulfilling. You can see the progression into self-development through the chapters of Pillar 1:

Self-Awareness → Self-Acceptance → Authenticity →
Self-Love → Self-Care → Self-Development

FLEETING PLEASURE VERSUS LASTING FULFILLMENT

Self-development feels uplifting, and yet, in the midst of a challenge calling us to change, it may not feel so good. We often find ourselves in a tug-of-war between wanting more and wanting comfort. The growth and effort that brings us long-term fulfillment is not as fast and sexy as the dopamine feel-good surges. Pleasure-seeking can be like filling a mere two-ounce cup and after drinking it up, we still feel empty. We become dependent on the next two-ounce cup and on it goes. I like to say we settle for fleeting morsels. This short-term fill-up requires no skin in the game, little to no effort, and certainly no self-development. There is nothing wrong with experiencing pleasure; in fact, we are here to enjoy life endlessly, but the problem is that the way we seek pleasure is often shallow and fleeting. Fulfillment, on the other hand, comes from the slow and steady process of expanding the size of our cup, endlessly larger—when we step up and work on ourselves.

THE POWER OF PAUSE

Growing the muscle to at least pause before seeking the instant urges that our brains are wired to seek is the first step on the personal growth path.

Consider this scenario: You feel the urge to lash out at your spouse for something they said that hurt your feelings. To protect your pride, you create a narrative where you MUST give them a piece of your mind, and it has to be now. Telling them off would be the instant pleasure, the "How dare you . . . you're so insensitive . . . you never this or always that." You'd get it off your chest, feel back in power, less vulnerable, more in control. But for how long? We all know what happens when we go after that itchy bug bite on our skin. We scratch till we make a bigger problem. The feel-good subsides and we are left with a mess. It's so important to appreciate the wiring in our brain that is constantly taunting us to seek instant relief, unearned pleasure.

In comes the power of the *PAUSE*. When faced with something that triggers you, give yourself a chance to slow down instead of going after the instant pleasure of reacting emotionally. Not reacting for a quick relief is one of the most strenuous things we do in life, and one of our greatest measures of success. We often need to remove ourselves physically to regroup. When you pause and wait until you're calmer to respond, this gives you the opportunity to turn on your capacity for self-awareness so that you can explore the opportunity this difficulty is presenting you. This is self-development. First, pause when you could just react. Second, reflect on how you're feeling inside, what this means for your personal growth, and what would be a wise response for the long term. Self-development is the ultimate in taking responsibility for our own happiness and well-being.

SELF-DEVELOPMENT IS WIN-WIN

Prioritizing a practice of self-development directly enhances your capacity for a close and happy relationship. It's how you create a win-win marriage. You benefit from your personal growth and your partner gains a more elevated version of you every time you work on yourself. With each positive shift, you create the potential to interrupt and transform the patterns that create friction and disconnect between you. Growth that benefits your relationship can come from building your confidence, learning to cope with stress, healing old wounds, addressing your anger, nourishing a purpose, becoming more flexible, harnessing your ADHD brain, learning to be a better listener. The sanctuary of your marriage is the biggest winner of all as you create an environment together where you can thrive and grow, laugh and play, and enjoy an ever-growing soul-to-soul connection.

BITS OF WISDOM ON SELF-DEVELOPMENT

Don't Mistake Self-Development as Perfectionism

When we look for what we need to change in ourselves, or receive outside feedback, we can feel depressed. This is certainly not the point. We want to feel enthusiastic about the opportunity to grow, not ashamed, discouraged, or sad about who we are. What helps to keep the journey light and rewarding is to distinguish between self-development and perfectionism.

None of us are meant to be perfect or think that we should be. Perfectionism is self-destructive, anxiety provoking, and an escape from feelings of unworthiness. Self-development is healthy striving, with plenty of room for the genius of our being to flourish amid the messiness of risk, experimentation, and trial and error. Self-development is less about the destination (which has many benefits for sure) and more of a celebration of the inner peace and joy gained from the growth process itself.

Take Hold of Your Own North Star

Whether it's a passion, calling, career, craft, volunteer work, or something else, pursuing a fulfilling direction and sense of personal purpose is an important aspect of self-development. How fulfilled you are will directly impact your well-being and how you experience your partner. You want to ensure that the energy you receive from life isn't relying too heavily on your relationship. The fuller you feel inside, the less likely you are to transfer responsibility for your happiness onto your partner.

Make Friends with Discomfort

There are a few things I say at the onset of my healing work with couples. One of them is, "Be prepared to be uncomfortable." I want to plant the seed with my clients that the difficulty they're facing is a call to grow both individually and as a couple. We tend to resist discomfort, and I want to reframe it as your best friend. Whatever you're facing in your relationship, ask yourself now, "How willing am I to go out of my comfort zone in order to turn things around?" Just as willingness is a precursor to change, so too is discomfort for experiencing real breakthroughs.

I like to use drawings with my clients because it helps couples visualize the process. Figure 4.1 is to help you reframe the pain and discomfort from whatever challenge you face and see it as a gateway to whatever better version of yourself and life that you seek. When faced with the discomfort of change, keep your sights on the *new you*. Your own joy and well-being are worth the effort.

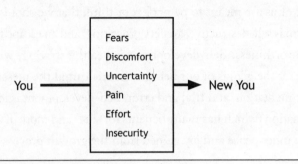

Figure 4.1   The Path of Transformation

Grow Your Consciousness Stronger than Your Feelings

To take advantage of any pain or discomfort as a gateway to something better, your perception will determine what happens next when you face darker times. Thus, strengthening and reframing your consciousness is essential for personal development. The extent to which you work toward accepting, trusting, and even valuing the lessons from the pain you go through paradoxically reduces the way you experience the pain. This is the power you tap into when your consciousness becomes stronger than your feelings. You lift yourself into a higher, bigger picture than your current strife and tap into the expansive energy of your soul. When you view your challenge as a gateway to something better, even if you can't see it now, this mindset can give you strength to endure what's uncomfortable. When we are in the middle of a growth process, we cannot yet see or feel the change we seek. *So we must develop the strength of our **mind over matter**, our perception over feelings*—not to suppress feelings but to grow our mind to lead the way.

IDEA INTO ACTION: WHERE IS YOUR GROWTH AREA?

By now, I hope you are more excited and eager to see where your growth opportunities can be found. A continuation of the exploration that comes with self-awareness and self-care, self-development involves getting more concrete about what you want to work on going forward, for yourself and your relationship.

Tips to get started:

- Be radically honest with yourself about your areas of growth.
- Resist creating a defensive narrative to protect your pride (aka insecurity).
- Remember that your areas of growth also contain your greatest virtues.
- Embrace yourself lovingly and joyfully as you commit to change.
- Remember the paradox: You're already whole and complete *and also* need self-development to find true fulfillment.

Part I: Below is to assess where you think your strengths and growth areas lie. Feel free to write directly in your book. I do it all the time and it can help you to digest what you're learning. Mark on the continuum where you feel you are among these qualities and then you can journal about which traits that stand out.

Patient	Less developed	Strongly developed
	1 ————————————+———————— 5	
Unconditionally loving	Less developed	Strongly developed
	1 ————————————+———————— 5	
Self-reliant	Less developed	Strongly developed
	1 ————————————+———————— 5	
Self-confident	Less developed	Strongly developed
	1 ————————————+———————— 5	
Generous-hearted	Less developed	Strongly developed
	1 ————————————+———————— 5	
Good communicator	Less developed	Strongly developed
	1 ————————————+———————— 5	

Motivated	Less developed	Strongly developed
	1 ——————————+—————————— 5	

Authentic	Less developed	Strongly developed
	1 ——————————+—————————— 5	

Manage emotions	Less developed	Strongly developed
	1 ——————————+—————————— 5	

Attentive	Less developed	Strongly developed
	1 ——————————+—————————— 5	

Respectful	Less developed	Strongly developed
	1 ——————————+—————————— 5	

Kind/compassionate	Less developed	Strongly developed
	1 ——————————+—————————— 5	

Forgiving	Less developed	Strongly developed
	1 ——————————+—————————— 5	

Playful	Less developed	Strongly developed
	1 ——————————+—————————— 5	

Humble	Less developed	Strongly developed
	1 ——————————+—————————— 5	

Approachable	Less developed	Strongly developed
	1 ——————————+—————————— 5	

Follow-through	Less developed	Strongly developed
	1 ——————————+—————————— 5	

Self-loving/self-caring	Less developed	Strongly developed
	1 ——————————+—————————— 5	

Appreciative	Less developed	Strongly developed
	1 ——————————+—————————— 5	

Part 2: Now you can identify your bad habits (with no guilt or shame) that block you from being who you want to be. A friendly reminder, try and be excited about what you discover. Our pride hates it, but our soul craves growth.

Consider the list of common barriers to personal growth below. Rank from 1-5 the bad habits that, when you're honest with yourself, you know to be true about you. 1 = I need little to no improvement 5 = This is a bigger issue, and I definitely need to work on this.

Anger	Little issue	Bigger issue
	1 ———————————————+————————— 5	

Blaming	Little issue	Bigger issue
	1 ———————————————+————————— 5	

People pleasing	Little issue	Bigger issue
	1 ———————————————+————————— 5	

Complaining	Little issue	Bigger issue
	1 ———————————————+————————— 5	

Addictive behaviors	Little issue	Bigger issue
	1 ———————————————+————————— 5	

Controlling	Little issue	Bigger issue
	1 ———————————————+————————— 5	

Self-doubting	Little issue	Bigger issue
	1 ———————————————+————————— 5	

Indecisive	Little issue	Bigger issue
	1 ———————————————+————————— 5	

Insensitivity/tactless	Little issue	Bigger issue
	1 ———————————————+————————— 5	

Critical/judgmental	Little issue	Bigger issue
	1 ———————————————+————————— 5	

Hold grudges	Little issue	Bigger issue
	1 ———————————————+————————— 5	

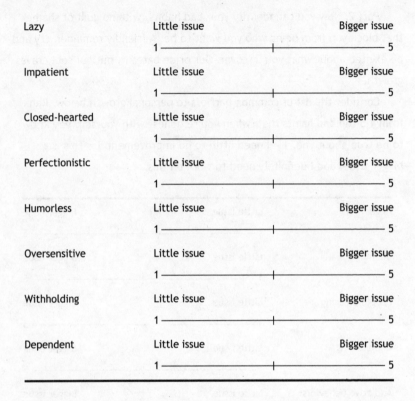

Lazy	Little issue	Bigger issue
	1 ———————————+——————— 5	
Impatient	Little issue	Bigger issue
	1 ———————————+——————— 5	
Closed-hearted	Little issue	Bigger issue
	1 ———————————+——————— 5	
Perfectionistic	Little issue	Bigger issue
	1 ———————————+——————— 5	
Humorless	Little issue	Bigger issue
	1 ———————————+——————— 5	
Oversensitive	Little issue	Bigger issue
	1 ———————————+——————— 5	
Withholding	Little issue	Bigger issue
	1 ———————————+——————— 5	
Dependent	Little issue	Bigger issue
	1 ———————————+——————— 5	

Part 3: Write about how this exercise was for you in your journal. What stood out? Remember to be patient and kind to yourself as you examine your growth areas.

Next, list 3 actions steps you can take to (1) develop your positive qualities and (2) transform your bad habits.

Growth

Growth

We Use Our Friction to Help Us Grow,
Individually and Together.

With Pillar 2 the focus moves from your relationship with yourself to your relationship with your mate. The order is deliberate, because we bring our ever-evolving connection with ourselves to every thought, word, and interaction in our relationship. In these next chapters, we are learning how to move from *"this is who I am"* to *"this is who we are"*; in particular, *"this is how we help each other grow."* Pillar 2 is where the ride gets bumpy. What you fight about, where you feel distant, what pushes your buttons, what hurts, where you feel stuck, what feels missing, how you fight, why there's resentment, what are your differences, how anger shows up, what's working, what's not, and ultimately how all of these come together with the magic ingredient for your best relationship, that is, *growth*.

By the time most couples land on my couch, it's their friction that has pushed them out of their comfort zone to seek counseling. They don't know how to take their conflict and use it soulfully to grow. We are not trained for this thing called long-lasting love, and the multilayers and facets to our committed relationship holds what is fundamental to our most precious dreams and desires in life. We even bring to the party our inner child who is perplexed why the same things keep happening. When we don't see or seize the opportunity to change and grow, chaos trends louder. Partners often feel stuck in a vicious cycle of fighting or distance or both, unsure how to connect to the force of forward motion. Their differences that may have once been attractive are not only no longer uplifting but taking them down. It's heartbreaking how few partners know how to find meaning and make good use of their conflict. When we don't understand the growth purpose of our relationship—that friction is here to benefit us, not hurt us—it's like finding ourselves in a maze without any map to guide us. Friction can be painful for sure, but suffering is avoidable when we are exposed to the growth paradigm, embrace it, and learn how to use our friction effectively.

GROWTH PARADIGM

A soulful marriage must have friction. This is why I introduce in the first session with my clients the growth paradigm I am sharing with you here throughout Pillar 2. I say to couples, and repeat again and again, "Your friction is a good sign." I see relief wash over them. I clarify, "*It's a good sign if you approach it properly and learn to use it for growth.*" We will be taking what we started in chapter 4 further and bringing your self-development face-to-face with your relationship. The soul nature in all of us loves to grow, and help others grow—especially "our person." You are creative by design. Through clashing with your mate, you open yourself to a wellspring of creative opportunities like (1) discovering the qualities you need to heal and work on, (2) deepening your capacity for unconditional love, (3) learning the joy of giving for its own sake, (4) becoming stronger and closer as a couple, (5) gaining deeper trust, and (6) growing from a relationship to a sanctuary. Through the process of growing closer to who we are capable of becoming, for ourselves and the world, we create a higher love. In a nutshell, as we grow, the love grows. As we see who our partner helps us become, the appreciation grows. On a deep soul level, we are all looking for a help mate who can help us shine and express the giving and loving light of our soul.

The purpose of growth, and the need for friction, in a soulful marriage is two-fold: (1) To help you mature into the most loving and giving person you can be and (2) to then create endlessly growing levels of love and appreciation, care, and closeness in your relationship. Embracing *the growth paradigm* is what allows the impossible, for two separate individuals to cleave as one and for the love to grow endlessly.

CHAPTER FIVE

Reframing Friction

A smooth sea never made a good sailor.

—Franklin D. Roosevelt

Most relationships start out with fantasy and expectations of easy, perfect love. These unrealistic ideals are simply not reality. Relationships can naturally surface issues and vulnerabilities which then create conflict. Rather than burying this conflict, it is important to realize that it can actually benefit your relationship. In a soulful marriage, growth ultimately means growing closer to an unconditionally loving and sharing being, as is the essence of your Source. To reach this version of yourself, you *need* friction in your relationship. Again, that's why "*your friction is a good sign.*" When we bump against one another in a close relationship, it's a fast-track to unearth what is blocking us from who we are capable of becoming, and the unity we are meant to experience. We all bring our unique individuality, childhood history, lineage, and past relationship experiences into our relationships. The decision to commit to an intimate relationship, it's as if we sign a contract giving our partner permission to push our deepest buttons. What makes all the difference is how we perceive this button pushing and what we do from there.

MIRROR MINDSET

When your partner pushes one of your buttons, consider viewing your beloved as your mirror—that is, try becoming curious about how they are helping you see yourself more clearly. This is very hard to do and counterintuitive. It's a spiritual idea because this means taking your vision beyond your five senses and in a quantum way, using the blemishes you're seeing in your partner to empower your own growth opportunity.* The father of psychoanalysis, Sigmund Freud, coined the term "projection": a defense mechanism that describes the human tendency to shield our pride and ego by highlighting unacceptable traits or impulses in others to avoid seeing these same attributes in ourselves. It's not just a spiritual idea.

Rest assured, seeing your partner as your mirror does not mean you don't address what's bothering you directly.

Your partner often mirrors two valuable areas of your growth:

- A trait they are displaying that is actually part of you—even if it's just a tiny trace. Such as being impatient, not following through, insensitive, anxious, a poor listener, self-neglecting, defensive.
- An issue, wound, or painful emotion that lurks beneath the surface until your partner pushes your buttons. Your partner's behavior could bring out feeling not good enough, lacking purpose, or fear of abandonment; or maybe it's a tendency to get irritable, blame, need to control, or not be present. Even if your partner is absolutely wrong in what they are doing or saying, you want to empower your own growth by first identifying what is being triggered or shown to you. Harville Hendrix, PhD, takes this idea so far as to say that "the unconscious is trying to resurrect the past . . . not a matter of habit or blind compulsion but of a compelling need to heal old childhood wounds."†

---

* Yitzhak Buxbaum, *The Light and Fire of the Baal Shem Tov* (Bloomsbury, 2005).
† Harville Hendrix, *Getting the Love You Want: A Guide for Couples* (Henry Holt & Co., 2007).

When our partners do or say something we don't like, what do we naturally feel compelled to do? Stay calm and look within for our own growth opportunity? Nope. This is not how our nature is wired. Our ego reacts. We blame, try to change them, shut down, feel victim, yell, judge, withhold kindnesses or affection, build resentment. Sometimes we try to people please or accommodate to avoid friction, but this is still the ego at play reacting and handing our power over to the external. Our instinct is self-preservation and to deem that our partners are responsible for the feelings we're having, especially about ourselves. Creating a soulful marriage requires rising above your reactive instinct when your partner does something you don't like and embracing the opportunity to do what your soul loves most, and that is to grow.

POINTS TO CONSIDER AS YOU LOOK IN THE MIRROR

- **It's Still Good to Argue**
  Looking in the mirror as an important action step doesn't mean you should never fight or express your grievances. Not at all. The idea is to keep the damage from arguments minimal and turn toward your own growth area *as promptly as you can*. Like when cleaning out your closet, the chaos looks way worse before it looks better than before. Similarly, after there's some kind of eruption of conflict or resentment starting to build, it's okay if it gets messy. Just make sure you're taking responsibility by being on the lookout for your own growth that the conflict is trying to show you. Like the closet metaphor, then you and the relationship can come back together better than before.
- **Don't Ignore What's Bothering You**
  Seeing our partners as our mirror doesn't discount the actual hurtful or inappropriate actions of your partner that may absolutely need to be addressed. You are not here to subjugate yourself and accept harmful behavior in your environment.

Looking in the mirror is simply step 1. There will be a step 2 and step 3 and so on to address conflict in a way that will bring you closer. I often say to my clients, you are both right and you are both wrong. Right, because each and every one of us has growth areas, so your concerns about your partner's behavior is likely spot on. Wrong, because you think that you could resolve the issue if you could just get your partner to change. That's like trying to change the mirror itself rather than the person who's looking in.

Turning inward and taking responsibility for your own growth opportunity makes room for a calmer, deeper, and more loving interaction when and if the time comes to address whatever issue you're having with your partner. This is a simple idea, albeit immensely difficult. It's a muscle you can build and requires the development of trust in the growth paradigm, in the process of life—that to best effect change outside of us, we benefit by starting to look inside of us. *Inward before outward.*

- **There Is Such a Thing as Too Much Conflict**
Too much conflict, explosive arguing, and ineffective approaches to handling friction: these all deteriorate your relationship and exhaust your nervous system. Friction is a good sign because you are here to grow and it's through opposition that you can create a new reality together. This means that the determining variable for using your friction for growth is the effectiveness of how you approach your conflict. You are going to love chapter 7, which is all about the methods for healthy, healing communication and conflict resolution.

Case: Meet Jarrett and Priyah, Looking in the Mirror
Jarrett had been married before, having a daughter with his first wife. He found himself in a stuck place with his new girlfriend, Priyah. They shared a connection and synchrony like he had never felt before,

yet Jarrett struggled with Priyah's habits and mannerisms, and lately she has been not as fun and loving as she was in the beginning. Having someone fun to be around was important to him, especially for his daughter. No matter how Priyah tried to accommodate Jarrett's particularities, he was increasingly pulling away. And, of course, she became less fun to be around too. As the sessions unfolded, we used their friction points as mirrors to see themselves more clearly.

Embracing the growth paradigm, Jarrett came to an epiphany that his irritability and lack of appreciation were recurring themes in his relationships, expecting his partners to work around his highly creative, sensitive self. If they could do so successfully and stay kind and delightful even when he became irritable or critical, then he would commit. An impossible feat, and a setup for a life alone or a miserable marriage. He shifted from the outer focus of how to get Priyah to be what he needed her to be to the internal work of managing his emotions and growing his respect and appreciation for the good woman Priyah is.

Priyah was able to see that her approach in relationships was to be as needless as possible, accommodating around her partner to manage her fear of being left and feeling not good enough. Futile as well. Priyah worked on not taking Jarrett's irritable behavior personally and dove deeper into building her sense of value from within. She began to express her feelings and needs more. She practiced setting boundaries that expressed her value and helped tame Jarrett's preoccupation with his own sensitivities.

This brought their relationship into a better balance and the fun returned because the tension melted away. Once Jarrett took ownership of his unrealistic expectations in a relationship, he began to use his creativity to find ways they can create work-arounds for his particularities. His personal growth revelations removed the barriers that had prevented their relationship from moving forward. In kind, Priyah gave herself permission to speak up for herself and express her opinions more. She realized that she would much rather face rejection than spend the rest of her life abandoning her own values, which is what tiptoeing around someone's particularities meant. The issue was never about finding the right match for either of them; it was that they needed to look in the mirror for the growth opportunity that was keeping them stuck in an infinity loop and killing the energy between them.

Case: Meet Nicole and Devon

Nicole had been coming to see me for several years, and during that time period she got married and had twin boys. Though she was coming to see me individually, we spent a good bit of time discussing her relationship with her husband, Devon. In one session, Nicole came in at her wit's end over how little responsibility she felt Devon took for child-rearing, household chores, and all the details their life together required. His grievance was that Nicole had no idea how stressful corporate life was, nor the emotional weight he carried by providing financially. If she did, he felt she would understand that he had nothing left in him at the end of the day. Nicole felt overwhelmed with her mental and physical load and was resentful that Devon did not understand that her job of raising their family was also hard and stressful. Her resentment was leaking out in angry bouts that were happening more often. They had had a huge argument the week before with no progress for how to move forward to a better place. Nicole's natural inclination, and I let her run with it for a while, was to lament on and on about Devon's insensitive way of devaluing her as a mother, judging her for not also providing on top of everything else she does for the family.

After validating that yes, Devon was not being sensitive to her needs, I asked her if she was willing to be in two places at the same time with me. That is, while keeping in mind that even though he's not showing her support, can we spend some time looking in the mirror, just to explore what might really be going on for her to address. I reminded her of the growth paradigm and that turning within is where she will connect with the center of herself and find agency to make changes. A self-aware soul, she agreed to go digging. Little by little we unpacked emotions and core beliefs that were just beneath the surface. Through what is called "laddering," we started with (1) her frustration about Devon, and we laddered down to (2) her frustration for allowing herself to be in a traditional marriage to (3) "I don't have any power" to (4) "I'm devalued" to (5) "I don't value myself" to (6) "I am lost with no purpose" to (7) "I am lesser for not providing" to (8) "I am not safe."

Nicole's whole countenance shifted when she got to the underbelly of her vulnerability and the feelings and beliefs she had about her herself and her life. She summed up her revelation, "I see now that it's my own perceived lack of purpose and insecurity at the root of my resentment toward Devon. I'm expecting him to fill in what I need to address in myself. Truth is, I am happy with my choices and my husband is a very loving man." While Devon does indeed need to work on his view of paid and unpaid work, by pointing the mirror toward herself Nicole found her center point of growth, some pesky core beliefs from childhood that she didn't even agree with. The pressure lifted, which empowered Nicole to shift into compassion for Devon's stress and approach this issue from a calmer, productive place.

BITS OF WISDOM: MAKE THE MOST OF YOUR FRICTION

Distinguish Love versus Need

As I mentioned earlier, we unconsciously confuse need as love. We become transactional. This is not real love, it's an ego reaction, a *what are you doing for me lately* mentality that leaves us unprepared to embrace and handle the times of friction, when our needs are not being met. Yes, of course, a loving relationship must include support and understanding of your partner's needs. However, growing unconditionally loving and giving for their own sake must come with the deep understanding that there is a difference between the experience of your needs being met (receiving) from the awakening of love in your heart for your mate and sharing that love (giving).

Consider love as a verb, a state you choose to enter with your thoughts, words, and actions. Not just a feeling to wait for and receive based on outside events. We create it. As Monica Berg says in her book *Rethink Love*, "There's only one way to receive love, and that's to give it away."*

Visualization

I would like to invite you to PBR—*pause, breathe, and relax*. Allow yourself to imagine what it would be like to let go of the need to change your partner, even just for this moment in time. Put that burden down and allow yourself to open your heart and simply love your mate. Place your right hand over your heart and breathe in the simplicity of loving. Imagine that your love is swirling around: simple, light, warm, and filling you with the joy of dwelling in a loving and giving state. If you have resisting or competing thoughts, just witness those thoughts with acceptance, notice them and put them aside, for now. Then bring yourself back to the loving aura you have created within you and surrounding your beloved. Use this when you are feeling particularly overwhelmed.

See Your Relationship as a Practical Instrument

A human being becomes whole not in virtue of a relation to himself [only]
but rather in virtue of an authentic relation to another human being(s).

—Martin Buber†

To let your friction lead you to a deeper connection, we all need to carefully examine how we view the purpose of our relationship and how we

---

* Monica Berg, *Rethink Love: 3 Steps to Being the One, Attracting the One, and Becoming One* (Kabbalah Centre Publishing, 2020), 13.
† Martin Buber, *I and Thou* (Scribner, 1958).

define love. At the risk of sounding cold, I see any committed relationship as a practical instrument for growth, individually and as a couple. Remember: *Love grows as we grow.* The more you understand that the fundamental purpose of your relationship is to help you grow toward the loving person you essentially are—that is loving of others, loving of yourself, loving of your Source, loving of your life—then the more you will run after the growth opportunities awaiting inside your friction.

The classic romantic idea of love, still alive and well for most of society, only causes us to resist and judge times of conflict. The focus is on what we are getting, not how we are growing. It's too easy to fall into thinking that everything will be resolved if I just had the right person or if my partner would just do and be more of what I need. Our consumer mindset encourages us to bypass the necessary skin in the game that the inner blessing of lasting love requires.

Embrace Times of Conflict as a Gift

Friction in the world creates great revelations in history. This is how the world evolves: There is a problem and something new is generated that is better. Solving problems requires effort but the exponential benefits are inherent in the system of the universe. We see the role of opposition, of adversity and discomfort, as the catalyst for the force of forward motion in all disciplines because it's a universal truth. However, we falsely think our relationship is supposed to provide for us and not require this same degree of challenge and work. When we embrace and trust the process of our times of conflict, rather than rush through, seek quick fixes or avoid, we gain the chance to approach our conflict soulfully, so that the new and better version of ourselves, and our relationship, can reveal itself.

Use Radical Acceptance as a Tool

The paradox for growth is that we must accept what is, right here and now, in order to make change. Because we are so naturally inclined to resist, judge, or avoid pain and discomfort, we need to get ahead of this inclination. Acceptance is a powerful tool to shift our consciousness, and it means to completely acknowledge and accept the reality you are in, that your relationship is in—including the pain or discomfort. Avoidance and rushing through conflict are some of the biggest mistakes I see couples make. Accepting the reality when there's conflict slows the process down so you can examine the friction and get to the root of your problems. This sets you up to create the kind of change that will lead to a better relationship.

Be Open to Feedback from Your Mate

Feedback from your mate will likely serve as a guide for what will help you in every area of your life, not just with them. You have chosen this person and by your commitment have joined your souls together.

Research conducted by marriage gurus John Gottman and Nan Silver have shown the positive impact that accepting influence has on our relationship.[*] Accepting influence means that you deem your partner's opinion and perspective valuable and open your ears and heart to their perspective as a result. Our ego pride wants to be in control, to figure things out ourselves and justify our bad behavior. When the dust settles after a fight, or when having a calm heart to heart, most couples I see realize that their partner has some pretty good insight into the habits and traits that hinder them and the relationship. Important influential messages from our partners could address how you need to (1) be more present and take better care of yourself; (2) seek help for your anxiety or addiction; (3) stop putting so much pressure on yourself and love who you are; (4) get support to heal your trust issues or money trauma; (5) work on your frustration tolerance and impulse control; (6) have better

---

[*] John Gottman and Nan Silver, *The Seven Principles for Making Marriage Work: A Practical Guide from the Country's Foremost Relationship Expert* (Harmony, 2015).

work-life balance; (7) listen to and trust yourself instead of giving too much power to others.

IDEA INTO ACTION: WHAT'S CONFLICT LIKE FOR YOU

Write your first thoughts about each of the following:

- Growing up, conflict in my house . . .
- My attitude about disagreements is . . .
- Today in my relationship, when there is something to confront, I . . .
- If I were to approach conflict in a more helpful way for my relationship, it would be to . . .
- If I were to accept and even embrace the opportunity for growth during times of friction in my marriage, I believe . . .
- What I fear most when we are fighting or distant is . . .
- I can tell I'm avoiding or resisting addressing something when I'm . . .
- When I'm upset about something with my partner, it shows up as . . .
- If I saw my partner as my mirror when we fight, then I would realize I . . .
- If I don't focus on changing my partner to meet my needs, I am afraid that . . .

Answer "Yes" or "No" to the following:

- I am the peacemaker and avoid and try to smooth things over. Y or N?
- I turn to anger when I'm hurt. Y or N?
- I tend to shut down and retreat when I'm upset or hurt. Y or N?
- I prefer to wait to talk about issues and not in the heat of the moment. Y or N?
- I can't stand not sorting something out right way. Y or N?
- I tend to take too much blame when we have a fight. Y or N?

- It's hard for me to own up to what I'm doing that's upsetting my partner. Y or N?
- It's easy for me to feel like a victim when we have conflict. Y or N?
- I tend to keep my feelings in and sometimes it builds and bubbles over. Y or N?
- I sometimes use my power to try and win. Y or N?

Now that we have built a case for embracing conflict and have reframed friction as a potential gift and a good sign, let's get into how friction is showing up in your relationship (chapter 6) and then how to best utilize it for growth (chapter 7).

CHAPTER SIX

The Problems

It is not a lack of love, but a lack of friendship that makes unhappy marriages.

—Friedrich Wilhelm Nietzsche

In the first moments with new couples, I like to learn how they met and when they "knew" this was the one. I want to know the seed of their relationship and help them remember the beginning as I prepare for the important next question, "Where do you need help in your relationship?" Often, it's a last straw incident added to a slow-brewing problem that inspired what most people dread and put off, finding a counselor. This chapter is about the problems that most couples experience, and the emotional pain they are struggling with. At first, I often hear a broad complaint like, "We just don't communicate," which typically means, "We fight like cats and dogs." As the dialogue unfolds, I find the pain and fear that motivated them to seek help, and the problem areas in the relationship at the root.

This chapter is divided into two parts. Part 1 will explore the emotions associated with the problems in your relationship. Part 2 will go over what I call the *eight friendships* of your relationship in which the problems tend to play out. It's important that you see yourselves in this chapter, how you are feeling in your relationship right now, and some of the pressure points that are creating the problems between you and your mate. Even though you are not sitting across from me in my office, I want to make sure you feel that I get what you're dealing with because how else could you feel hopeful that I can offer you solutions?

PART 1: HOW DO YOU FEEL IN YOUR RELATIONSHIP?

Don't be afraid of your uncomfortable feelings: embrace them as a tool, a guide map for change. Feelings are here to teach you something. They might take you to a deeper root as it did for Nicole as she looked in the mirror in chapter 5. Getting to know how you feel in your relationship can give you clarity about yourself, which is an essential step for taking a healing path with your partner. It can be difficult to identify and be present with your more vulnerable feelings, much less putting words to them. This is essentially why I wanted to provide some thought starters to help you discover and put words to your own experience.

Identifying your feelings in the relationship is not for the sake of building more fodder for the case against your partner, or to deepen resentment and lack of appreciation. Rather, knowing yourself and your feelings is a stepping stone to using your conflict for growth. *You cannot solve a problem if you cannot identify and understand your own heart, and then ultimately your partner's.* Further, naming your feelings should be calming. Inner knowing brings a connection inside yourself that can make you feel more in control and centered. In turn, you can more effectively address a problem with your partner.

Find Your Emotions: Let's Start Here

This chapter is not about solving or elaborating on the problems in your relationship, but rather identifying them as a first step. Solutions for the pain in your relationship will be addressed as you continue to move through the pillars toward a fulfilling relationship.

Step 1: *Taking your Emotional Temperature:* Take a look at the list below of the most common emotional struggles I see in therapy. See which ring true for you.

- Angry and sad because my needs are not being met
- Overwhelmed by the fighting
- Unheard because my partner won't listen or change
- Unjustly blamed for the problems in the relationship
- Feeling unwanted or loss of interest in sex
- Unappreciated for all I do and who I am
- Controlled and judged for wanting to express myself
- Crushed by the betrayal of a secret relationship, addiction, or abuse
- Not respected from frequent criticism, blame, and contempt
- Missing the connection, spark, and communication once shared
- Bored, lacking fun—intellectually, spiritually, and sexually
- Frustrated from differences in personality, lifestyle, attachment style, values, or goals
- Lonely because my partner is emotionally unavailable
- Stressed from life's responsibilities, leaving little room for me or time as a couple
- Inadequate because I can't seem to make my partner happy
- Fearful about our future together

Step 2: *Your Partner's Emotional Temperature:* With your partner's feelings in mind, read through the list of challenging emotions a second time. What have you heard from your partner about how they feel? Try and sense what maybe they haven't told you directly? Expanding out of oneself and building empathy is a necessity for a soulful bond.

Self-Reflection

After reading through these common emotional struggles:

- Which stood out and resonated with you?
- Which emotion(s) feels most important to address in the following pages?

- Next, reflect on which emotions you sense are most prominent for your partner.

PART 2: WHAT SETS OFF THE PROBLEMS

You have narrowed in on your feelings in the relationship, and did your best to imagine your partner's, so now let's talk about the relationship themes that bring on friction and these painful emotions in your relationship. Here are the broad-based areas that I see which bring relationship problems to the surface: (1) Communication, (2) Sex, (3) Betrayal, (4) Domestic vs Paid Work, (5) Attachment Style, (6) Overall Desire, (7) Money, (8) Religion/Spirituality, (9) Parenting, (10) Lifestyle, and (11) In-laws.

The Eight Friendships in Your Marriage Wheel

In Figure 6.1, you'll see what I call the marriage wheel, including the *Eight Friendships* (spokes) that make up the well-being of modern-day committed relationships (seven for those who do not have children or pets). Just as the wheel leans on its various components to turn effectively, marriages run on a similar principle of interconnectedness. When one or more of the friendships are not functioning well, friction and all those painful feelings come rushing in. Sometimes one weak friendship spoke can be absorbed by other strong ones. More often, because of the notion of connectivity, when one friendship is weak and off-balance, eventually, other spokes of the relationship are impacted. Furthermore, just like a wheel that is designed for continual movement, the spokes of long-term committed relationships must account for constant change to keep the relationship alive and well. As the famous Buddha quote reminds us, "Everything changes, nothing remains without change."

What is the main message for partners when one or more of their "friendships" are weak or off-balance? *They are being called to grow!* That is, if they want their marriage to remain and in such a way that is

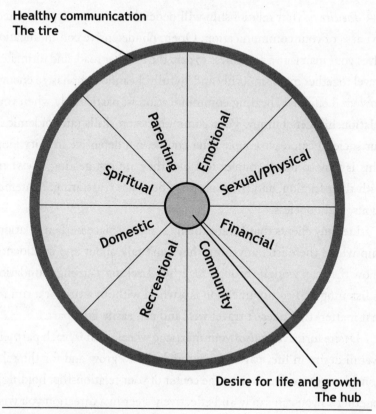

**Healthy communication
The tire**

Parenting
Emotional
Spiritual
Sexual/Physical
Domestic
Financial
Recreational
Community

**Desire for life and growth
The hub**

Figure 6.1   The Marriage Wheel

alive and fulfilling. Again, making friends with growth is the primary message for all the chapters in Pillar 2.

The Tire and Hub: Communication and Desire

Before we dive deeper into the eight friendships, please take notice of the two other components in the image above, the tire and the hub. These are both vital for keeping the eight friendships of your marriage wheel balanced, moving forward, and growing strong. So much so that without the tire and the hub, improving any of the eight friendships becomes almost impossible.

The tire of your relationship will depend on the quality and effectiveness of your communication. Open, nondefensive communication gives your marriage a sturdiness to grip the rougher road, and ultimately travel together more smoothly and joyfully. I cannot emphasize enough how vital effective, healing communication is, particularly when your relationship gets bumpy. Poor communication skills (an epidemic in our society) can leave couple after couple in a defensive infinity loop. This is why so many couples feel like they are not getting anywhere with their friction, and then marriage becomes frustrating, contemptuous, and hopeless.

I tell my clients that I want them to get to a place in their relationship where there isn't anything they can't talk about and confidently know they can work it through together. Lacking a strong foundation in listening and communication is a wheel without a tire (or a rim for that matter) that doesn't travel well and can easily fall apart.

Desire forms *the hub* of your marriage wheel. That is, each partner's overall desire in life, particularly the desire to grow and for the relationship to grow. Desire is at the center of your relationship, holding it together so you can safely and effectively steer in a direction you wish to go. To the degree that both partners desire more out of life, desire each other and the relationship, and are willing to put in the effort it takes to grow, the marriage wheel can move forward and upward, especially during more difficult times. You can't inject your desire into someone's lack of desire, but you can elevate the relationship by the work you do within yourself.

As you read through the eight friendships, begin thinking about your compatibilities and the differences between you that cause conflict and emotional struggles.

- **Emotional Friendship**
  A strong emotional friendship means couples share a sense
  of intimacy and vulnerability together where communication

abounds. There is a deep rapport, appreciation, and respect for one another, replete with private jokes and affection for their idiosyncrasies. Couples feel warm, safe, and connected. Partners know and trust that they are a cherished priority and their well-being and happiness are cared about for its own sake.

Partners who are emotionally intimate friends show their love through knowing their mates well and attuning to one another with positive regard. They willingly take care of each other when they are sick or need extra support. They trust one another and take feedback to heart, even things that are hard to hear. Couples who have opposing attachment styles, or some variability on the continuum, can have a harder time navigating their emotional friendship. Some people simply have a harder time with emotional connection, whether that be from falling on the avoidant or the insecure/anxious side of the scale. Our early relationships with our primary caregivers have great influence on our attachment style, so they are very deep rooted. You can still grow your emotional friendship with differing attachment styles by working on understanding the vulnerabilities of each style and by creating a social contract that considers the needs of each partner.[*]

• **Sexual/Physical Friendship**

A strong sexual and physical relationship mean two different things, although they can overlap. Having a strong sexual friendship means an erotic and sensual one. Partners who value their sexual friendship appreciate the fundamental communication that their sexual connection provides. They care about their partner's sexual satisfaction and their

---

[*] Stan Tatkin, *Wired for Love: How Understanding Your Partner's Brain and Attachment Style Can Help You Defuse Conflict and Build a Secure Relationship* (New Harbinger, 2024).

generosity is expressed sexually. Even at times if they feel lazy or not naturally aroused, partners with a strong sexual friendship make time to be creative and enjoy this very special experience together. Partners navigate their differing sexual drives with respect and openly communicate their needs, desires, fantasies, and preferences.

The physical friendship includes affection and touch. Partners with a strong physical friendship rub each other's shoulders as they walk by, or maybe rub a special place that only they save for each other. They hold hands, snuggle, hug slowly, and feel something missing when they don't kiss good morning, or when their beloved is not beside them in bed. When feeling ungrounded or dealing with conflict, those with a strong physical connection can regulate emotionally by physical touch, perhaps a hand reaching out, a gentle brush of the cheek, catching their scent, or a long hug.

- **Financial Friendship**

A strong financial friendship means couples are generally on the same page about how money is spent, saved, donated, and valued. The communication is open with no secrets, hoarding, or white lies. They involve each other in the big picture, and if desired, in the small picture of their financial hygiene and goals. They consider their finances "ours" and not "mine." Each partners' contribution is accepted, valued, and appreciated with an expanded definition of the currency, beyond dollars and cents, that makes their lives together whole and sound. Any resentments, sense of unfairness, or betrayals are communicated openly without blame and for the sake of growth and creating a healthier connection.

- **Community Friendship**

The community friendship most valued is the children and family they created together. A couple who shares a strong community friendship appreciates being part of a collective and adding value to the larger group they belong to together. This communal experience yields a deep and unique fulfillment and is a friendship that leans most couples who have marriage doubts toward trying to make it work. For some, leaving the marriage can even mean risking estrangement from the children. Community friendships also involve the shared experience of the families from which each partner was born (aka in-laws), and/or a friendship group, neighborhood, charity, social club, or a religious or spiritual community.

Some partners struggle with the community aspect of their relationship when they don't agree on parenting, don't deal with conflict effectively, or if they have differing attachment and recreation styles from the rest of the family unit. Being good community friends means that in-law issues are dealt with in consideration for the priority that the marriage holds. Partners who have a strong community friendship enjoy the version of their mates, and the connection they share, in the context of the larger group.

- **Recreational Friendship**
Now we are talking relaxation, laughter and *fun*. Couples who have a strong recreational friendship are great playmates and view relaxing in the same way. They enjoy some (not necessarily all or most) shared hobbies and avenues for leisure and playtime. They have a similar relationship to the need for fun and can relax enough together to laugh and even be silly (depending on their personality of course). They might enjoy traveling together, going out to eat, playing golf, hiking, or skiing, going to museums, throwing dinner parties, beach time, camping, reading, trying new cities, biking, going to concerts, or even a favorite Netflix show. If you take a Sunday, a vacation, or a day off and see how couples handle

that open time, you can get an idea where they stand in their recreational friendship.

This is where lifestyle and work-life balance come into play. Some couples have the same idea of the kind of life they want to live while others are quite different. Couples with a strong recreational friendship are naturally aligned with many of their interests and lifestyle choices, and when they are not, they genuinely support their mate's happiness. They make sure to find common ways to have fun together as a couple. They express their needs and desires respectfully and listen to their partner because they truly care.

- **Domestic Friendship**
  Our domestic friendship introduces the least fun part of many couple's relationship and can be fraught with friction and can even be an eroticism and joy killer. Of all the friendships, this one has become a growing inferno of importance to the couples I meet with, especially the younger couples and the more seasoned folks who are rethinking the traditional roles. Where the roles were once clear and defined, they have become open, expansive, and blurred. Overall, this is huge progress for domestic democracy and support, mutually involved parenting, and balance for all human beings—but boy does this transition create waves.[*]

The behind-the-scenes, never-ending thinking and emotional tasks needed to manage a household (aka invisible labor or mental load) are pressing their way into the currency of a relationship as our society has increased the awareness and appreciation for the uneven and overwhelming strain that many partners (often women) face. Partners who have a strong

---

[*] Eve Rodsky, *Fair Play: A Game-Changing Solution for When You Have Too Much to Do (and More Life to Live)* (Penguin Publishing Group, 2021).

domestic friendship (1) talk about their expectations about shared domestic life, (2) negotiate and delegate tasks (inside and outside of the relationship), (3) do not lose sight of what they appreciate about their partner, and (4) make room for fun in their relationship, not just dividing chores.

- **Parenting Friendship**
  Often an extension of the domestic friendship, couples who have a strong parenting friendship are comfortable with the way parenting responsibilities are shared and divided. They appreciate being partners together for an endeavor they agree cannot be matched in importance—raising happy, healthy children into self-sufficient adults. The parenting friendship includes so much more than the tasks required to get the job done at the end of the day. A strong parenting friendship means sharing the love and joy, the pain and concern, the surprises and humor, that no one else in the world could possibly feel as the two of you do. A strong friendship as coparents means being filled with gratitude for the beautiful soul(s) that you are raising.

  Some couples really struggle when they have differing parenting styles. For example, how children are disciplined, the way sleep and food are handled, what is expected of them at school and in sports, and what privileges they are given: these are top triggers for friction among parents. Ignorance, lack of self-awareness, and relying on the way we were raised seem to be the biggest culprits for haphazard parenting that can lead to emotionally charged differences and not enough couple time. Regardless of baseline differences, strong parenting friends appreciate the input from their coparent and turn to neutral and agreed-upon parenting experts to learn the most effective approach for rearing young people into balanced adults. They make sure to balance time spent on their own amid the demands of parenting, making their partner and their marriage priorities.

- **Spiritual Friendship**
Couples who share a spiritual friendship first and foremost appreciate that there is *no coercion in spirituality*. From this fundamental idea, good spiritual friends give one another space to find their own unique path whether that be a religion, connecting with nature, yoga, meditation, living their values, charity work, the journey to their higher self, their best self, or whatever resonates with them. Spiritual friends might inspire or invite one another closer to a path or spiritual idea, but it's very dangerous to impose our religious or spiritual agenda onto our partner. Each soul has a unique desire and path for connecting with something bigger than themselves and to the higher and better version of who they are. Couples who have a strong spiritual friendship honor their own spiritual path and their partner's free will to do the same.

That being said, nothing can take a relationship to a deeper and sweeter level than growing more spiritually connected, especially finding a wisdom or path to share together. A spiritual connection is the key to creating a soulful marriage. I define a spiritual friendship as a bond that a couple builds together through how they live their spiritual values and beliefs and support one another to become who they are meant to become.

Many of the couples I meet with, who feel unhappy or empty in their relationship, don't realize that it's a spiritual friendship they are missing. Whether it's through our traditional affiliations or our spiritually minded practices, bringing purpose or the divine into our relationship is the secret sauce for keeping our relationship perpetually alive— because we are connecting the relationship to endlessness.

Case: Meet Sarah and Todd: I Don't Feel Emotionally Connected

Sarah began coming to see me when the last of her four children flew the coop and went off to college. For her husband, not that much changed because his work demanded so much of his time and focus. For Sarah, who stopped practicing law years ago, her whole world and sense of purpose went out the door with her children. Left in the wake was Sarah's realization that the connection in her marriage was based on their parenting, community, and domestic friendships with a wide-open chasm for their emotional and spiritual friendship. They had some degree of recreational friendship because they loved hiking together but that had atrophied as the years went on. They were getting a crash course in the lesson that the marriage wheel is always turning, and that without change their wheel was being compromised. Their problem with emotional connection became an invitation to grow, more of a two-arm push forward because they were terrified of losing their whole marriage wheel, which they treasured.

Case: Meet Sam and Lance: Is This Relaxing to You?

These partners love to take vacations, but their idea of vacation differs greatly. Sam considers it a vacation to enjoy long mornings in the hotel room, relaxing and savoring the experience. Then, maybe around noon, he likes to venture out and enjoy the beach or town experience. Lance, on the other hand, sees the hotel as a launching pad, a place to sleep. But he can't get out of there fast enough to explore all the sights and culture of wherever they go. This same couple has a totally different definition of relaxing when they are at home as well. Sam defines relaxing as sitting on the couch reading or watching something together. Lance, on the other hand, finds sitting still on the couch anything but relaxing. It makes him feel restless. He prefers to do stretches on the floor or write alongside

Sam while he watches something. For Sam and Lance, their lack of compatibility over how to have fun led to fighting, each feeling a lack of connection and pressure to be someone they're not. They are an example of partners who before they strengthened their recreational friendship were at risk for a bad outcome. Their bickering over leisure was bleeding into their sexual, domestic, and emotional connection as well.

IDEA INTO ACTION: JOURNAL EXERCISE TO ASSESS YOUR MARRIAGE WHEEL

Consider the eight friendships of the marriage wheel in Figure 6.1, as well as the tire (communication) and the hub (desire).

Step 1: Answer the following question about your eight friendships:
Which friendships are stronger, and which are weaker? That is, where do you find the most compatibility and where do you find the most of your differences?

Step 2: Answer the following questions about your communication (tire) and desire (hub):
How do you and your partner handle communication, especially when there's friction? Do you get somewhere better and closer after a fight?
How would you describe your level of desire, from weaker to stronger, about what you want in life and especially your desire for a better relationship and the effort and growth this entails?

Step 3: Ask your partner to take a look at the marriage wheel, and ask them to answer the same questions above.

CHAPTER SEVEN

Solutions Begin with Soulful Communication

Being heard is so close to being loved that for the average person, they are almost indistinguishable.

—David Augsburger

BEGIN WITH PREPARATION

These next few chapters are *all about soulful communication*, that is, self-aware and compassionate communication, with an eye toward growth and connection. Bringing in the marriage wheel, you might recall that the quality of your communication is so all-encompassing that it forms the tire itself, determining whether you travel at all and how you handle the rougher terrain. Growing and going anywhere good or better in your relationship begins with open and respectful communication.

It's important to keep in mind that even the most skillful, emotionally intelligent communicators don't necessarily make their way to a fulfilling marriage. For that, you need all four pillars. But soulful communication is a beginning and a profound gateway for making the most of each pillar, especially this one: growth.

Now let's dive in to making the most of your communication. The first step is preparation. To pave the way for mutual solutions, ones that bring you closer, you must prepare yourself before even uttering a word.

This chapter will focus first on building a case for the importance of investing effort into your words and dialogues, more than we naturally tend to, and the preparation required to have more productive conversations. It's beneficial for each partner to take on the responsibility of becoming a better listener and communicator, but even when only one partner does so, this can make a big difference.

The What and the How

When couples start coming to see me, I make sure to explore and help them differentiate between the *"what"* of their problems and the *"how."* The *"what"* means what are they fighting about, what is provoking them, which of the eight friendships are stronger, and which have gaping holes? Does their friction center around parenting, in-laws, sex, insulting tones, or all of the above? Are they unhappy with how they are treated, the lack of a spiritual connection, broken trust, how tasks are divided in the household, or are they not having enough fun?

The *"how"* refers to the process. What approach are partners using to address their friction or emotional struggles; mostly, are they talking things through, and how? Most couples report they stink at this part. They get defensive with each other, shut down, don't feel heard, feel dismissed, see no possible solution, and start to pull away. Emotional space leads to the need for physical space because the nervous system can't handle the strain of another failed, unproductive argument. Remember my soapbox about adding communication and listening skills into our school systems? We must realize that we are not well trained for one of the most important ingredients for success in life, and especially in our relationships. We think communication is saying what's on your mind. That's a small percentage of being effective and even smaller when it comes to communicating soulfully.

The inability to gain forward motion, mostly because partners are not really hearing each other, is often why couples come to counseling. This is exactly why I begin the healing journey with preparing couples and training them to have compassionate, vulnerable conversations. The key is for both partners to feel heard and validated. This is the *"how"* that makes all the difference. Better communication patterns must come first to give the marriage some traction as partners deal with their issues together. Some couple's issues resolve on their own once they improve the skill and quality of their communication. The destructive communication patterns themselves are the dominating problem. For many others, better communication provides a much-needed gateway to address their perpetual friction with an open heart. They feel closer in the process because that's what feeling heard does and they are able to find simple solutions through their thoughtful dialogue. Without improving the *"how"* when it comes to our friction, we don't stand a chance for creating something better, which is the whole point of the friction to begin with.

Creating a Sanctuary Environment

Partners who want their relationship to be a *sanctuary* in their lives must learn how to create an environment in which they and their partner feel secure and comfortable. Not meant in a necessarily religious way, but just like a sanctuary that is sacred, we are the ones responsible for creating an atmosphere where everyone is seen and valued. In a sanctuary, we are more likely to find respectful words and voice tones, kindness and warmth. Each person in the sanctuary is responsible for creating this refuge of peace and safety. Extending that to our relationship, partners want to be able to trust and confidently say, "We can talk about anything."

Communication holds the power to build or destroy our sanctuary. Even if the quantity and quality of your communication doesn't break you up as a couple, it will still directly impact whether your relationship grows more joyful and loving. The environment you create by ineffective and hurtful communication, or the mere lack of, can reduce your relationship into mediocrity, emptiness, and even contempt.

The Power of Feeling Heard

After learning to use effective communication tools, one of my clients grasped the power of hearing his partner and feeling heard. He told me, "Being heard feels like being loved to me, like a warm pool to slide into versus fighting and stomping my feet, demanding, 'love me!'" I watch the magic unfold right in front of my eyes, time and again, when I work with couples to help them "hear" and be heard. Partners' more vulnerable and authentic selves can come out, and you can visually see their bodies soften and relax as their hearts open into a peaceful smile. This is where the unexpected solutions to your problems reveal themselves.

Six Truths about Listening

- Fixing is not listening.
- Deep, compassionate listening does not mean you agree or require that you agree.
- Effective listening is not just something you're born with; it takes effort and is a trainable skill.
- We often think we are better listeners than we are.
- We don't naturally grow better at listening the older we get.
- No gender is classified as a better listener. Although, generally speaking, with some exceptions, women seek communication for connection, cooperation, and expressing emotions. Men place higher value on facts and can feel uncomfortable with highly personal and emotional subjects, especially for long stretches.

Know Your and Your Partner's Communication Style

It's important to learn what good communication sounds like and to also identify what you do in your communication style, especially when there's friction, that creates defensiveness and builds a wall. Partners need to self-reflect and identify key words and gestures that either set them off or make them feel safe and calm. It's important to talk with each other about what works and what doesn't, especially when you argue. Better to share your preferences not while in the heat of an argument, but when it's neutral so you can more calmly negotiate your arguing style. For example, some partners prefer direct language and it's not a problem if voices get raised, while (most) others need calm and a softer approach. Some like to talk while on a walk and others need the privacy of no one around. Certain partners need some time to collect their thoughts while others want to dive in spontaneously. It's also important to become emotionally intelligent about your and your partner's "hot" or activating words, phrases, tones, volume, etc., to avoid them.

Soulful Communication

What makes our communication soulful? The intention. When you direct your desire toward growth and healing—and ultimately toward a closer bond, you are primed for soulful communication. With this intention, you are more likely to see and speak to the essence of goodness and light within your partner, and in so doing, connect to the same in yourself. Caring about growth and unity in your communication requires personal responsibility, self-awareness, courage, an open heart, and tremendous patience. When you are coming from this higher place within yourself, you are better able to find calm and perspective. There's more room to consider your dreams as well as your beloved's and look at whatever you face from a win-win perspective, versus a I win, you lose. It's about us, not just about me.

I give fair warning, when your emotions are flying high, being measured and compassionate is one of the hardest things you will ever do. Once the human ego gets rolling, it can feel like stopping a freight train at full speed. In those reactive moments, it's harder to remember that your partner is a spark of holiness, filled with goodness, just as you are; and your desire for healing and growth can fly right out the window. The urge to take control and get your own point across becomes all-consuming, overshadowing the love you truly feel. Each and every one of us needs all the tools we can get our hands on to become more proficient in communicating—*especially listening*—heart to heart, soul to soul. Otherwise, we become one beast-like ego clashing into another's. In an office setting I put a quick stop to escalations when they erupt, because they are not who these partners really are or want to be. At home, you and your partner will need to be extra cautious of these moments.

The biggest enemy when fighting isn't one another, it's defensiveness. This is the body's fear-based survival nature protecting our pride, inclined to blame, needing to be right, jumping to conclusions, seeing only our view, resisting ownership of our part, and seeking to feel better NOW. Soulful communication is non-defensive communication and the path forward to have healing conversations, albeit sometimes difficult ones.

Negative Communication Is Better than No Communication

Not to encourage negative communication here, but I want to highlight the danger in not communicating. When couples are not fighting at all, this likely means they are not communicating, not engaging. John Gottman's research[*] on relationships revealed much insight on this topic. His research found that after three years into a relationship—when by this time our warts and bad breath are fully exposed and the dopamine rush from infatuation has come down into reality—if partners are not fighting, even about the little things, it's a sign of disengagement, distancing, and stagnation. This lack of real, engaged talking is particularly toxic and damaging for a relationship, and the hardest to work with in couples counseling. When I'm meeting with couples, it's not only a good sign when couples tell me about their complaints and fighting because of the growth opportunity, but this also tells me they

---

[*] John M. Gottman, *The Marriage Clinic: A Scientifically Based Marital Therapy* (Norton, 1999).

still care. Desire is the hub on your marriage wheel. Arguing indicates engagement and that your desire is alive.

Many people cope with distressing emotions by suppressing their feelings and distancing themselves rather than addressing their pain points through speaking up. The emotional conversations can feel overwhelming, so withdrawal becomes their go-to response. Whether they are people pleasers or avoiders, the inclination to "not deal" or resist making waves carries on, until one day they've had enough and their distance leaves nothing left to repair.

Case: Meet Gerardo and Nina

One such sad scenario comes to mind between Gerardo and Nina. Gerardo was drawn to his wife because of her strength, beauty, and surety in herself. She was not as warm as he would have preferred, didn't express her love in words much either, but he accepted the love she gave in her own way. Whenever he tried to express himself or his needs, not an easy task for him, he would cower to her point of view all too quickly. Over time, he stopped even considering the idea of changing their marriage style and withdrew. They never fought, so Nina was stunned by how unhappy Gerardo had been. At some point, over decades of supporting each other's career and raising a family together, Gerardo began to have secret relationships. By the time they came to see me, Gerardo was finally ready to tell Nina how unhappy he was, but by then he had checked out almost completely. Therapy was merely something to check off his list, so he didn't feel as guilty about leaving the marriage. I quickly realized he was not in a place to really care enough to work on the relationship. He let his desire for his marriage dwindle down to a pulp.

Gerardo and Nina represent what can happen when you avoid your issues and don't have those difficult, but necessary conversations. We have patterns that run deep, and avoidance is one of the most destructive to long-term love. Even if you are afraid about opening up, it's important to take a step to receive the support you need to overcome the barriers that keep you from being honest and authentic with your feelings and needs. It was too late for this couple, so I did my best to help each of them take their lessons forward in their lives and referred them to individual counseling.

Takeaway: It's Okay if It Gets Heated, to a Point

I share this sad story to make sure it's clear that truthful communication can mean we are not always calm, and that tensions can rise and fly out of our mouths. First of all, always being calm is not realistic. We are made of flesh and blood, not stone and steal. Let yourself, even make yourself, engage. Share what's bothering you; it is okay to sometimes let it get messy and hot. The most important thing is to not allow your initial anger, frustration, finger-pointing, victim energy, or lashing out be your predominant and persistent communication style. The blowup should be temporary and followed up with the necessary prep work to go back to it, once you're ready to create a more objective and productive experience. With time and practice, you will find that your preparation stage for having impactful conversations will build momentum and come more naturally and quickly. This will begin to eliminate the blowups as a means to get the sludge moving. Nonetheless, in the long term, it's better to engage than to distance and withdraw.

What Preparation Looks Like

Creating healing communication, and a sanctuary environment in which to do so, requires preparation. While it's not always realistic to have long preparation time, every bit that we do accumulates and sets up for a better outcome. In brief, getting yourself ready for a purposeful conversation is a four-step process:

Step 1: Pause, to regulate your emotions.
Step 2: Get in touch with yourself.

Step 3: Move into the right state of consciousness.

Step 4: Honestly address the issue.

Step 1: The Power of Pause

The first tool I want fighting couples to take home after their first session is the almighty pause. Whether it's stepping away, going outside, PBR (pause, breathe, relax), developing a silly code word together to shut the reactivity down, whatever it takes to elongate the space between your reactive feelings and acting or speaking them out. To help appreciate the importance of the pause, please consider the research by professor and psychologist Daniel Kahneman. In his book *Thinking, Fast and Slow,*[*] Kahneman explains that we each have two distinct thinking systems. System 1 is automatic and fast thinking, and System 2 is slow and intentional, hence the title of his book. Much of our error-prone decision-making we later regret, especially in relationships, stems from using our fast-thinking mode, which operates automatically with no effort and no sense of voluntary control. In this mode, we are reactive and self-centric, and we don't take the time for the big or long-term picture. This is biologically our most common go-to. Our slow-thinking mode generates more conscious, well-thought-out responses and decisions. This mode requires more effort and opens us to a more compassionate consideration of our partners needs and feelings and for how our behavior might impact them. Slower thinking System 2 gives us a better perspective for problem solving.

The pause is the quickest cue and path to begin *s l o w i n g* down. Sometimes this could mean a minute, five minutes, or five days. This slowing down mechanism benefits us greatly so we are less prone to the snap judgments and words, the irrationality of thinking System 1. Pausing and preparing internally takes great strength because we are

---

[*] Daniel Kahneman, *Thinking, Fast and Slow* (Farrar, Straus and Giroux, 2011).

resisting our primal urges. System 2 allows us to awaken our soul nature, which paves the way for a more effective, soulful conversation.

Emotional Regulation Zone

When I work with couples, they love when I show them a chart much
like Figure 7.1 below, because it visualizes what is happening to their
nervous systems when they are taken over by the emotional stress of
life or in the relationship.

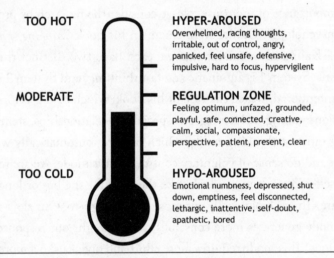

TOO HOT

HYPER-AROUSED
Overwhelmed, racing thoughts,
irritable, out of control, angry,
panicked, feel unsafe, defensive,
impulsive, hard to focus, hypervigilant

MODERATE

REGULATION ZONE
Feeling optimum, unfazed, grounded,
playful, safe, connected, creative,
calm, social, compassionate,
perspective, patient, present, clear

TOO COLD

HYPO-AROUSED
Emotional numbness, depressed, shut
down, emptiness, feel disconnected,
lethargic, inattentive, self-doubt,
apathetic, bored

Figure 7.1   Emotional Regulation Zones

Notice the three temperatures: too hot, too cold, and moderate.
These correspond to your nervous system in a state of hyper-arousal,
hypo-arousal, and when you are in the regulation zone, respectively.
When you feel emotionally distressed, you have your unique bandwidth
for how much you can comfortably tolerate and absorb. This is your
regulation zone, which can also be called your window of tolerance.* In

---

* Daniel J. Siegel, *The Developing Mind: Toward a Neurobiology of Interpersonal
Experience* (Guilford Press, 1999).

your relationship, you have everything good to gain by learning how to bring yourself toward your regulation zone in order to more effectively address your friction.

Some of the biggest mistakes couples make is to duke it out when they are emotionally dysregulated, either too hot or too cold. When life stress rises, our nervous system overload kicks us into hyper-arousal, which can trigger feeling overwhelmed, anxious, irritable, racing thoughts, and a more urgent feeling of "I have to fix this feeling now!" Another response to stress is feeling numbed by it, as you see with hypo-arousal. Hyper- and hypo-arousal are both indicators that the emotional stress triggered in our bodies is literally more than our nervous system can handle. Take the time to read through the descriptors next to each nervous system state and see which you recognize most about yourself—and your partner.

In comes the almighty pause. Whatever it takes to regulate yourself is the first and most important step you need to take. Regulation is your responsibility. Sometimes couples can coregulate together. For example, I'll invite some couples to sit closely, knee to knee, each putting their hands on their partner's heart across from them. Then they PBR, pause, breathe, and relax, together till they begin breathing in the same rhythm together. Physical touch can co-regulate partners, like a hug or a hand reaching out, and so can listening with compassion.

When couples fight openly and get defensive or withdraw and shut down, this indicates the stress they are experiencing is out of their range to tolerate. This is where the chaos takes place. On the other hand, when you and your partner are in your regulation zone, this is where the good stuff happens. You feel full versus empty, calm versus racing, engaged versus checked out, safe versus panicked, alive versus numb, connected to yourself versus dead inside. When you are in your optimum zone, you can think and feel at the same time. That is, you can fluidly go back and forth between fast and slow thinking to give you the power to choose the best way to handle whatever situation or conflict you are facing.

The work before you open your mouth is the most important and influential part of having conversations that heal versus destroy your sanctuary. Pausing and preparing is about connecting within for energy before you reach for energy from your partner. We are all in training here.

Steps 2 and 3: The 5 Ws

Once you have paused and calmed the emotional storm, at least to some degree, now it's time for steps 2 and 3, that is, *getting in touch with yourself* and *moving into the right consciousness*. These steps elongate the pause and further prepare you for a soulful interaction. I use five W questions to consider before speaking up: (1) Why, (2) What, (3) When, (4) Whether, and (5) the Way. I know all these steps may sound like a lot of work, just to have a conversation, but the effort you put in on the front end literally will make all the difference for a better outcome and save you effort on the backside. Rest assured, this process goes faster and becomes more second nature each time you practice pausing and do the work inside yourself before you address the problem.

- *Why*
  Why do I want to say something?
  This inner question is to awaken self-awareness. We so often lash out before we really tap into the real issue underneath. Taking responsibility for your relationship with yourself is the first step. You'll want to explore your inner agendas and needs, where you might be feeling stressed, empty, or unfulfilled. I know for me, I am always more likely to say things I regret to my husband when I feel anxious, insecure, or out of control. Asking why questions reels in the reactive tendency to seek energy outside, brings you back inside yourself and your regulation zone where you can access your slower thinking mode.
  To gain greater self-awareness amid your friction, asking yourself *"Why is this issue so important to me?"* is another

angle to take. Maybe there's a dream, need, or desire that is
particularly important to you with this friction point, and
you're seeking more support? Perhaps you dream of more
travel, a more loving environment, or want to finish something
important in your life. Maybe you're afraid what will happen if
this issue isn't addressed? Some other questions might be: "Do
I feel responsible for changing my partner?" or " Is this issue
bringing up something painful inside myself, maybe from
childhood?"

Why do I want to say something? also points us toward our
intention and is vital for bringing our minds into the right
state of consciousness. If you express being upset, are you
trying to bring your relationship closer in this moment, or are
you needing a place for your own frustration to land? Do you
want to vent your anger? Maybe so, but do you also want to
understand yourself and your partner better? Do you want to
grow closer from what just happened? Or do you need to be
right? What is the intention of your ego here and what if you
listened to your soul's intention?

Asking "Why" can help you remember to look for growth.

Becoming clear about your why can also help remind
you to be on the look for the growth opportunity, which is
very difficult to do when you're upset. Try pausing and asking
yourself:

"Why is this challenge here to benefit my growth in some way?"
Maybe this challenge is here to help you see something you
need to work on or heal in yourself? Keep the mirror mindset
handy from chapter 5 because you want to be curious within,
more than without. Look for patterns. Maybe you feel
unappreciated, overlooked in your relationship. While your
partner might very well be treating you that way, examine first
how you might be overlooking yourself. Maybe this challenge

is here to help you debunk the belief that you are only worthy when someone is recognizing you. Only you know the whispers of truth within, but the key is to take the time and care to ask yourself why.

The moment we hit on our lesson from this why question, so much of the emotional distress that makes us feel wronged dissipates. Anger subsides and leaves more room to see the good. When we seek and find our growth message, it's empowering because we are able to open ourselves up to change.

- **What**

What is the core message I want to communicate? What am I truly feeling and needing? Do I have a request? Do I need to be heard? What do I want my partner to understand and what are the words I can use that will keep them receptive? Without knowing what you want to say from the depths within, you leave yourself at risk to lash out when the negative, judgmental part of you takes over and says damaging things. For example, your ego may want to lash out with, "You're so bad at this," "You're so rude and insensitive," or "You never listen to me." When in reality, if you come from a place of owning your feelings and inner experience, your core message might sound like, "I feel angry, alone, and overwhelmed when you don't put things away. It feels as if you are waiting for me to clean up after you from room to room. I don't want any distance or anger in between us, so I don't know the best way to express how important this is to me so you can hear me."

- **When**

When would be the best time for a conversation to go well to bring us closer and to grow? Waiting till you are not emotionally dysregulated is best, as long as it's not avoiding. Avoiding is another form of reactive communication. The *when* question brings us back to the power of pause. When we are neutral and calm is best: honest but not reactive, reflective versus reactive.

The human ego seeks instant gratification, which for many it's to say something when you're feeling it. Like we will never address this, and it's going to go on forever unless I say something NOW! This is a delusion. The truth is just because you are feeling it doesn't mean you need to say it right then. In fact, often it's best to wait. When you are feeling distressed or in a need state, it's best to pause and connect to yourself from within; and then from there move to a place of more conscious choice to share what's on your mind.

Timing is so vital. We can and are often best to go back to issues when we are more grounded and prepared, clear about our intention for addressing the issues.

The decision to bring something up must also consider how frequently you and your partner are fighting and how frequently you have negative interactions. It's not just when to bring something up but also the frequency of negative comments or complaints we need to be tracking. Spread out your grievances: You will have another opportunity to share what you need or are observing later. Sometimes I suggest for a partner to postpone addressing something when there's been a lot of friction in the relationship. To balance things out, it can be helpful to focus on what is working well. Letting some things go allows for the right time to emerge and for the times that are heavier to be more manageable.

Regulating Your Nervous System

I encourage you to refer to the thermometer diagram above whenever emotions begin to feel overwhelming. Just the visual alone can remind you that you have the power and choice to regulate your own nervous system. Your body is a profound part of your relationship, influencing how you will react to conflict and emotional distress. When you fortify yourself with your glimmers, what you know helps you feel centered— in mind, body, heart, and spirit—you access the power you have to be in charge of your body reaction. This groundedness sets you up to pick the wisest time to address an issue. This takes practice.

- *Whether*

  You ultimately need to ask, *Is this something I should bring up at all*, at least for now? Will this encounter help me, my partner, and we as a couple grow? Am I putting too much weight on my partner for my happiness and well-being? The pause allows you to decide whether it's really worth bringing up. Without falling into avoidance, don't be afraid to wait days, weeks, or months if it means gaining clarity on your why, what, when, whether, and ultimately the best way. Ironically, a good way to know you're coming from your soul is when the urgency to talk about it has lessened. Instead, you might find a deep sense of knowing that having a difficult conversation is the best thing to do.

  The *whether* to bring up an issue overlaps with the *when* question because, with some time passing, you might realize that while I'm sensing that one of our marriage friendships needs some serious work, now when I'm still too angry or unsure what the growth is for me, makes this not the right time. If you allow yourself to make room for a *whether* question, you are taking the power of the reactive part of you out of the equation. When you consider the "whether" to bring something up or say something, this leaves the option that "hmm, maybe I will be okay if I don't say something." In so doing, you take the power out of the reactive self and move from need to love, from "you are responsible for my feelings" to "I am responsible for them and I am now in a position to be a true giver," even if it's to tell your partner how they have hurt you.

When you entertain *whether* to bring something up or make an issue of something, you can imagine what it might be like to let this go, or maybe just for now. Maybe you are not ready yet. Maybe they are not. Maybe your relationship needs a break from so much focus and friction. Time, and a pause that is pregnant with a *whether* question, might bring the realization that there are so many other more important traits and gifts your partner brings and if you do need to bring up this issue in the future, you want to make sure that you are in a consciousness of fullness and appreciation, versus lack and what's missing.

Caution: The Anger Bucket

Something we know about anger is that when it builds up, desire for the relationship goes down. This means sex, being close, spending time together, working on the relationship, doing loving things, seeing the good, and on and on. As we talked about earlier in this chapter, how negative communication is better than no communication, I want to reiterate the caution to not let things build up. Consider picturing a bucket where all of your hostile, frustrated, angry, irritated, resentful, disappointed feelings toward your partner go. You must take care of your own bucket. You do this in two ways: (1) Speak up when the time and mindset are right, and (2) embrace your partner as they are, with unconditional love and acceptance. They are BOTH important and one without the other can create a huge imbalance in your relationship.

IDEA INTO ACTION: JOURNALING FOR YOUR WHY, WHAT, WHEN, AND WHETHER

Step 1: Think of something that is bothering you about your partner or your relationship and write about the scenario or incident. Something that you either need to address and haven't felt ready to or perhaps something you've avoided or overlooked.

Step 2: Now, with the possibility that you'll communicate with your partner about this, consider first the following questions from above. That is:

- Why do I want to bring this up (for what purpose)? Why is this scenario coming to help me grow, or our relationship grow, in some way?
- What is the core message I want to communicate? What am I truly feeling and needing?
- When might be a good time? Am I ready? Am I avoiding? When will my partner be most receptive?
- Whether to bring this up, is this a topic that would benefit me and our relationship for me to address? What does our relationship need right now most?

Note: For a past argument that went poorly, you can use the above W questions to gain insight on where you could have approached it better. Going back to a previous argument, and assessing what would have been a better approach, can open up so many lessons as a couple. Remember, there are no mistakes, only learning.

Step 3: The fifth W, *the Way*, will be about having a conversation with your beloved about this or any issue. Chapter 8 and the remaining chapters of Pillar 2 will be your guide map for making the most of your conflict for the sake of growth and deeper connection.

CHAPTER EIGHT

The Way to Grow Closer through Your Conflict

When two people relate to each other authentically and
humanly, God is the electricity that surges between them.

—Martin Buber

THE FIFTH W, THE SOULFUL *WAY* TO FIGHT

Now, it's time to take your personal preparation to the next level. This chapter will introduce ways that you and your partner can prepare yourselves together for more soulful conversations when there's friction—and ultimately take what you learn into practice. We have entered into the fifth W of soulful communication, the Way. These next few chapters will be loaded with ideas and tools, tips and exercises that may feel like a lot to take in. Please take your time, digest, try some things out and then come back, again and again—whatever it takes because this is how instrumental healthy communication is for a relationship. Remember fighting is not a problem; it's actually a good sign. However, and this is a big however, the *way* you approach the friction can either mean you grow and grow closer, or you move apart and build walls and resentment.

Partners in a loving and happy marriage build what they share together in large part through growing more proficient in communication skills and habits—the kind that can turn their conflict into closeness. How? By truly listening to one another, with their hearts open. We think we are listening, but often we have an agenda. We use leading, conclusion-based questions (that are not true questions at all) and we wait for a point to jump in and tell our side. This is the ego wanting to rush in with our own needs, fearing everything isn't going to be okay for us otherwise. Further, we simply overlook the importance of building better communication skills, which are absolutely essential for the satisfying relationship we seek.

Breakthroughs

We grow as we learn to become better communicators and speak and listen more consciously. Becoming a more evolved communicator and listener is practical for the outcome of a better relationship, but the process has its own value for our growth journey. While our comfort-craving ego nature resists this, our soul wants to grow, wants to have empathy, wants the taste of unconditional love, and most of all is thrilled to come home again by the oneness you create together. In a soulful marriage, these safe and sacred conversations make way for breakthroughs within you and together. Healthy and compassionate communication creates a refuge so you can dig a little deeper, to learn something important that might be at the root of the conflict.

Maybe you learn something you didn't realize about your childhood relationships and how they are impacting you today, make some headway with your trust issues, or have an aha moment about yourself from your partner sharing with you something that bothers them. I see this all the time. For many, working through conflict to a better, closer place helps partners break cycles of relationship dysfunction in their lineage and puts new tools in their hands for future generations. Learning opportunities and awe-filled awakenings are endless when we keep defensiveness at arms-length and build one of life's most powerful skills—*diplomacy*.

Spiritual Diplomacy: I and Thou

Effective communication is the foundation of diplomacy. Not just for nations or political groups, diplomacy has its place at the head table of a close relationship. It can come off like a cold concept, but the opposite is true. To soften the term with my clients, I use "spiritual diplomacy" because it better relays the idea of growing more thoughtful and intentional in our dialogues.

Martin Buber, an existential philosopher, is known for his theory of a dialogue. In his epoch-making book, *I and Thou*,* Buber distinguishes an *I and thou* dialogue from an *I and it*. In our daily lives, we are more inclined to see others as objects for the sake of our own benefit. This is harsh, but honest about the human self-centric inclination. The *I and thou* mindset brings you to recognize the unique and whole being each person is and see them in a positive light. Buber had an intimate relationship with God and at the heart of his theology was the idea that only when you develop a genuine and intimate relationship with another do you move from an intellectual understanding of God and into a personal one. Engaging in more *I and thou* dialogues moves you away from a need-based relationship into an intimate loving one, with your partner and with your Source.

Spiritual diplomacy in your interactions builds warmth and a soul-to-soul connection because you are in receiving mode and giving mode at the same time: receiving mode because you have something you need to address, and you have a stake in how this relationship unfolds; giving mode because you know you can't get to where you want to go without viewing and treating your partner as a holy human being whose happiness you value equal to your own.

You want to see your relationship as one whole, think from a win-win perspective versus win-lose. If your partner goes down, you both go down. This collective mindset is how you build a true sanctuary. With

---

* Martin Buber, *I and Thou* (Scribner, 1958).

spiritual diplomacy, you move into giving mode by way of sensitivity to your partner's needs and being open to their perspective. You use intentional language based on what will help them receive your message best. This means putting effort into the *way* you use your words with democracy at the top of your mind, negotiating the issues in a balanced way, keeping both of you in mind.

When you are diplomatic, you are using calm, tactful, and respectful language. You are actively listening (not just actively communicating), which is the heart of effective, soulful communication. Further, you are not just listening for the words, but you are listening for the emotions, fears, dreams, and desires your partner is trying to convey or that you might sense beneath the surface. You can negotiate best when you try to see the world through your partner's eyes. Deep empathy is not easy because, for example, you can't feel your partner's headache when they have one. The effort to understand your partner is transforming you at the very foundation of your body nature.

Myth-Buster

Partners often think they should be free to say what they want, when they want, and how they want with the people closest to them, especially their spouse. Diplomacy can sound stiff and formal, like too much work and not natural. I receive pushback much like this so many times: "If I have to put so much thought into what I say and how I say it to my partner, then I'm not being true to myself. It's not only exhausting, but it's not genuine." That's a total illusion and I love dispelling this myth for the people I meet with. I share with them that even after thirty-eight years with my husband, I know that I am responsible for how I speak to my husband, that I need to put effort day in and day out to make sure I'm approaching him with spiritual diplomacy, treating him as my *Thou* and not my *It*. If I want things to go well, I need to be conscious of his buttons and what I have learned about him that helps us fight for more closeness, not fight for a personal win. This takes the F-word—effort, constant effort. We must all embrace this reality if we want to create a lasting and growing connection with our partner.

HOW TO BRING THE SOUL INTO THE ARGUMENT
(AKA TURN CONFLICT INTO CLOSENESS)

Spiritual diplomacy often needs to begin with some simple dos and don'ts. So many of our natural practices are downright harmful to healing during times of conflict. We make it worse instead of better. I often give partners who are newly coming to see me a handout like the one you see below. It's a first pass and overview of some universal *dos and don'ts* when it comes to lovingly and soulfully addressing any issue. Couples usually chuckle as they identify right off the bat some of the "*don'ts*" they are doing all too often. Please consider the list below and know that we will deepen these concepts throughout this chapter and the next.

THIRTEEN DOS AND DON'TS TO FIGHT PURPOSEFULLY:
RECOMMENDED RULES OF ENGAGEMENT

- **Select a good time and setting to talk about the issue.**
  Preferably not after 8 p.m. Consider your and your partner's circadian rhythm. Ask when a good time would be. Outside is better than inside. Sober helps, dare I say it's essential!
- **Sit eye to eye, knee to knee when discussing issues.**
  Open body language prompts the *I and thou* mindset, aka our hearts.
- **Use a language you know your partner will hear best.**
  This takes caring and emotional intelligence about your partner. Does your partner hear facts best or emotions? What words are less triggering? Do they like direct or softer talk? Do they like reassurance or appreciation before hearing a complaint?

- Do not play psychologist, especially about childhood or past relationships.
- Do not bring up past arguments or issues. Focus on one current issue or grievance at a time.
- No silent treatment. Do not refuse to talk.
- Pause and calm the emotional storm.
  If you're too angry or emotional, tell your partner you need some time to get calmer because you care about the relationship. Then you need to follow up.
- No name-calling, putting down, character assassination, or physical attack.
- Use a warm start-up, and avoid biased language and the blame game.
  Warm versus cold openings set the tone and direction of the argument or issue.
  ○ *Start with acknowledgment or appreciation.*
    Show your partner you have perspective and see the good in them.
  ○ *Use "I" messages that describe how you're feeling:*
    "I feel _____ when you _____ because _____."
  ○ *Avoid accusatory "You"-statements.*
    Avoid "You make me feel . . . ," "You are . . ." Turn these into "I" messages owning your feelings.
  ○ *Refrain from generalizations, such as using the words "always," "never," "should."*
- Use active listening skills.
  Reflect, validate, and show empathy. Ask open-ended questions.
- Focus on healing, not winning.
  Most fights come with one or both partners in pain. Allow room for underlying vulnerable feelings with an eye toward healing.

> • **Share and commit to what you will work on to do better next time.**
> • **Close with appreciation.**
> Share with your partner what you appreciate about them, what they shared, and how glad you are that they opened up to you.

Your Couple's Conflict Constitution

A foundational tool to prepare together for loving communication is to create your *conflict constitution*. This will be your Idea Into Action at the end of this chapter. Including the thirteen dos and don'ts above, I recommend that every partner reflect within themselves, then come together to create the customized dos and don'ts for your relationship—to navigate friction in the most productive, meaningful way.

Why is creating a conflict constitution so important? *Couples need to communicate about communicating.* Discussing your preferences for how to handle conflict is a vital way to respect your unique relationship and to create an *I and thou* spiritual connection. When couples decide together how they prefer to handle conflict, they feel a sense of partnership and shared responsibility. Knowing ahead of time the plan for how you will handle these tense moments makes them less frightening. In the language of Dialectical Behavior Therapy (DBT),* this is called a coping ahead skill and reduces the stress when face-to-face with an emotionally distressing situation. This conversation about the *how* you argue needs to be ongoing as you experiment and learn from each encounter.

Negotiating Cooling-Off Time

Couples tend to have a different style and need for timing when it comes to addressing their friction, meaning whether to talk about it right then

---

* Marsha M. Linehan, *DBT Skills Training: Handouts and Worksheets*, 2nd ed. (Guilford Publications, 2014).

or pick it up later when some time has passed to reflect and cool down. This preference has a lot to do with each partner's neurology, attachment style, family history, and comfort with emotional and sometimes difficult conversations. Some can't bear when issues are not resolved right away. They find it literally intolerable when there's something heavy blocking their connection, and don't have the tools to deal with the big emotions that come with a fight and the unresolved conflict. Others feel so overwhelmed when the fighting gets too hot, they can't even get their thoughts together and need to step away. They can feel frightened by their partner's dysregulated behaviors and words. They would much rather reengage later to listen to one another.

I often hear from couples that a stepping-away gesture from their partner to cool down can feel like a rejection or abandonment—especially when it's abrupt, reactive, or aggressive. I recommend for couples to come up with an agreed-upon understanding, with prepared-ahead phrases or code words that signal in a comforting way that it might be best for a stepping-away period to cool down. Consider the example below.

In the heat of the moment, instead of:
"I just can't deal with this right now!" Followed by walking away, storming off, or leaving the house.

In the heat of the moment, try this:
"I'm reactive and maybe you're reactive, so I want to talk about this later when we are calm, and we can have a deeper conversation about this topic. I promise we will get back to it."

When it's neutral, try this:
"In general, when I walk away or say I need a minute, this means I'm feeling out of control. I might even have irrational feelings, so I don't want to react. I need some time to calm my emotions, to get some perspective before we talk."

Be Careful of These Extreme Don'ts

1. *The Silent Treatment (or stonewalling)*

   Some never want to come back to the issue at hand, period. This is different from a cooling off period and more in the realm of withdrawal and distancing. When the withholding goes so far, this is what we often hear as the silent treatment. Make no mistake, withholding communication and warmth during times of dissatisfaction and conflict is a less mature approach to conflict and in some cases an indication of abusive tendencies. Silence can be used for shaming, revenge, and manipulation. If this practice occurs with the couples I meet with, I emphatically recommend this to be top of their "don'ts" list.

2. *Tirades (aka disrespectful communication)*

   On the flip side, some partners feel full permission to let it rip when they are hot and bothered. They lack the appreciation for how flooding and long-term damaging their long string of violent, emotionally charged words are. Often filled with criticisms and accusations, tirades typically overwhelm the partner and trigger a natural trauma response. From a personal growth perspective, if your partner yells a lot or brings up grievances frequently and in a critical and accusatory way, it's okay to have boundaries. Actually, boundaries are vital in any relationship for everyone involved, and certainly for building a true sanctuary. I encourage everyone to reach a place of self-love and self-care where you can say and live by, "I never let anyone talk to me like that." Some very real, honest conversations, and even ones that are painful, can be had without yelling or filled with explosive communication. Partners can establish with their mates that while they want to hear what is bothering them, they will only do so under these conditions: (1) it's balanced with times of positive words and gestures and (2) when their partner is calm, ready to take responsibility for their feelings, and share what's bothering them from vulnerability, not rage and assaults.

Teaching Our Partners How We Like to Be Talked To

Besides the extremes just shared above, we have many other important and often subtle preferences for how we like to be talked to and listened to. Taking responsibility for your own happiness and well-being includes the self-care component of relaying to your partner how you want communication to go. You need to teach your partner. Even the most attuned and caring partners can't always read your mind for the words and style of communicating that works best for you.

In kind, it's important to make it your priority to grow more and more emotionally intelligent about your mate. This means playing "I Spy," that is, listening with your heart to pick up on cues of what activates your partner and what makes them feel relaxed. Asking open-ended questions are part of the game of learning about your partner's style. To come up with the rules of engagement that work best for the two of you as a couple, you and your partner should talk about the following:

1. The words or phrases you prefer and what helps you hear their message best
2. Your trigger words or statements to stay away from
3. Your tone of voice preferences
4. The kinds of affirming words or gestures that reassure and soothe during conflict

Case: Meet Steve and Angela

Speaking of teaching our partners about upsetting words, meet Steve and Angela. Amid a structured listening exercise that I was facilitating, Steve halted the flow. He had to clarify a word that Angela kept using that was shooting him out of his regulation zone every time. It was making it hard for him to listen to his wife. Angela referred to his behavior from the night before, "when you *'yelled at'* me about . . ." The words *yelled at* upset him, having put so much energy into trying to be calm when he approached her. Steve much preferred "when you *'engaged'* with me about . . ." because it reflected his softer tone. This one-word adjustment can sound petty, but it's not at all. The words *yelled at* signaled an aggressiveness that bothered Steve. Steve explained to Angela that he was sensitive about being an aggressive person. Someone he had worked with, in his past, used that word, and it is a trait he is working so hard to heal and overcome. She knows this about him and was happy to adjust her wording mid-conversation.

It's important to be on the lookout for how you might unconsciously slip biased words and dramatic tones into a conversation to justify yourself or prove a point. One word or tone can throw harmony off course in a split second.

Discuss Your Underlying Expectations Ahead of Time

Similar to teaching your partner how you like to be talked to, a powerful tool to prevent conflict is to openly communicate about the expectations you have ahead of time, whether it's about how an evening will be spent, a weekend, a trip, a celebration, or holiday, or what a romantic evening might mean. We have a dream or vision for how the connection will look and feel at all junctures in time and for all our life experiences but, unfortunately, we are naturally inclined to keep our expectations inside our minds. Brené Brown, in her book *Atlas of the Heart,** calls these

---

* Brené Brown, *Atlas of the Heart: Mapping Meaningful Connection and the Language of Human Experience* (Random House, 2022).

expectations *"stealth expectations"* because of the concealed visions we keep in the recesses of our minds. We unrealistically want our partners to just get us and know what we need. It's vulnerable and brave, and takes effort, to put yourself out there and share your desires and dreams, even for how a Sunday might look. When your vision is not actualized, this can create a lay-up for disappointment and to blame your partner for taking your hoped-for experience away from you.

Case: Meet Jeff and Me

I can recall one particular Sunday when my husband and I got into an argument because we kept our expectations to ourselves. We were empty nesters by then and so our Sundays now had less structure. I had in mind that we would organize the house, maybe even take a stab at the overflowing basement. He had an entirely different idea in mind. He wanted to relax, go for brunch together, maybe go for a hike. When we started our day, each with this opposite plan in mind, it didn't take long for the clash. I began to resent him not participating and he felt trapped in the doldrums of no fun. I remember that day vividly because that's when I realized that our problem was that we were not sharing the expectations we had now that we were freer for our weekends together. Since then, we try to start each Sunday with, "So, honey, what did you have in mind for the day?" Once we started asking that question, our weekends filled up with connection and partnership, whether we were playing or getting stuff done. I really didn't care what the focus was, I was just so grateful for the full feeling of being connected and close.

Reassuring Statements

A close cousin to spiritual diplomacy, reassuring statements can temper hurt and vulnerability when we are having a dialogue about something sensitive. Being compassionate with your partner during difficult conversations is treating your partner in an *I and thou* versus *I and it* manner. You can do this by offering statements that both soothe and qualify what might be hard to hear. It's like wrapping your words in a warm, cozy blanket. It's not fake or ingenuine fluff as an excuse to sneak in harsh criticism. Reassuring statements are true and real and give your partner mercy and kindness at a difficult point in a conversation, or at a difficult time in their life.

Reassuring statements are like a treasure chest filled with glimmers of love. We all benefit from identifying reassuring statements and finding out what helps our partner feel more safe and secure.

Partners might need reassuring statements when:

1. We choose to step away and cool off when there's friction. This can feel threatening or abandoning to some. *Reassuring statements could sound like:*
   - This isn't me pulling away from you, it's me pulling myself to my center.
   - I need to calm myself, so it will go well when we get back to it.
   - I want both of us to feel heard and understood. Let's wait until we are not so reactive.

2. Actively arguing and one or both partners feel scared. Are we okay? *Reassuring statements could sound like:*
   - Don't worry, we are okay.
   - I trust this is for our benefit, even though it's really hard now.
   - I know we will grow stronger from this.

3. If your partner is struggling with self-love, they might need reminders of the good you see in them and their inherent value. *Reassuring statements could sound like:*
   - You're such a special person to me.
   - Remember who you are.
   - I am proud of everything you are.

4. You are healing from a secret relationship, abuse, addiction, or other trauma or betrayal. The one betrayed will need ongoing reassurances. *Reassuring statements could sound like:*
   - I'll do whatever you need to rebuild your trust.
   - I will make our marriage my priority.
   - I am deeply sorry for hurting you.
   - I take full responsibility for my actions.

5. Giving feedback of some trait or habit that you see in your partner that they need to work on. *Reassuring statements could sound like:*
   - I'm bringing this up because I want to be closer.
   - You're amazing and loveable and so special to me, but there's this little thing.
   - I know you can do better with this. I believe in you wholeheartedly.

6. You make a choice to do something against your partner's wishes, maybe solo, that makes your partner feel disappointed and unimportant. *Reassuring statements could sound like:*
   - How can I make it up to you?
   - I will miss being with you.
   - Your happiness is my utmost priority; this decision was so hard for me.

7. Your partner made a mistake and is beating themselves up or afraid something bad will happen to your relationship. *Reassuring statements could sound like:*
   - You are my person and I'm not going anywhere.
   - I know you had good intentions.
   - You are human and we are supposed to make mistakes.

The Extreme: Over-Seeking or Over-Giving Reassurance

Balance is always key for everything to flow in our lives, as it is for reassuring statements. Be on the lookout for taking this need for reassurance, or the responsibility you feel to reassure your partner, too far. Through the lens of attachment theory,* we can understand ourselves more clearly when it comes to the need for validation and reassurance in our relationship. The idea is that our earliest relationships, usually with our caregivers or early romantic partners, shape the way we view and bond with others in our adult life. While I encourage you to use reassuring statements in your relationship, we need to also be on the look-out for how much might be too much.

To mitigate going too far with seeking outside validation from our partner or feeling overly responsible for holding our partner's north star, consider reflecting internally for the roots of why the need for reassurance is so important for you or why you feel it's your job to make your partner feel whole and secure. What feeling about yourself is this trying to protect you from? What are you afraid of if you don't get the reassurance or if you can't help your partner feel secure? Ultimately, a person's growing ability to reassure themselves can be the most powerful endeavor, for their own well-being and for the soulful bonds we are born with a need to forge.

Code Words (Silly and Lighthearted Tone)

Code words or phrases are a fun tool for bringing us into our regulation zone and the temperature of our conversations to a productive, soulful level. Some use "waffle" or "banana" or "hedgehog" to serve as a lighthearted cue to each other as if to say, "Hey, we are starting to go down a bad path, so let's break and get back to it later." It's a reassuring statement with one word because partners pick the word (object) together and give it a warm and loving meaning with no hint of accusation, judgment, or stonewalling. Picking the word together is important, and one that's a little silly is recommended so you're even

---

* J. Bowlby, "Attachment Theory and Its Therapeutic Implications," *Adolescent Psychiatry* 6 (1978): 5–33.

inclined to a shared chuckle. Laughter and lightheartedness create a fast pass to calming tensions before they rise, as they rise, or that have already gotten out of hand.

Codes can also come in the form of short, simple ways to express your current bandwidth. Particularly regarding how stressed or overwhelmed you are. Inspired from Brené Brown, I like to recommend to clients that they ask each other, "What's your number?" 1 = depleted with nothing in my tank; 10 = full and ready to engage and help. This simple question in and of itself tells your partner that you see them and want to know where they're at emotionally. *"What's your number"* can intercept the emotions that can turn any shared experienced into a nightmare. This is often a great exercise when couples are getting home from work, after picking up kids from daycare, or at the end of the day with the kids at home: any time adults are at risk of feeling depleted, overwhelmed, and stressed.

Case: Meet Ali and Joan

I started meeting with Ali and Joan because their arguments were not only unproductive but also leaving such a chasm that they were questioning their relationship. Joan had big feelings about their fertility journey, as she had found Ali late in life and she was terrified about not being able to conceive. Ali had children from a previous marriage to a man, and now only recently having discovered the love of her life in a woman, she wanted to have the experience of bringing children into the world with Joan. As they began their fertility treatments, problems began to bubble up in their relationship. Ali had a more difficult time with emotional conversations and with Joan's emotional swings from all the procedures. She wanted to smooth over any problems—fix it for Joan so Joan could focus on getting pregnant, but Ali was only making Joan feel worse when she tried to resolve things in her usual "controlling" way. When they tried to talk about anything they were struggling with, emotions ran high, they would fight, and then shut down. We worked together to help regulate their emotions when their fights became overwhelming. They loved the "what's your number?" and this became their code and cue to be sensitive to each other's bandwidth and to use better communication habits.

In the end, they were not able to conceive, but they have handled their grief gracefully and are comfortable in their relationship. At a recent session, you could see the soul-to-soul connection all over their faces as they came into session smiling, and sitting close together on the sofa.

IDEA INTO ACTION: CREATING YOUR CONFLICT CONSTITUTION TOGETHER

Now that you've read through this chapter, I invite you to begin creating your Couple's Conflict Constitution with an eye toward making your fights more loving and soulful. You can start with refering to the thirteen universal dos and don'ts above to help prompt you to write your own dos and don'ts for fighting and resolution. Next, I have created these questions below for you to write down and discuss with your partner. They are based on the most common and important aspects of arguing successfully so you can get more specific in developing your conflict constitution as a couple.

1. Do you like to talk about issues right away or later when you've had some time to reflect or calm down?
2. How can we let each other know that we need some time to get calmer or if we are getting overwhelmed and need a break until later? Is there a code word we can use, something light and playful, that gives us a safe pause when we are getting too emotional?
3. What's our stance on getting back to issues we weren't ready to address at an earlier time?

4. How about tone? Do you need it calm? Are you okay if it gets heated at times?

5. When is the best time of day or day of the week to talk about our relationship?

6. Is there a particular setting that works best for you?

7. What's the best way for me to tell you I'm not happy about something? What words would you like me to use?

8. What should I never say to you?

9. Do you like direct or softer, more sensitive language?

10. How do you feel about fighting in front of the kids?

11. What do I do that you like when we are fighting? And that you don't like?

12. Do we need to address any silent treatment, stone walling, or tirade behaviors between us?

13. What reassuring, loving statements resonate with you most, when we are fighting or any other times you need support?

Now we will move on to the heart of soulful communication—learning to become a compassionate listener.

CHAPTER NINE

The Love Seat Listening Method and Co-Journaling Exercise

We think we listen, but very rarely do we listen with real understanding, true empathy. Yet listening, of this very special kind, is one of the most potent forces for change that I know.

—Carl Rogers

When clients tell me about their friction points in our sessions, and especially when the tension erupts right in front of me, this is my cue that it's time to add structure to the interaction. We can't listen well or grow from our friction when our ego reactivity is in command. I introduce them to what I affectionately call *The Love Seat Listening Method*. I use this approach with clients 95 percent of the time and most of this chapter will be laying this out for you to use directly in your relationship. It's a loving version of being in the hot seat, where partners hear each other one at a time in a neutral, structured way using a script. Yes, a script.

When you are in the Love Seat, your partner's job is to take off all their clothes (metaphorically) and put yours on. They are the listener and their job is to create a nonjudgmental environment, like a sanctuary, for your intimate thoughts and feelings to be freely expressed—and for you to feel heard. Then, at some point, you will switch seats.

The second method which you'll see toward the end of this chapter is a *Ten-Question Co-Journaling Exercise.* This even more structured approach can be used when there is a profound gridlock or for topics and times when **tensions run high**. I use and recommend this even more scripted approach that first helps you halt the contentious dialogue by co-journaling the same ten questions, followed by reading what you've written to each other.

WHY A SCRIPT?

Listening well is not easy and is typically what a good therapist will help facilitate. We often need a more intentional experience, along with a communication script, to slow us down and thwart off defensive and interrupting tendencies. Typically, we are *talking at* each other, trying to force our view into our partner's ears that are blocked because of their own emotions and trying to force their view into ours. We fall into an *I and it* dialogue by default instead of an *I and thou*. We can trick ourselves into thinking we are asking a real question when it's not a question at all. Rather our questions can really be cleverly wrapped statements of our opinion or view, or words trying to interrogate or lead our partner to our own perspective.

With the scripts you will see below, I am here to help you get started with what can be the most powerful ways to bring your heart and soul into your arguments. When partners take turns being heard, validated, and understood, the shift from ego to soul, from feeling cut off to connected, is visual and palpable. This allows solutions to come open-heartedly and organically. These kinds of healing interactions cannot happen by default. They are born by going against our nature to create an opening for the force of love to flow.

When couples are in my office, they have me there to guide them. For you reading this now, since you are on your own, this script will walk you through this communication strategy. Don't worry about it feeling forced. That's okay; it's meant to help you open up to each other and it will become more comfortable over time. You will grow to rely on this structure and incorporate pieces more naturally into your day-to-day interactions—especially once you have experienced the success it brings for repair and closeness. Then you will be in a better position to address your issues right away, calmly and productively, rather than burying them until they blow up.

THE LOVE SEAT LISTENING METHOD

The Love Seat Listening Method is a structured communication model I use with my clients inspired by three of my favorite and accredited methods that share a similar process—Imago Dialogue,* Gottman Dreams-within-Conflict,† and Clean Talk Communication.‡ They all provide a method for taking turns between speaker and listener. They promote an atmosphere of equality, compassion, and nonjudgment to express your grievances with ownership of your own feelings.

Over time I have created my own approach and script that I use with my clients to help them navigate their conflict constructively. Drawing from these three methods, I have adapted and combined the best features of each model and added some elements that have worked throughout my practice and in my own marriage: *not just to get through it but grow through it.* The script will offer you and your partner several prompts to choose from, which will combine active listening, empathic listening, open-ended questions, and will help guide you to express yourself cleanly by owning your perceptions and feelings. You will also have a chance to help each other discover growth and breakthroughs.

Before we move into the *Love Seat Listening Script,* I want to talk a little about **active listening,** which you will see incorporated throughout

---

* Harville Hendrix, *Getting the Love You Want: A Guide for Couples* (Henry Holt & Co., 2007).
† J. Gottman, *The Seven Principles for Making Marriage Work* (Orion, 2000).
‡ See https://shadowwork.com/clean-talk/ by Cliff Barry of Shadow Work.

the script. Then I'll share some ground rules for when you're in (1) the Love Seat Mode and (2) Listening Mode.

Active Listening

Active listening is very important because it lets your beloved know you care enough to enter their reality. It will help you each feel connected—and clarify the intended meaning in your words and what your challenges are. You don't have to agree with your partner to listen well to them, which will mean responding with words that reflect, normalize, and show empathy.

Reflection, that is, paraphrasing or even sharing word for word what you heard your partner say, will be the most critical element of this exercise. It's important to reflect to listen for the words, and to listen for the feelings. It's best to be tentative in your reflections because your beloved is the ultimate authority on their experience, and you want to check with them to see if you have accurately understood them.

Normalizing means you let your partner know that their perspective, and their feelings, make sense based on how we as humans respond to things like this in life. Normalizing takes "I understand you" even deeper with "It's understandable how you think and feel the way you do."

Empathy takes reflecting your partner's feelings to the level where they know you feel what they're feeling *with them*. Not at a distance, which is more like sympathy. Even if you've never experienced the same situation, you can show empathy, which will bring you even closer to an *I and thou* dialogue than any of the other skills.

When you get to the script, you will see these three active listening skills set up for you with sample prompts. Again, this may feel forced, but it will help you get to the heart of what you need to get to in your relationship, learn what will make it better going forward, and help you remove what is blocking your connection. You will remove barriers and grow your bond through the dialogue itself. Don't worry if you're not an expert at these listening skills. Any effort will make a difference, and practice is the name of the game.

SOME GROUND RULES

When You're in the Love Seat

Your job is to be honest and express yourself. PBR, that is, pause, breathe, and relax, then share what's on your heart and in your mind. Owning your own experience with "I" statements, you'll be telling your partner the way you perceive the situation, the needs you have, and the feelings you're experiencing. You're not here to talk your partner into agreeing with you or to make accusations with "you this" or "you that" statements. Rather, you want to focus on helping them understand what this issue means to you, what you're struggling with, what you wish for, what you need going forward, and where there's an opportunity for growth. Be vulnerable and dig a little deeper as you feel safe to do so. Let your partner into your heart and soul.

When You're in Listening Mode

Your job is to help your partner feel safe by mindfully listening to understand. Remember, you are creating a refuge, a sanctuary, together. You start doing this with your body language, that is, facing one another, making eye contact, opening your heart and body posture to show that you are really paying attention and that you care. Make your goal to understand your beloved as deeply as you possibly can. Think of yourself as an empty bowl, and you want your partner to fill it up with what it's like in their reality. You will be using the active listening skills above. Resist the urge to be thinking of your own defense or trying to jump in and fix it. There will be time for you to share your side, and for solutions later. You don't need to agree with anything you hear. It's not relevant right now. Just let go and enter your partner's reality. Remember, you will be in the love seat next.

Note: It's so important to use your partner's **body language and facial expressions** to assess whether you've hit the sweet spot of being heard. You'll see you're on the right track by the physical relief that will wash over your partner's whole body. In particular, you might notice your partner's head nod, eyes open wider, body relax, face soften and even smile, shoulders come down, and you might hear a nice deep breath.

GETTING READY

Step 1: Invite your partner to have a dialogue and ask them when would be a good time? Make sure you are both open to this intimate conversation. If you force a dialogue when they are not ready, and you are not in a good head space, you set yourselves up for failure.

Step 2: Together, pick a physical location that feels good for both of you and where you can have privacy and you can be in close physical contact. A park bench, on a walk, at the kitchen table, in your backyard, or literally on the love seat in your house. It's best to be able to see each other's eyes and be able to reach out with a hand or a gentle touch.

Step 3: Decide who will go first, knowing that you'll switch and take turns. In my office, I notice that it works best for the one who has a lot on their heart to go first. This can defuse that partner's more intense emotions, which will then prepare them to actively listen.

Step 4: Each partner will review the script, get acquainted with the flow of the dialogue, and scan the prompting questions to see which feels most natural to them. Keep the script handy and refer back to it as often as you need while you're having a dialogue. Before you begin, it's important to remember that it's not *just* about getting your point across but creating a deeper, closer relationship through the interaction. This may sound or feel forced at the beginning but enter this dialogue with an open mind and open heart. You will find that the script will help you get started but also begin to get at the root of the problems you and your partner are experiencing.

Step 5: Begin the dialogue using the script below.

THE SCRIPT

Dialogue Step 1:

The Listening Partner is the person who you have decided will listen first. The listening partner begins by asking a soft, open question to invite a gentle, caring environment. Here are some sample soft start-up questions:

- I'd love to hear your thoughts and feelings about this issue.
- Tell me what's on your mind and in your heart?
- I'm all ears . . .

The Love Seat Partner is the one speaking first. It's important that you begin with owning your feelings and thoughts. You do this by using "I" statements, such as:

- I feel . . .
- I believe . . .
- I need . . .
- I'm worried because . . .
- When I heard you say . . . , I thought . . . because that meant to me . . .

Dialogue Step 2:

The Listening Partner **reflects** back what they just heard to make sure they are truly entering into their partner's reality and not tangling up their own emotions and hearing what they want to hear. Here are some sample prompts to reflect back what you've heard:

- What I heard is . . .
- So, what you're saying is . . . ?
- It sounds like when _____, you felt_____, because _____.
- Did I get that right?
- Is there something else . . . ?

The Love Seat Partner **confirms, clarifies, and elaborates** on what the Listening Partner reflected, staying with "I" statements, such as:

- That's it . . .
- That's close to what I meant, but it's more like . . .
- Not exactly, it's more like . . .
- I'd like to add . . .
- It feels good that you . . .
- The hardest part is feeling . . .

Dialogue Step 3:

The Listening Partner **reflects** again what they're hearing in words, again checking for facial expressions and body language as well to see if you're understanding them. Note: *You'll see that there are a lot of back and forth clarifying rounds here which may feel redundant but are in fact important so that two things happen: The Listening Partner has in fact heard what the Love Seat partner is saying and that the Love Seat partner feels thoroughly understood.*

- Are you saying that . . . ?
- So, I'm hearing that . . .

The Listening Partner *reflects with empathy.*
Here are some sample prompts:

- It seems like you're feeling . . .
- You must feel so . . .

- That would be hard because . . .
- I imagine you might be feeling . . .
- I want to make sure I understand how you feel . . .
- If that happened to anyone, they would feel ____ too.
- You're right, this shouldn't have happened . . .

The Love Seat Partner **clarifies** whether their partner is grasping their feelings here with prompts like:

- Yes, that's what I'm feeling . . .
- You got it.
- Well, not exactly, it's more like . . .

The Love Seat Partner can **elaborate** on their feelings with simple words like sad, angry, shame, lonely, afraid, happy, hopeless.

- When I'm really honest with myself, I notice I feel . . .
- I am also feeling . . .

The Love Seat Partner **acknowledges** and **appreciates** their partner's efforts. This is important because we want to feel we are having some success even if we're not master listeners.

- I see you are really trying to understand me and that means to me . . .

Dialogue Step 4:

The Listening Partner can now take it deeper with any of these **open-ended questions** to bring out their partner's dreams, needs, and desires—as well as lessons or growth opportunities for them and as a couple.

- Tell me why this is so important to you?

- What are you afraid might happen or not happen?
- What do you need most from me going forward?
- How do you see this as a chance for you to grow?
- How might this help us grow as a couple?

The Love Seat Partner **opens up** from their heart and soul with answers to the above questions:

- This is important because . . .
- This reminds me of . . .
- I'm afraid that if _____ then _____.
- It would help me so much if you could remember to . . .
- I think I am being given a chance to grow in this area of myself . . .

CLOSURE BEFORE SWITCHING SEATS

Now share with each other how this process felt. Was it hard being the listening partner? Share what you appreciate about your partner and how it felt to have them listen to you in the Love Seat. Give positive feedback. Focus on the good part of the experience because even if your partner did only a so-so job of listening, we want to make this experience feel successful. We want our partners to be willing to continue this kind of communication going forward. The more you practice, the better you can become—and the closer and happier you can feel together.

Now switch seats and repeat.

WRAPPING UP THE LOVE SEAT LISTENING EXERCISE

After you have both finished this scripted dialogue as speaker and listener, you will hopefully feel calmer and closer but you might also feel exhausted. Real listening takes emotional and mental effort. Make sure you leave enough energy for appreciation of your partner for whatever effort they gave and care they showed. If you're up for it, share your takeaways with each other. See if there is something you learned to make your connection more fun and less contentious going forward. How can you listen better next time? How might you prevent similar clashes or disconnects? If you feel saturated and cooked, stop and let the experience sink in. Often partners will take what they learned from a real and intimate dialogue like this and apply it going forward when faced with the same scenario. Don't pressure one another; go at your own pace.

Case: Meet Trent and Maura, Using the Love Seat Listening Method

Trent and Maura are newly married, Maura for the second time. They came in for their first session very self-aware—which unfortunately wasn't getting them anywhere. Trent still lost his temper and Maura continued to walk on eggshells, and sometimes blew up herself. Maura's two teen daughters were living with them—which he had agreed to—yet Trent struggled with the lack of contribution and responsibility these young women were showing as household members. Maura's permissive style with her girls stemmed from their earlier aggressive and chaotic environment, about which she felt guilty.

In their second session, I felt they were ready for the Love Seat Listening Method. They came in ready to discuss a fight they had just had earlier in the week and every time throughout the following week that they tried to revisit the encounter, Trent and Maura would each get angrier and shut down respectively. Below is how their interaction unfolded.

Dialogue Step 1:

Trent: I'd love to hear your thoughts and feelings about the other night when I asked if the girls left the food and dishes on the counter.

Maura: I feel scared every evening that there might be something that you don't like about what my kids have done or not done.

I'm never sure what you are going to react to, and I just want the house to be peaceful.

Dialogue Step 2:

Trent: So, do you think that it's right for your daughter and her friend to leave a big mess for someone else to clean up?

Dr. Glik: Trent, I understand that you have your own feelings about the scenario. You will soon share your perspective. At this point you are trying to understand Maura's, so simply reflect back on what you just heard Maura say. Use the questions on the script under Dialogue Step 2 for the listening partner.

Trent: So, I heard you say that you want things to be peaceful and don't like it when I lose my temper. Did I get that right? Is there more?

Maura: Yes. I don't think I have told you what it does to me. When I see something that might upset you, waiting for you to react to it like what happened last night, my whole body starts to shake and I panic. I'm already such a people pleaser. Your moods are really hard for me.

Dialogue Step 3:

Trent: So, what you're saying is that it's worse than you let on. You even shake like I see you doing now. Our conflict has been very difficult for you. Especially as a pleaser. You just want things to be peaceful.

Maura: Yeah, it has been difficult. I grew up with parents who fought all the time, and it was loud and scary for me. I was always on edge waiting for the next blow up, which was always around the corner. I promised myself I would do better when I had my own family.

Trent: What's the hardest part about worrying if I am going to get mad at your kids or at you?

Maura: I feel lonely. Like I have to deal with things by myself and that you don't understand what my daughters have been through with their dad.

Dialogue Step 4:

Trent: If there is a past wound from childhood this is reminding you of, what might that be?

Maura: Oh my gosh, yes (tears running down her face). I mentioned this earlier but to be honest, this is what my entire childhood felt like. Afraid and alone.

Trent: That would be so difficult and I'm sorry you had to grow up like that. What do you need most from me going forward?

Maura: It would help me so much if you can talk to me the way you are talking to me now. I can feel that you are with me and that means so much.

Note: *By this point Trent has his hand on Maura's knee and his other arm on her shoulder. They are connected and calm, which created an opening for a deeper step, exploring the personal growth opportunity this incident might be awakening.*

Dialogue Step 5: Growth Opportunity

Trent: How do you see this as a chance for you to grow?

Maura: This is really hard for me to tell you what I need and to think I'm allowed to do that and that you will respond with what *I* need not your own. I don't think I have felt worthy, and I've always tried to make everyone else okay, hoping it would bring peace. So, I think I need to work on my confidence and rather than waiting for the next shoe to drop, assuming it will, I need to ask you to be patient and kind with me, especially about the issues with the boys.

In Sum

Maura let herself be vulnerable with Trent and underneath it all, he found capacity to show empathy and tremendous love and warmth.

When they switched and it was his turn to be in the Love Seat, what came from the dialogue was that he wanted to be appreciated for how hard he is working to manage his anger, and that night in question, he actually never lost his temper. Maura was just so afraid that he would that she became accusatory off the bat. With Maura's active listening, Trent also had the chance to share how exhausted he was from working, and then when at home, he felt like he needed more help. And that he felt he wasn't a priority to her. Her girls' well-being and needs always felt more important than his. Together, they were primed for some brainstorming together to find solutions that would help each of them grow and have the kind of experience they were really looking for. They also agreed to see a counselor who specialized in stepparenting to help them create a healthy dynamic amid the new family they were forming.

SCRIPTED EXERCISE #2: STRUCTURED CO-JOURNALING, TEN QUESTIONS

When couples come unglued in my office, and each word opens another storm, I increase the structure even more. At these embroiled moments, I split my clients up from any interactions with each other. I hand them a note pad and pen and give them a set of ten self-reflecting questions to journal about in their notebook. I have each partner connect to themselves—through writing. I call it structured co-journaling. In most cases, this can really help partners begin to calm their nervous systems. I send these questions to clients reaching out in a pinch outside of their sessions, for when they are gridlocked and spiraling out of control.

This co-journaling method came about years ago when I couldn't stop a couple from really going at it in my office. Now, I use this all the time, not just for high conflict moments. When tensions get that crazy, no progress is being had by anyone. Through these ten questions answered in a co-journaling format, I discovered a method to calm the spiraling storm. Not only that, but this communication exercise keeps the positive momentum going, lowers the walls around your heart, and helps you deepen into the more vulnerable issues running beneath the surface.

How and When to Co-Journal with Your Partner

If it gets too hot between you and your partner, that's your cue you need to stop talking. I recommend journaling these ten questions privately, which could mean side-by-side or taking some space on your own. Then you can work your way back to a love seat listening interaction *eventually*. There is a pause built into the private writing exercise which, together with the empowering questions themselves, helps you move from the downstairs emotionally charged part of the brain to the upstairs calmer part, the part that has *perspective*. For most couples, I marvel at how this writing exercise stops the chaos, begins to regulate their nervous systems, and relieves the inner wounded child from taking charge of the interaction. From this calmer state, they are ready for a new level of repair and growth.

Step 1: *Halt!* Maybe pick an object, even get a yellow flag or a caution sign as your cue that you don't want to continue when it's this heated. This cue can also come to mean *"Let's do this better and we need some help"* (aka the ten questions).

Step 2: *Invite your partner to co-journal with you about whatever hot topic you're fighting about.* Even if it's not an erupted argument, you can use this when you're feeling in gridlock about an issue. Pull out the ten questions you see below.

Step 3: *Grab a notebook and pen.*

Step 4: *Take your time writing out your answers to the ten questions.* Some clients take several days. They are deeper questions, and they need to be. There is typically a gold mine waiting beneath the surface of our friction—for self-discovery, healing, and a more compassionate understanding of the root of the issue. An understanding that eventually will be greatly beneficial for our partners to know about.

Step 5: *Read through your responses with your partner* **when you're both ready.** You will mostly use only one listening tool: loving eye contact and open body posture. You can also add reflection, normalizing, and empathy as long as your hearts are truly open. Sometimes, as in cases when it's risky to brew up another storm, saying less or nothing at all is best. Then you will switch.

Step 6: *Give positive feedback to one another.* After you both have shared your responses to the ten questions, you answer and share this final question, "When I listened to my partner's responses to their ten questions, I was happy to hear them say . . ."

The Ten Questions: From Blow Up to Breakthrough

Here are the ten questions. You can use this communication technique anytime. But most especially, pull these questions out when you're raging out of control.

- How do I perceive this encounter?
- How am I feeling based on my partner's words and actions; what am I feeling within me?
- When something sets me off like this, I react by . . .
- I think this issue is so important to me because . . .
- To be the kind of person I want to be, I would respond to the situation of _____ by . . .
- This scenario brings to my attention what I know I need to work on in myself, which is . . .
- If my feelings in this encounter bring to the surface something in my past or childhood, it might be . . .

- What I would like to ask to help me feel supported would be . . .
- If I were to receive my partner like the gift they are and come from the love I feel for them, then I would approach this challenge between us . . .
- Referring back to question six with what I need to work on, I can take these action steps to move forward with this growth area of mine . . .

Case: Meet Alice and Carlos, Using the Ten-Question Co-Journaling Exercise

I had been seeing Alice and Carlos for several months as their fighting escalated. Their most recent fight was over a boys' trip that Carlos decided to take. It was tricky because they had a young baby at home and had stressful full-time jobs. They were both quite depleted. During our session the arguing and defensiveness became over the top and I resorted to the ten questions in an attempt to calm the session down and get to the root. After they took some time to journal on their own, we were able to go through the questions together and they calmly shared their responses. The intensity they experienced began to dissipate and they were able to get to the root of Alice's concerns about Carlos's trip, and why the trip was so important for him. They were able to reflect rather than react.

Alice realized that deep down she actually wanted Carlos to connect with his friends, but him being away completely overwhelmed her. She tapped into a familiar painful feeling of frequently being left alone growing up. Her mother died when she was a teenager and her father was often away trying to create a new relationship. As independent a person as Alice is, she can still easily feel abandoned. She could rationally understand the need for Carlos to take this trip, but she had trouble controlling her anxiety, which resulted in blaming and angry language.

The questions helped Alice get past her lashing out reaction to understand and express her fear underneath. The journaling helped Carlos put into words and then share with Alice how this particular group of guys allow him to be completely himself, something he didn't have in his youth. From Alice sharing her more vulnerable feelings (instead of rage), Carlos saw that he needed to be more sensitive to what his wife was going through. Understanding each other better paved the way for a calmer, more loving exchange and, ultimately, a mutual solution. They took these ten questions seriously and found connection, compromise, and even some breakthroughs.

When to Seek Counseling

These heartfelt conversations are tough, especially if the anger and escalation require more help than a pause and structured co-journaling can defuse. These communication skills are not an overnight study, and if you're not able to move things forward, this could be a good time to seek a therapist. At any point as you are reading this book, if you feel the inclination to consider the help of a trusted couple counselor, I would listen to this voice.

This book is not to replace therapy.

Repairing Trust from Damaging Communication

Our communication dynamics in a close relationship can in and of themselves create problems and damage to the relationship. Things can be said that you can never take back, and chronic bad listening and toxic communication can deeply damage trust and the foundation of your relationship. What could be a sanctuary for some in a relationship can feel like a cold prison for others. Chapter 10 will cover how to repair wounds, of all kinds, and to guide you on a path forward toward healing and rebuilding trust.

CHAPTER TEN

The Wounds That Need Healing

Even loss and betrayal can bring us awakening.

—Buddha

In this chapter, I will go over the ten types of relationship wounds I see couples face. Things can get a little heavier here as I go over the wounds and betrayals we incur, so please stay with me, because fully grasping all the blatant and subtle ways we cause harm to our mate and the relationship is a first and essential step toward growth and repair. Beyond the well-known and excruciating pain from sexual betrayal, there are so many other breeches of trust. Many of these other types of betrayal go unacknowledged and therefore unrepaired.

POST-TRAUMATIC GROWTH AFTER BETRAYAL

I want to put out a friendly reminder that we are in the heart and center of the growth pillar. The kind of growth we are entering now is called Post-Traumatic Growth (PTG).* That is, the positive changes and growth that research has shown can come in the aftermath of life crises and challenges. We often overlook how trauma can lead to growth, and it can sound insensitive when the wound is raw. Like a tree that is pruned and appears dead and barren, eventually it rebuilds stronger and more

---

* Richard G. Tedeschi, "Growth After Trauma," *Harvard Business Review*, July–August 2020, https://hbr.org/2020/07/growth-after-trauma.

beautiful. This is much like we as human beings when we face challenges and major life crises. With more than twenty-five years of data, the PTG Research group* describe post-traumatic growth this way:

> It (PTG) is a positive change experienced as a result of the struggle with a major life crisis or a traumatic event. Although we coined the term post-traumatic growth, the idea that human beings can be changed by their encounters with life challenges, sometimes in radically positive ways, is not new. The theme is present in ancient spiritual and religious traditions, literature, and philosophy.

As you read through these distressing scenarios below to see if any ring true for you, it will be more important than ever to remember that the healing path toward a soulful relationship is paved by treating friction and strife as a calling to grow personally and closer together. This is not a guarantee; there are so many variables. However, I can guarantee that change is possible; and that by investing in personal growth, and healing your relationship, it will be a win-win, for your own journey and potentially for a stronger relationship.

NINE MOST COMMON BETRAYALS OF TRUST

Below are the wounds and betrayals of trust I have seen working with couples over the years. I will go over each one and share some case examples, but I first wanted to give you the list at a glance.

IDEA INTO ACTION UP FRONT: THINK ABOUT YOUR RELATIONSHIP AS YOU READ THROUGH THE CHAPTER AND ASK YOURSELF, "HAVE I EXPERIENCED BETRAYAL OF THIS KIND TO SOME DEGREE IN OUR RELATIONSHIP, AND HAS MY PARTNER?"

- A secret relationship (infidelity)
- Lying

---

* See the PTG Resource Center at https://ptgi.uncc.edu/what-is-ptg/.

- Addiction or abuse of uses
- Financial infidelity
- Broken promises
- Emotional coldness, absenteeism
- Avoiding physical and sexual intimacy
- Disrespectful communication
- Making your top priority something or someone else

If you can relate to any of these, and to the degree that you can, the first thing I want say is that I'm sorry you've had to go through this. I deeply feel the pain of my clients, sometimes heartbreaking, that can come with all types of betrayal—discovering a secret relationship being the most excruciating. Your own self-care will be essential, especially if the wound is fresh and the betrayal trauma more serious.

Regardless of the severity, I have seen couple after couple who never thought they could recover from their marriage trauma not only do so, but in a way that made them a much happier, stronger couple. You will hear me say this again and again—disloyalty can be healed and even create a better relationship. I usually expect my clients to throw a pillow at me, or worse, when I plant this seed, but I say it anyway, *"Someday you might even see this as a gift."* Since awareness is a first step for growth, let's dive in to understand the ins and outs of the nine most common betrayals that need repair. These will include some case examples of couples I met with who ultimately healed from the disloyalty.

Secret Relationship

Affairs of one kind or another are the most prominent and painful betrayal I see in my practice and what often motivates couples to seek my help. For the healing of all of types of betrayal, I draw on what I've learned from helping ailing couples navigate the dark waters of romantic and emotional infidelity. While the healing all of kinds of betrayals will follow a similar repair process and vary depending on severity and the state of their foundation, couples trying to heal from a secret relationship require special tools, tremendous commitment, and guidance. Make no mistake, these betrayals of intimacy I've listed below all qualify as cheating and can awaken the same pain and trauma response—and serious investment to repair—that a secret relationship is known for. If these are relevant in your relationship, don't dismiss the impact on your partner, that is, if you would like to heal and move forward together. Secret relationships can include:

Physical cheating
- Serious sexual affair with romantic and emotional intimacy
- Casual detached sex—paid or unpaid—one time, or recurring

Emotionally intimate affair with no sexual intimacy (yet), including friends your partner doesn't know about.

Cyber affair, emotional and/or with sexual engagement, i.e., sexting, sex talk, meet up or romantic fantasies or internet sex

Micro-cheating, e.g., flirting online or in person, leaving wedding ring at home, and other subtle messages of sexual openness or interest

Porn that impacts your relationship negatively—either by impairing emotional and physical intimacy, done secretly or against your partner's wishes, or it is becoming a gateway to other forms of betrayal

Case: Meet Craig and Lori: Casual Sex Betrayal
Craig and Lori adopted two children, then conceived on their own. They were thrilled with this surprise for their family. Soon

after their third baby was born, Craig began to seek out one-night stands through an app designed for this kind of hookup. He knew everything about this was wrong. Addicted to porn and masturbation since he was a young teen, Craig used this all-too-common dopamine surge to cope with emotions that he had no idea how to navigate. As it does so much of the time, his porn habits weren't doing the trick anymore to escape his angst, so he needed to up the dose by an in-person experience. My first session with Craig and Lori was soon after these casual hookups had started up, and the day after Lori found out.

Case: Meet Martin and Scott: Emotional and Fantasy Cyber Affair

Martin loved his husband Scott but formed a romantic fantasy relationship with a man he met through work who lived in London. He was a workaholic and didn't have good coping skills for handling his stress. Sexting with this man who accepted him exactly as he is became his escape. He justified that he wasn't cheating on Scott, because there was no sex; they were not even in the same continent. When Martin discovered Scott's relationship through intimate text exchanges, he was devastated and feared the marriage was over because he thought he would never be able to trust Martin again.

Case: Meet Phil and Nancy: Serious Sexual Relationship

Days after Nancy shockingly discovered Phil's affair with a colleague at work, they both slouched onto my couch desperate for help. Married for thirty-two years, Phil adored Nancy and knew she was his lifelong partner. Nonetheless, amid decades of the grind of corporate life, he lost himself. "I can't find my soul," he confessed. Nancy thought that Phil was the kind of man who would never betray like this, not in a million years. Until the affair, he thought that about himself too.

Case: Meet Claire and Bob: Micro-cheating

Bob and Claire started counseling because Bob had found some emails that sounded too personal and intimate for a neighbor. Claire kept her flirty relationship a secret from Bob, because she knew he would get upset and she didn't want to stop the attention she was getting from her neighbor. Growing up insecure about her looks, Claire realized her insecurity from being rejected and unconsidered as a love interest for her entire youth was still influencing her today. She was spending the rest of her adult life trying to fill that hole. In addition to flirty emails, she finally admitted that she liked lunches with men because it allowed her to have the same hint of sexual openness even though that's as far as she ever planned to take it. Flirting as harmless is a huge myth!

Lying

Lying associated with affairs

When partners have had an affair of any kind, the lying is the most damaging and painstaking part to heal. I hear again and again, *"It's the lying that broke my trust in you more than anything else. Before I never thought twice about trusting you. Now that I know you're capable of hiding such unthinkable behavior from me, how will I ever trust you again?"*

Tiny, chronic fibs

The damage from lying isn't always about the big things but can come through the tiny little stretches of truth to avoid conflict or shameful feelings evoked when your partner is displeased with you. Even if your lies are uttered from a desire to maintain peace, they are still a breach of trust. Common with people pleasers and a hard pattern to break, these small lies told over time can disrupt a marriage as much as a big one if you don't learn to curb this tendency. Many people learned in childhood that to avoid harsh judgment or to look good they needed to lie to protect themselves. Fibs are like death by a thousand cuts. Partners just want to know they can't count on their beloved being straight with them, even about the little things, and even if they are not going to be happy about it.

Lying by omission and hiding

For those who are engaging in behavior they know their partner would be uncomfortable with, and they aren't ready or brave enough to address it or make changes, they become good at keeping secrets and avoiding. These include secret relationships and the addictions and abuses of uses you'll see next.

Addictions, abuses of uses—with or without hiding

Loving an addict can come with great trauma, personally and to the relationship. This is where we find the most incidence of *broken promises.* Addictions can undermine the trust in a relationship, which potentially leads to destroying the bond altogether. Sometimes inappropriately understood as being codependent, the partner in relationship with someone addicted to a substance experiences the same sense of betrayal as the wound from a secret relationship. This can mean hypervigilance, anxiety and depression, rumination, easily triggered, irritability, need to control, and shutting down emotionally.

Here are the most common addictions and abuse of use which are even more wounding when there are secrets, hiding, and broken promises.

Problem drinking
Drug or steroid abuse
Porn and sex
Gambling

Excessive shopping
Compulsive phone use
Eating disorder or food addiction

Case Meet: Dominic and Penny: Problem Drinking

Dominic always felt he needed to drink to fit in and feel more secure about himself. Besides, it's what everyone in his family did growing up and continues to do today. Penny grew up in a religious family who didn't drink much, so this was new to her. She was fine with it until the drinking made her feel that she had lost a partner and gained a child to take care of. Penny's mental health began to decline, especially when she discovered that Dominic had a sexual affair at work while drinking. For Penny, unless Dominic could take responsibility for his drinking problem, she was unwilling to consider the process for healing from the affair. Dominic promised countless times to regulate his drinking, and yet each time, he would eventually lose his free will and over drink. The two betrayals intertwined to form an almost fatal traumatic wound to their marriage.

Financial Infidelity

The damage from financial infidelity is widely swept under the rug, yet this situation can cause as much damage to the relationship as a secret relationship can—sometimes worse because of the potential financial issues lingering long past the turnaround or the end of the relationship. How does financial deceit look?

- *Undisclosed debt.* Some partners find out about their partner's debt only after they got married. The implications can impact their financial future.
- *Hidden income.* Financial infidelity occurs when you hide how much you earn, or what's in your savings, to avoid sharing it or discussing it for joint decision making.

- *Secret spending habits.* This can include spending considerable money through secret purchases, using money allocated for bills toward something else. Even when not in secret, some spend down joint accounts on big purchases or compulsive spending that adds up.
- *Hidden accounts.* Some secret purchases come from unknown credit cards or bank accounts.
- *Financial gifts to others.* When a partner secretly gives to a friend or family member. Whether their joint finances are impacted or not, they are diminishing the partnership and trust in their relationship.
- *Chronic poor money management.* Some partners end up needing to carry the burden of handling finances when a partner makes chronic poor choices, even if they are not in secret.

Financial deceit can stem from an unconscious desire to coerce or control, poor communication around money, or more common than we realize, unresolved trust issues around money.

Broken Promises

Similar to a lie, a broken promise can range from not changing a behavior when you said you would, perpetually not coming home when you tell your partner, and not keeping to an agreement made in the relationship. It's okay and normal if things change in life that inspire you to reevaluate a promise you have made. The key is to acknowledge the promise you've made and discuss the reasons why the promise was broken, and when and how you will handle it together.

Case: Meet Kim and Oliver: Broken Promise Betrayal

Kim and Oliver married later in life as established adults. Before they married, Oliver offered to Kim that he would be the primary financial provider. As the main financial supporter to her kids from a previous marriage, Kim was excited to take a job that was purpose driven which meant that it was less financially rewarding. Unilaterally, twelve years into the marriage, Oliver decided to stop working, calling it an early retirement. They were not financially secure when he made this decision, so Kim had to quit her job and take on a more pressure-filled one to now become a sole provider. Because Oliver had never discussed how desperately miserable he was at work and made a decision that impacted them both alone, Kim held an underlying resentment toward Oliver even though she loved him and cared about his happiness. Her resentment unaddressed grew until they talked about it and cleared the air.

Emotional Coldness and Absenteeism

Intangible distance and coldness can hurt as much as a physical betrayal. The wound from emotional detachment must be taken seriously if you want to heal and move forward in your relationship. Sometimes the emotionally shut-off partner only realizes they need to do something about the way they're showing up for their partner when that partner is getting ready to leave. Often it can be too late, if the betrayed partner has shut down so deeply.

Yes, we have different attachment styles and not every partner is comfortable with emotional intimacy in the same way. Nonetheless, in an overall healthy relationship, partners must have warmth and emotional presence, and ample physical time spent together. I recommend for those who have the tendency to be on the cold side emotionally to try to appreciate the damage this causes their partner. Coldness and detachment can look like:

- Lack of sharing day-to-day experiences, thoughts, feelings, desires
- Lack of empathy and basic consideration
- Avoiding deeper conversations

- Silent treatment
- Lack of affection in words or actions
- Perpetually distracted
- Overworking
- Not sharing physical space, seeking to be alone.

Case: Meet Jill and Grace

Jill and Grace began seeing me because Jill felt disconnected from her wife of many years. She felt lonely and diminished. They were both doctors with busy schedules but at the end of the day, Grace didn't open up or show any warmth toward Grace. Grace was raised in a stoic environment and felt that Jill was just too needy. Even when they were together, it seemed to Jill that Grace was somewhere else. Jill knew Grace was more private and less emotional, but things had been light and fun at the beginning of their relationship. Everything changed with the responsibilities of a household and children. It was important for Grace to understand that while unintentional, her emotional detachment felt like a betrayal to the marriage, a breach of trust. While Jill might need to grow more emotionally independent, Grace would need to wholeheartedly understand why Jill felt let down for any real repair to take place.

Avoiding Sexual Intimacy

After years of marriage, it's normal for sexual intimacy to change. Avoiding or withholding sexual intimacy, however, can become a more serious matter, leaving one or both partners feeling hurt and that a promise has been broken. When you feel, or hear from your partner, a sense of loneliness, emptiness, and as if you have become roommates, this could be a sign that your sexual intimacy, or lack of, is causing harm to one or both of you, and to your overall connection. Some couples are still satisfied in the relationship even when the sexual connection tapers or stops. If you're the one who desires sexual closeness, what makes withholding feel even more like broken faith, is when your partner dismisses your pain and emptiness and doesn't show concern for making your sexual relationship more of a priority. This doesn't mean ignoring your own preferences for frequency and style of erotic connection. The key is to appreciate sexuality as a vital form of communication between partners. Withholding sexual intimacy can limit your closeness, harm the soulful bond, and be felt as a broken promise and breach of trust.

Reasons partners withhold intimacy range from (1) unresolved personal issues, (2) distraction due to work, (3) punishing or seeking control, (4) laziness, (5) resentment and anger, (6) lack of sex drive, (7) sexual dysfunction, and (8) selfishness.

Disrespectful Communication

We can't take back our words, or tone of voice once they've left our mouths. Some couples have a hard time repairing trust that was broken during embroiled and ugly fights, and others have lost a sense of trust by the sarcastic digs, eye rolls, constant retorts, interrupting, belittling, or other ways they feel disrespected that can seem invisible or harmless. They're not.

So many of the couples I meet with are simply not seeing how their words and body language, even if they are not yelling or nasty name calling, are disrespectful and leaning toward *I and it* kind of dialogue versus *I and thou*. It's vital to examine the kinds of communication that go under the radar as disrespectful, even coined violent by certain communication theories. While these words can seem innocent on their own, over time this treatment can leave a partner feeling diminished and unloved.

Disrespectful communication* can look and sound like:

---

* M. B. Rosenberg, *Nonviolent Communication: A Language of Life*, 2nd ed. (Puddle Dancer Press, 2003).

Humiliating your partner, name calling, or speaking disparagingly—directly or to others in public

Examples: *"Really, second helpings?"* Or *"Oh, he always does that. Don't pay attention to him."*

Sarcasm and mocking tones intended as insults

Examples: *"Great job on yelling at the kids."* Or *"Is that what you're wearing?"*

Manipulative language that twists reality

Examples: *"It didn't happen that way."* Or *"I never said that. You're taking it wrong."*

Moralistic statements that insult, correct, criticize, demean, diagnose, label

Examples: *"You spoil him way too much, because your mother spoiled you."* Or *"You're so selfish."*

Blame shifting

Examples: *"I hate yelling, but you just frustrate me so much."* Or *"You're making me feel guilty."*

Blocking compassion by advice, interrogation, one-upping, or correcting

Examples: *"How come you didn't talk to me about this sooner?"* Or *"Why don't you just ignore her?"*

Making Your Top Priority Something or Someone Else

This form of betrayal happens when you allow a third entity to come between you and your beloved. This could be in-laws, your children, an addiction, your work, a friend. When you turn to your parents, siblings, or friends before your mate, especially with someone who is not necessarily a friend of the marriage, this creates a divide between you and your partner. You create a bigger chasm in your trust with your partner if you consider this other person's needs and opinions as holding more weight than your partner's, and if it's a pattern. You might also confide in your parents or an outside confidant about private matters you know would make your partner feel betrayed, not a priority, or hurt. Over time, this can make a partner feel, well, not like a partner at all.

Case: Meet Marko and Tricia

Marko had to flee his country as a young adult and was very close with his mother. I began working with Marko because his wife told him that in their decades-long marriage she doesn't feel like she has a true partner. He was confused about how he made her feel that way. Eventually, Tricia joined for marriage counseling and clarified that it all started early on in their marriage when Marko turned to his mother first and sometimes exclusively when it came to decisions and sharing of news. Tricia reported many examples where his mother's well-being had been regarded more important than her own. Her decades of hurt came right back to the surface when Marko asked several of his friends for guidance on an important family matter that directly affected her. The old wounds of him turning to anyone before her made her reconsider the commitment of the relationship.

Whatever wounds or broken faiths you might have in your marriage, know that identifying and naming the betrayal or wound is one of the first steps toward repairing. Acknowledging the source begins the healing process that comes next.

CHAPTER ELEVEN

Repairing Wounds and Rebuilding Trust

For only when faithfulness turns to betrayal and betrayal into
trust can any human being become part of the truth.

—Rumi

For your relationship to be one that is happy and growing, repair must become an essential component—for the smaller cuts and most certainly for the bigger bleeds. Most couples lack the tools to heal their wounds and the appreciation for how vital repairing is—whether that's after a fight, an insensitive moment, or a bigger trauma betrayal. Don't feel badly if you aren't sure how to heal forward in your own marriage. We are just not trained in navigating conflicts, missteps, and relational crises, particularly in ways that lead to healing and a closer bond.

Truly, it's the whole of the four pillars in this book—responsibility, growth, priority, and purpose—that creates healing for couples long term. However, there are phases to healing our relationship. In the immediate crisis of a deep wound or even the chronic betrayals that have built up plaque over time, couples need special tools and guidance to navigate and begin healing from the inside out. I will be walking you through the way that I help couples whose trust is damaged, predominantly from infidelity, using a model of *the three key healing elements*—for both partners on either side of the wound. While there are some differences in the repair process depending on the type and degree of trust betrayal, the healing approach I use after the discovery of a secret relationship will apply for any of the disloyalties you would have read about in chapter 10. I will be pulling forward some of the same case examples to help you see how their healing process unfolded.

TURNING YOUR WOUNDS INTO GROWTH

Last chapter, I introduced the well-researched and heartening phenomena of Post-Traumatic Growth (PTG), which is defined as positive personal change and growth that follows traumatic life events. Researchers[*] have tested whether Post-Traumatic Growth can apply specifically to infidelity in a marriage. They found that partners are not only able to heal from the trauma of this kind of betrayal but that forgiveness and even positive growth can take place. Keep this idea close at hand if you are in the midst of healing a deep wound in your marriage. It is possible to turn whatever darkness you've experienced, or caused, in your marriage into growth and meaning—and potentially a deeper love and closeness in your relationship than you had before.

Case: Phil and Nancy
Let's bring back Phil and Nancy and talk about their healing journey. They are the couple who had been married for several decades when Nancy discovered Phil was having an affair with someone at work. As they sat sullen on the couch, I said to both of them right off the bat:

> What you're facing is one of the most excruciating life experiences I witness. Please know this is normal and we are about to go on a journey—a growth and healing journey. It's hard to

---

[*] Heintzelman, N. L. Murdock, R. C. Krycak, and L. Seay, "Recovery from Infidelity: Differentiation of Self, Trauma, Forgiveness, and Posttraumatic Growth among Couples in Continuing Relationships," *Couple and Family Psychology: Research and Practice* 3, no. 1 (2014): 13–29.

imagine now, but when approached in the right way, you can heal from this. You will not always feel this trauma like you do now. For couples, this kind of crisis can be seen as a wake-up call (of the most painful kind) for the growth and change that has been needed but ignored. I've seen it, again and again, if you lean into a repair process where you (1) take *accountability*, (2) make a *commitment* to change and to prioritize your marriage, and (3) learn how to *communicate* compassionately, you can heal AND build a deeper, stronger bond.

Telling the Story Is Part of the Healing

Phil and Nancy began telling me the story of what happened, because telling the story is part of how we turn trauma into growth. For Nancy, it was to tell how she found out by stumbling onto some confusing and unthinkable texts on Phil's phone. In that moment, her world went dark and blurry, and her body fell under siege from the shock and trauma. For Phil, the story was how he had lost himself. He didn't know who he was anymore, and he felt like a robot climbing the corporate ladder and was dead inside. His guilt consumed him along with the terror of losing the love of his life, the broken woman right there next to him. Phil couldn't explain much why he did what he did and was a bit in shock that he had become this kind of person. Nancy just wanted answers and for this whole nightmare to go away.

Guidance for Phil (the Role of the Betraying Partner)

After a great deal of empathy and validation for Nancy's pain, and to Phil who was suffering too, I turned to Phil and said the following:

> Nancy will be the focus for a while as the hurting partner. Yes, there will be a phase when we will explore your unmet needs or feelings of neglect, and what may have been going on in your

marriage dynamic that made you vulnerable to an affair. But not yet. For now, you must become a healing ally in helping Nancy with the trauma. Here are the three key elements for you to become a force of healing for Nancy, to soothe and support her and to begin rebuilding the broken trust.

Become a Healing Force

What I will share next is the wisdom and guidance I offered to Phil through the course of our sessions, starting with the early crisis stage, which is most fragile. With Phil causing the serious breach of trust, I knew from experience that, as quickly as possible, he needed coaching on how to begin making things right again—to become a force of healing. After a discovered betrayal, many partners make mistakes at the get-go, which only prolong and worsen the damage. The key elements to become a force of healing include: *Accountability, Commitment,* and *Communication.*

Accountability

Own It!

In your words and actions, show Nancy you take full accountability for the hurt you caused. This will give her something to lean on when

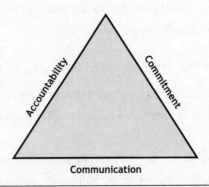

Figure 11.1 Key Elements of Repair

she feels no ground to stand on. It's tempting to blame, make excuses, or avoid, but now is not the time for any of these. Be brave and keep owning it. She will need reminding that you take responsibility for what you have done, over and over, long past your need to tell her or show her. Don't worry about being redundant. The trauma will mess with her mind and she will likely require frequent touchstones.

Show Your Remorse

Feel the pain you have caused Nancy and show her your remorse. Apologize with depth and sincerity. Many partners keep this inside because of their shame, or they already feel beat up and don't want to open the gates for another bashing. As long as you don't make it too much about you, you should absolutely share the torment you feel for hurting Nancy like this and for your own disappointment in yourself.

Accept the Consequences

Taking accountability also includes tolerating whatever emotional mood Nancy finds herself in. She might want to be close to you for comfort or she might want you far away, and it can change on a dime. She's grieving and the emotional roller coaster will be the predominant reality for some time. Of course, I'm not suggesting you accept abusive behavior. But it's natural for there to be angry days or moments, sadness, shock, fear, and doubt. She will be more vulnerable and insecure. Nancy expressing these to you are a profound healing tool to turn her trauma into growth. More on this when we talk about how to use your communication as a healing tool.

Commitment

Commit to Fight for Your Relationship

Express your *willingness* to do whatever it takes. The willingness is what makes all the difference. I hear consistently that more than the healing action itself, it's the willingness that matters most for repair—whether that's to cut a trip shorter, change jobs, share all passwords, check in extra, keep a live camera on when you're out of town. Nancy will be feeling very insecure, and unwanted. She wants to know you are willing to fight for the relationship, even if there's been years of other issues never addressed. If you're having trouble finding the desire to fight for your relationship because of your own doubt, then commit to giving your 100 percent to this healing process. You can get to all of those unresolved pain points in your relationship, and you should. But first lean into and express your commitment.

Commit to Prioritize Your Marriage

We unconsciously presume that our relationship will stay healthy and strong, and sustain us, without making it a true priority. Commitment has to mean rearranging your priorities and you need to say this and show this to Nancy, consistently. Not just during this intense time of crisis but establish new patterns that can nourish your connection going forward.

Commit to Change Through Personal Growth

Your transformation will be the most important healing element for rebuilding trust. When Nancy sees you gaining insight into the root cause of what made you vulnerable to fall as low as you did, and that you are addressing the underlying issues, she will see that you are making true change from the inside out. *This is what will allow her to trust you again—experiencing the more evolved, stronger person you've become through this.* A more self-aware person, who understands their feelings and how to care for their well-being, becomes a stronger, more trustworthy person. Once again, Pillar 1, taking responsibility for your own happiness and well-being is fundamental to a soulful marriage and certainly for becoming a force of healing. Your betrayal was weak and selfish, and Nancy needs to see that you are doing the work to get stronger and more in touch with your soul—who you really are.

Phil, it's time to do some digging to discover why you were so unhappy and depleted, what made you vulnerable to an affair, what fears and insecurities you have, where were you caught up in your ego and body desires versus what really matters in life? How is the quality of your relationship with yourself? In addition to marriage counseling, seek individual counseling to help you with your inner struggles and growth, with your relationship issues, and to explore your upbringing and how that may have impacted your view of yourself and expectation of marriage. When the time is right, open up and be vulnerable with Nancy regarding what you are learning and realizing about your mistakes and what caused you to betray her: not as an excuse, but as a way for Nancy to see that you're getting to the root of what led you astray.

Phil's Personal Growth Takeaway

What Phil realized early on in our sessions, with Nancy right by his side, was that he had been keeping his feelings suppressed inside of himself. He never asked for what he needed and felt he was here only to please—his wife and kids, his parents, his bosses and coworkers too. Phil realized that he held in his feelings in large part due to the critical environment in which he was raised. Phil was drawn to the other woman at work because she was not someone he needed to please. She was in a position in the company where he could be the focus and she made him feel good about himself, no strings attached. She was attentive and made him feel like he mattered, more so than he felt in his life with Nancy. Nancy had no idea that Phil didn't feel valued at home because he never opened up.

Commit to Forgiving Yourself

Yes, your remorse has a place in becoming a force of healing, and it's important for Nancy to genuinely feel yours. At the same time, your continued guilt and lack of self-forgiveness will only hold you back and keep your wife stuck. The first stab that made you fall was the betrayal itself, okay it was a big mistake. Next, you need to be careful of getting lost in the second stab, and that is guilt, which can keep you from climbing out of this hole even more than the mistake itself. You must believe in your fundamental goodness and your ability to change. Especially because it's a lack of self-worth that was at the root of your betrayal. You can say to yourself, *"Okay, I made a mistake, a big one, and I own that. But that's in the past and now, NEXT. What can I learn from this that will allow me to become the better version of myself I know I can be?"*

Communication (Soulful)

Listen and Attune

Let Nancy talk about it, *as frequently as she needs.* Allow her to talk intimately about her feelings, ask you questions, share what she's going through. Use the active listening prompts from the Love Seat Method in chapter 9 to create an environment conducive to intimate conversation. This will help her more than you think. Feeling heard and validated creates connection and builds trust, in and of itself. Nancy needs to know you're grasping her pain and that you care enough to see her perspective. Otherwise, it can feel like she's on an island and she'll have no logical reason to trust you again.

Be patient and don't rush her to feel better and safer on your timeline. Resist the urge to "fix" her feelings. She is grieving, which is a roller coaster of emotions—not a steady linear path forward. She will always want to talk about it more than you will. She might repeat herself, but that's normal (at least at the earlier phases) because the healing journey is an iterative process. Ask her what you do or say that helps her the most. You might be very clear in your commitment to be loyal and desire to move forward, but it's harder to trust that when you've been betrayed. The emotional storm she's dealing with is normal.

Reassure

Through words and actions, be liberal with reassurance. Communicate she is a priority and that you want to make this right. This could mean giving thoughtful gifts, doing nice things for her, more frequent check-ins, or whatever you know about her love language that will make her feel good inside. These are all forms of communication. Words are important too. Even if you've said it once, twice, three times, or more, keep repeating things like:

"I'll do whatever it takes to gain your trust in me again."
"We will get through this as a couple."
"You are the only one I want."
"I am committed to making sure I will never do this again."
"Seeing how much I have hurt you is the biggest pain of my life."
"I hope you'll let me spend the rest of our lives making this up to you."

Be an Honest, Open Book

The lying is the most damaging, even more than the actual sexual behavior or other kind of betrayal. The willingness to be honest heals and restores trust and builds hope for honesty in the future. If there's any question of you telling the truth from here on forward, Nancy will spiral with doubt and trauma.

Allow full access to all passwords, phones, Facebook, etc. She might not want to check, but again, you should demonstrate your commitment by your *willingness* to forgo privacy or the feeling of personal freedom for the sake of not causing any more pain to Nancy. You can let Nancy know where you are at all times. It's not what I'll recommend long term, but for now she needs open access to where any secrets could be stored.

Guidance for Nancy (the Role of the Betrayed Partner)

Once I made sure that Phil and Nancy understood Phil's role as an ally for Nancy, and their marriage, it was time to turn to Nancy to further soothe her and help her understand her role. While the repair process will depend on your unique scenario with certain elements taking precedence over others, I am sharing here the essential aspects for repair, and growth, as they most commonly unfold.

Let's bring up the same golden triangle as I shared above for Phil. Nancy's role will include the same three elements as Phil's, in some overlapping ways but mostly in ways that are obviously unique for her betrayal trauma in the relationship.

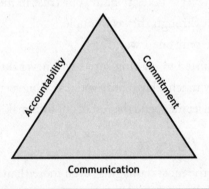

Figure 11.2 Key Elements of Repair

The Key Healing Elements (for the One Betrayed)

When it was Nancy's time to learn about her role, something like this is what I shared with her:

> Nancy, you have experienced a profound trauma. You are not alone in feeling devastated, humiliated, insecure, and broken. I just want to normalize the impact of what you have just discovered. Though your marriage may not be over, you are still facing a deep loss, a

disillusionment, which means you will be going through stages of grief. You have every reason to expect your partner to do all the heavy lifting to heal this. At the same time, your role right now is to prioritize taking responsibility for your own feelings and self-care. This is mostly what *accountability* will look like for you. I will also be letting you know what *commitment* will mean for you, and the *communication* that will be essential if you choose to move forward to build a renewed faith and a better future.

Here is what accountability, commitment, and communication looked like for Nancy:

Accountability

Captain Your Own Healing Ship

Owning your part at this point means not running from your pain, being gentle with yourself, and getting the support and tools you need to lovingly navigate the agonizing waves of grief. Mood swings are completely normal, and this trauma of unfaithfulness might bring up some unresolved feelings or issues from your past. Phil must serve as your ally in the process, and I'll guide him as best I can. Nancy, you are still the captain of your own healing ship. The sooner you own your role, which is to choose you by taking care of your own well-being, the better you will fair personally and the better able you will be to build a better future together.

Stabilize the Emotional Storm

Amid the devastation and roller coaster of insecurities and emotions, you'll need tools to self-soothe, build your resilience, and handle the invasive thoughts. It's vital that you embrace your feelings as they come while also managing them when they are throwing you overboard. Fight to stay in the present moment, because after all this is a crisis. We all cope with crises best when we don't get ahead of ourselves in time. You can manage one day at a time, one moment at a time when you keep your mind in the present, right here and right now.

Your fear of future betrayal, or what's at stake to lose if you can't rebuild the trust, is completely normal. However, these thoughts might be falling into the category of cognitive distortions, such as catastrophizing and overgeneralizing, particularly if the facts are telling you that Phil is committed to building your trust back. Yes, be on the lookout for signs of mistrust; you owe that to yourself to make a wise decision that will be in your best interest. At some point though, you will need to build a mindset where you "assume good news," whether you decide to continue or end the relationship. Otherwise, you will thwart your potential for healing, within yourself and the relationship. Appreciate and use the power of your thoughts to help you create the reality you desire most. One of the darkest feelings that comes with betrayal is insecurity and shame. Don't believe the ego voice that makes you feel unwanted and unworthy. Try this instead: "I am inherently lovable and valuable. No human can change that fact about me."

For all of these emotional pains and fear-based thoughts, you will need tremendous support. Don't think it's weak to ask for help, especially when the betrayal triggers old wounds. Support can come from a trusted friend or family member, a spiritual advisor, or an individual therapist. I recommend all of the above.

Create Your Map of Glimmers

Whatever practices you have that elevate you, center you, calm you—whether that be with Phil, with other people or animals, or on your own in nature or at yoga—now is the time to invest in what makes you feel as grounded and *in the present* as possible. Some people like to go sit in church or do extra baking. Work on a puzzle, move their body more than usual and in a way that they like. Being of service to someone else, even if just for five minutes a day, can be the best way to help yourself and connect to your essence. No matter what happens around you or to you, the more you take responsibility for your feelings and your life experience, the more empowered you will feel, which is especially important at a time of crisis like this where everything can feel out of your control.

Commitment

Commit to the Process

You are not committing to a lifetime at this point, but simply to give 100 percent to the process. I know it's hard to imagine now how this pain could subside and how you could feel at peace and trusting again in this relationship. If approached in this proactive way that I will be guiding you through, yes it will take time, but know that *it's possible* to start to seeing some light of hope in this darkness sooner than you think. Nancy, I highly discourage you from making any big or final decisions about this marriage based on how you feel now. Try to not even go there with the "should I stay or should I go" kind of ruminating. The jury is still out and committing to a second chance at this point means postponing a reactive decision and leaning into this healing journey we are embarking on.

This will be the hardest time in your marriage to fight for it, Nancy—but it's possibly the most important time to do so. When you can't see or imagine how it can be better, lean on my experience of watching couple after couple repair and even grow stronger. Don't talk to the wrong people about your trauma. Yes, it's a must to seek support, but it's better to not seek out those who don't believe healing is possible and who will only amplify your resentment and doubt.

Commit to Prioritize Your Marriage

Similar to what I suggested for Phil, commitment to making your marriage a priority is the only way to heal forward and to sustain a close relationship. For now, the focus will be more on your marriage than ever. This can be hard when you're filled with doubts, which are natural. You can still invest in making your marriage a priority, because it's a win-win. Either way, you will feel proud of yourself that you gave it your all.

Part of this commitment to prioritize your marriage as you are healing will include evaluating where you and Phil have stood over the years regarding the priority you have placed on each other and the marriage. For the long term, you want to do everything you can to keep a healthy fear of losing what you have, or what you will be rebuilding. The next pillar, Priority, will be a perfect next section for the growth and transformation that you will likely need for this chapter in your marriage.

Commit to Self-Understanding and Personal Growth

Though you are not responsible for Phil's hurtful actions, the sooner you can open yourself to how you may have contributed to the weakness in your marriage, the more you will be able to accelerate the recovery process. Remember, we are all here to grow, especially in our relationship. Even though you didn't deserve this kind of pain, now that it's here, try and see what this pain is here to teach you. Where do you have latent or blatant insecurities that you need to address? Where do you devalue yourself or need to grow more self-love or sense of purpose? Where might you have been part of cocreating a dynamic that left your marriage weak and vulnerable? Where did you sense something was off, even years ago, but didn't trust yourself to rock the boat? These self-reflective questions need to come when you are ready, and they don't mean you should blame yourself. Committing to your personal growth is not about blame but taking responsibility, for your own happiness and well-being, and the health of your relationship. It's about using whatever you face to free you from whatever blind spots that are holding you back.

Nancy's Personal Growth Takeaway

As the sessions unfolded and Nancy grew stronger emotionally, she began to have greater insight into her own lessons amid the betrayal. First and foremost, her level of self-doubt and insecurity hurled to the surface. That never feeling good enough feeling had been with Nancy as long as she could remember, though try as she might to run and hide from this pesky and deep wound. While it's completely normative to have insecurity triggered when your partner has an affair, Nancy was quick to realize that she could no longer afford to keep the vulnerable part of her that carried the burden of her inner shame isolated and alone. She sought individual counseling and invested in healing her sense of self-worth. Nancy also had body image issues that had been preventing her from freely being sexual with Phil. In her hiding from herself, she had been closing off the marriage from a very sacred form of connection.

Nancy also realized she had neglected the marriage. Still not taking the blame for Phil's actions, but she owned how much her focus had been on the kids, putting them first like she thought she should. She didn't realize how Phil had felt less important to her, when in reality that was never the case. She admitted that sometimes even when she knew that Phil was needing more one-on-one time with her, that she got lazy. It was easier and more natural to pour all she had into the kids.

Commit to Understanding Your Spouse Who Betrayed You

Many become instantly obsessed with wanting to know *why* and *how could they*. A rational explanation is often difficult to absorb or be satisfied with. While obsessing over wanting an explanation can be destructive, it can be helpful in healing to begin a process of understanding your partner. The sooner you can have empathy and understand what your partner is struggling with, or needs to overcome, the more quickly you will gain some detachment and perspective. The commitment to understand your partner needs to happen when you're ready to do so. But only at that time will you begin to rise out of victim feelings, see the betrayal as something your partner has mostly done to him- or herself, and take steps forward for healing.

Commit to Learning How to Forgive

I want you to consider that forgiving Phil is for your sake, first and foremost, most especially because it's the way you grab hold of your power to heal and to live with true inner peace. This doesn't mean you forget or deny the painful things he has done or minimize your hurt. At the same time, dwelling obsessively on how you were wronged will only cause you more pain and suffering. So out of self-love, please consider learning forgiveness. Yes, forgiveness is a trainable skill—a choice to protect the joy in your life and to become a hero instead of a victim. Science backs this up with some of my favorite research by Dr. Frederic Luskin with the Stanford Forgiveness Project.* Learning forgiveness empowers you with a mindset that bad things may have happened, but they will not ruin my experience going forward or who I want to be. You get to write the narrative here.

Blame is the first boulder on our back that allows other painful emotions to pile on top, like sadness and resentment, shame and hopelessness. Once you lift the boulder of blame off your

---

* Frederic Luskin, *Forgive for Good: A Proven Prescription for Health and Happiness* (HarperOne, 2003).

back, including self-blame, you will feel lighter and better able to appreciate the good in your life. The more you approach this loss and trauma with an openness to your own growth, while of course tending to your deep pain, the easier it will be to stop blaming Phil for how you feel. Because even though you are not responsible for the choice Phil made, like all of us, you are responsible for how you feel and how much mental real estate you give to your hurt.

Here are some mantras to make room in your mind for soothing and empowering thoughts and to help you move into a mindset of forgiveness:

- "I did not cause the affair, but I can always decide who I want to be."
- I choose to use this adversity for my own growth and to see how we can build a stronger marriage."
- "I am responsible for my feelings, no matter what is happening to me or around me."
- "I choose the calm and freedom that arises when I acknowledge human imperfection with an open heart."
- "I choose to forgive because this is who I want to be and how I want to live my life."
- "I let go of my self-justified anger and blame because they don't make me feel good inside. I care about my emotional well-being more than anything else."
- "I will assume good news."

Communication

Be Open and Vulnerable

Share your feelings

You're grieving. Don't keep your feelings inside. Do your best to put your feelings into words. Let him know if something has triggered you, and what kind of day you're having. Some days will be better than others, and Phil might not know when you've had a dip, whether that be feeling sad or angry or bad about yourself. When you share with Phil, do your best to use "I" statements, as in the Love Seat Method. For example, I feel ___; I wish ___; I'm scared that ___; I'm struggling today because ___.

Ask your questions (cautiously)

If you have gnawing questions for Phil, then ask him. These might include questions like

"How do you feel about me?" "What actually happened?" "What were you thinking at the time?" "Are you still attracted to me?" "Was the affair happening on this date when we were ___?" Please, before you decide to ask any question, keep in mind that you will then need to carry the burden of the answer, the image, and all that goes with that. You can't unlearn what you discover. So, Nancy, you will need to decide how much you want to know. There are no steadfast rules about this in my experience. But I do want to caution you with asking questions you may not want to live with or need to know about. Moving forward is the most important investment of your energy. However, many partners find that the not knowing is more difficult than knowing, even if what they learn devastates them.

Ask for what you want and need

If Phil misses a cue that you need a hug, don't hesitate to let him know. If you need space, same thing. Maybe you will need to be reminded and reassured of his commitment to do whatever it takes, even though he has said it time and time again. Tell him what you need, please do not hesitate on this. To know what you need means you need to tune in to your inner thoughts and feelings. This will be new for you, Nancy. Your survival mode has been to ignore what's uncomfortable inside. You communicating with Phil what you need, which can change minute to minute, will bring you closer and help you heal.

Listen and Attune

I know you might not feel like it, especially when you are in so much pain from Phil's deep betrayal, but the sooner you can bring yourself to open your heart and really hear what he's been struggling with the better. Ask open-ended questions to help Phil explore his feelings. Normalize his feelings and do your best to show compassion and empathy. The two of you need to get to the point where there isn't anything you can't talk about, that intimate conversations are welcome and somewhat commonplace. This is how you heal forward and grow closer than ever.

COMMUNICATION: LET'S TALK ABOUT SEX

The final stage for many couples who are recovering from sexual betrayal is bringing sexual intimacy back into the relationship. For some couples I've counseled, however, the fear of losing what they have together awakens their erotic desire to be close. For most others, they have a hard time reengaging sexually from feeling terrified to let themselves be vulnerable again or from the horror images that flood forward about them being with someone else.

As a way to gradually warm up to re-engaging sexually again, couples can begin to talk about sex and ask each other sexual questions. Sometimes the questions can make partners giggle a bit and the playful tone can help override the dark and heavy association that had formed around the topic. Talking about sex is a good stepping stone so it doesn't feel so foreign and scary after betrayal. I recommend making this new ritual of talking and asking questions about sex something to adopt long-term. Couples who communicate outside of the sexual encounter improve their sexual friendship, which means more satisfying and meaningful sexual experiences. Here are some sample questions you can ask:

- What are some of your sexual fantasies?
- What are some dos and don'ts for you sexually?
- What positions do you prefer most?
- Do you like aggressive or gentle stimulation?
- How can I initiate sex that you find exciting?
- Tell me your favorite way that I touch you?

The Healing Journey Will Be Ongoing

Healing from betrayal trauma is a multitasking process of navigating the intense emotional storm while gaining understanding about how you as a couple, and each of you individually, arrived at this point. Repair is about moving forward with the golden triangle of *accountability*, *commitment*, and *communication* to rebuild trust and make the changes that left the sanctuary of your relationship vulnerable in the first place. There will be many iterations and phases that will keep evolving, hopefully leaving more and more room for the experiences that bond you and bring you happiness and meaning as a couple. While this chapter took a deeper dive into the wounds from a secret relationship, consider this golden triangle model as a guide map for healing the rest of the ways you may have betrayed your partner or been betrayed.

Not Always a Happy Ending

Not all marriages can and should survive the breach of trust and hurt they have faced, especially with partners who are not willing or ready to invest in the healing process. With a second-time betrayal, be prepared for a greater investment in the golden triangle than for a first-time misstep. For some couples, their unresolved issues have built such thick walls between them and the foundation is simply too weakened to withstand the pressure of a healing journey. Further, everyone responds differently to betrayal, and for some, it's either too late or the desire, which is the hub of the marriage wheel, has grown too weak. We will discuss factors to consider when deciding whether to stay and invest or to leave your marriage toward the end of the book in Addendum B: Should I Stay or Should I Go? Regardless, committing to the healing and growth process typically yields a positive outcome, either by way of growing while leaning *in* to the relationship or as you grow while leaning *out* of the relationship.

IDEA INTO ACTION: RESTORE AFTER BETRAYAL

- **Keep talking.**

  Use the Love Seat Listening Method to have ongoing, healing conversations with honesty and tolerance for the roller coaster of emotions. If you feel you're ready, start talking about your sexual preferences and asking each other questions. You can find a variety of sex questions in John Gottman's book *What Makes Love Last?*[*]

- **Refer to the golden triangle.**

  As a reference, check in with the elements of the triangle—accountability, commitment, and communication—to see how you're doing. Where can you continue investing in being an ally of your partner's healing and the captain of your own?

- **Allow for some light and fun time.**

  Step aside from the hard parts you're facing right now and find some time where you can remember, even from before the kids came, what did you do for fun when you were first in love. Try to enjoy as best as you can. This will be important for your healing. Many couples find that things are so heavily focused on the trauma and pain, that they have forgotten about all the other good parts of the relationship. Imagine

---

[*] John Gottman, *What Makes Love Last?: How to Build Trust and Avoid Betrayal* (Simon & Schuster, 2012).

putting your woes in a container (you can always pick these back up later) and have a little fun. You won't be ignoring your issues but giving yourselves a chance to not take yourselves so seriously. We all need this.

- **Consider specialized books.**

Here are some books I trust and recommend:

More Than Sorry: Five Steps to Deepen Your Apology after You Have Committed Infidelity by Dr. Deborah S. Miller, LPC

Transcending Post Infidelity Stress Disorder: The Six Stages of Healing by Dennis Ortman, PhD

Forgive for Good: A Proven Prescription for Health and Happiness by Dr. Frederic Luskin, PhD

- **Seek individual and marriage counseling if you haven't already.**

It can make all the difference to have a therapist help you navigate this sensitive time.

CHAPTER TWELVE

Navigating Your Ongoing Differences

What counts in making a happy marriage is not so much how
compatible you are but how you deal with incompatibility.

—Leo Tolstoy

W e don't need a deep betrayal to suffer from relationship conflict and strife. I see a lot of couples who struggle day-to-day with how to navigate their everyday differences, ranging from personality to lifestyle, sex drive to how feelings are talked about. This is normal for couples. In fact, from over forty years of research,* Dr. John Gottman found that 69 percent of what couples fight about stems from a dissimilarity that is so fundamental that it's not resolvable. It's easy to fall into the illusion that a different partner would make your relationship life more fulfilling or easier. I remind my clients that with a new person, they would likely be trading in one set of perpetual problems for another. As Dan Wile wrote in *After the Honeymoon*,† "Choosing a partner is choosing a set of problems." The good news is that you don't need to be conflict free; happy couples can and typically do have perpetual differences.

---

* John Gottman, *Seven Principles for Making Marriage Work: A Practical Guide from the Country's Foremost Relationship Expert* (Harmony, 2015), 138.
† Dan Wile, *After the Honeymoon: How Conflict Can Improve Your Relationship* (Daniel Wile, 1988), 12.

From a spiritual perspective, living in harmony is inherently difficult for two separate human beings. It's part of the design so we can engage in the journey of joining souls. We each have our own unique needs and self-centric realities, so to truly merge with another in a long-lasting romantic relationship can seem unachievable. This is why we need to embrace our friction and adopt a mindset of growth to achieve true harmony.

Unless your differences are extreme or slice through a harder boundary of yours, they are not even a bad sign, just as friction isn't as well. The key is how you talk about and manage your differing needs and desires, and the extent to which you keep an eye out for turning your conflict into greater connection and growth.

EXPECTATIONS

We all have our own ideas of what we expect our relationship to look like in order to fulfill our needs. For example, some assume or want a more traditional type of marriage, which will certainly impact the nature of how they share domestic responsibilities. Others will be more companion-based, others more sexually oriented. Those who view their relationship mostly as a financial or a parenting marriage will have very different expectations than those who either want it all or who seek an emotional and spiritual one. These are often concealed expectations that only exacerbate the conflict when our realities and needs clash.

NAVIGATING YOUR DIFFERENCES

The key to handling your differences is the *HOW*. Below are five proactive steps to help you navigate your differences so that the positive thoughts and feelings you have in your relationship will outweigh the negative ones.

1. Assess your compatibilities and differences in your marriage wheel.

2. Establish your harder and softer boundaries.

3. Talk about your desires and differences soulfully—you're on the same team.

4. Seek compromise with generosity, embracing each other's needs with true care.

5. Grieve, grow, appreciate the relationship you've been given.

STEP 1: ASSESS YOUR COMPATIBILITIES AND DIFFERENCES

The Marriage Wheel with the Eight Friendships

It's time to bring back the marriage wheel. To assess your compatibility and your differences, below are pointed questions within each of the eight friendships.

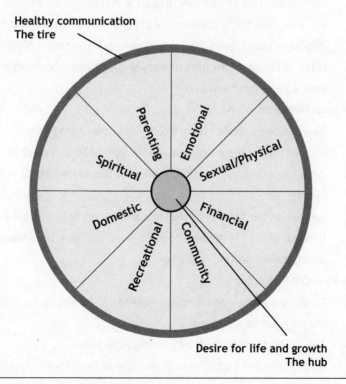

Figure 12.1   The Marriage Wheel

IDEA INTO ACTION

Now is a good time to pull out your journal to answer the questions below. The main idea is to identify where you're already aligned with your partner and where you have gaps that cause conflict. You can consider some of the questions as thought starters. Once you have reached the last of the eight friendships, write your first thoughts out on paper, for what you learned and your takeaway.

- Emotional Friendship
  - *Do you have a similar attachment style?* That is, do you share a similar degree of desire to be close and emotionally intimate, to have personal space and alone time?
  - *Are you married to your best friend?* Is that important to you?
  - *Are your personality preferences, communication styles, and love languages complementary?* Such as introverted versus extraverted? Planning ahead or being spontaneous? Round-about or direct in your style of communication?
- Sexual/Physical Friendship
  - Do you share a similar sex drive? Style? Sense of frequency?
  - Are you touchy feely, affectionate, snugglers? Do you need more space and feel uncomfortable with touch? How about in public?
  - Are you on the same page talking about sex while you're not in the heat of it or in the bedroom? Do you each share the same idea about communicating during sex?
- Financial Friendship
  - Do you get along when it comes to finances? Do you agree on how money is spent and saved?
  - Are you comfortable with who manages the money?
  - Do you trust each other even if you have different ways you relate with money?

- Community Friendship
  - Do you see eye-to-eye with the role and importance that extended family, neighbors, friends, and other community members play in your life?
  - Does your style of relating to your family bring you closer or cause friction?
  - Is there someone in your family or partner's family that causes an issue in your relationship?
- Recreational Friendship
  - How do you like to play and relax? Do you have fun and laugh together? Do you play in the same way? Are you an active type or a stay at home on the couch type? Do you like to travel? If you differ, what extent does this cause friction in your relationship?
  - How important is play and relaxing to you, and to your partner? How is your work-life balance and how does this work in your marriage?
  - Do you balance recreation time that you do together with that which you do on your own? Are you happy with how that works in your relationship?
- Domestic Friendship
  - Do you have rhythm and peace around who does what around the house and for your joint life together?
  - Is there one or both partners who feel they are overloaded mentally and emotionally in a way that causes tension between you and your partner? Do both of you have a good system for keeping the lines of communication open about shared responsibilities?
  - Do you agree on what should be delegated and what you should take care of on your own? How important is domestic equality to you?
- Parenting Friendship
  - Do you share the same values and approach to parenting? Does your parenting together bring you happiness and closeness or friction and distance?

- ○ Do you discipline in the same way? Do you come to terms with an agreed-upon balance of mercy and kindness with tough love and boundaries?
- ○ Do you feel appreciated for the parent that you are and a sense of being on the same team? Do you feel like you are true partners here, or do you feel there's an imbalance of effort, time, or priority?
- • Spiritual Friendship
  - ○ Do you and your partner see the world and something bigger than yourselves in the same way? Are there other values where you align or have differences, such as politics, being charitable, or how you spend your resources like time, money and talent.
  - ○ Does your approach to spirituality or religion bring you closer or does it leave a gap or even tension?
  - ○ Do you and your partner feel connected by way of a common purpose? Is this important to one or both of you? Do your desires to make a difference in life align, in scope and direction?

STEP 2: IDENTIFY YOUR HARDER AND SOFTER BOUNDARIES

To negotiate your differences in a balanced way, it's important to first get clear about what needs are core to you. Some of this will unfold through your dialogue, but coming in with self-awareness better prepares you and ensures that one partner doesn't sacrifice too much.

You have certain fundamental needs with little to no room for compromise in order to be true to yourself. I call these your *harder boundaries*. You have other areas that are more bendable, not as black and white. I call these your *softer boundaries*. Softening your boundaries doesn't mean you are betraying your needs and desires, but just being more open to adjusting the frequency, timing, and method for achieving what your core self needs. It will be best to keep your harder boundaries as few as possible and be prepared to share them with explanation to your partner so they can understand what they mean to you.

Unconditional Love ≠ Unconditional Environment

A soulful relationship is *not* one where you sacrifice so much that you betray yourself. Don't confuse unconditional love with unconditional environment. A relationship is an environment. You can love someone endlessly, but this is different from the environment the relationship creates. You have a responsibility to be conditional about the quality of your environment. It's the free will you've been given and has a direct impact on your capacity to find joy and self-actualization.

Certain harder boundaries won't come with much compromise because they are about protecting your environment. For example, perpetual lying and neglect, substance abuse and disrespectful communication, financial infidelity or repeated secret relationships: These are fair game for harder boundaries. Don't be afraid to set parameters and *choose you* if you feel your well-being and self-respect are not honored.

Table 12.1 on the next page shows some examples of harder boundaries and softer boundaries.

What Are Your Harder Boundaries?

To connect with what truly matters most to you, you'll first need to quiet the noise and find the inner calm inside of you. This will open you to the voice of your *core self.* As author Mary Pipher wisely said to me during a visit in my thirties, "Slow down to speed up."

Visualization: Listening to Your Core Self
(to reveal your harder boundaries)

Allow yourself to get a little more comfortable and relaxed in whatever position you're in. Now take yourself through a few rounds of *pause, breathe, and relax* (PBR). You can soft-close your eyes in between reading through the words here at any time. Now, gently place your hand on your heart, connect with your core self. That still and quiet voice that has known you the longest and who knows your heart best of all, who knows what you need to be true to yourself.

- What do you need to feel connected to your partner?
- What makes you feel deeply loved, and loving?
- What are the things you do or experience that without them, your life doesn't feel right?
- What is never okay for you?
- What would be too big of a sacrifice?
- What is most important to you that fulfills what you've always dreamed of?

Harder Boundaries (black and white)	Softer Boundaries (gray)
I need some quality time to talk in the week.	I'm flexible about what day or time of day.
I don't let anyone raise their voice at me.	I will hear your concern when it's calmer.
I need some time to go out together socially.	I understand you're not as social, so I can go out on my own sometimes.
It doesn't work for me to do all the tasks at home on my own.	Let's talk together about a solution that takes the pressure off of both of us, and our marriage.
I am not okay with you flirting with others.	I will agree to showing more affection and flirting with you myself.
I need sex regularly to feel close, loved and fulfilled.	I can be patient and adjust my expectation for how frequent.
I must have money allocated for vacations and excursions.	I can bend when it comes to how many times a year.

Table 12.1   Harder and Softer Boundaries

IDEA INTO ACTION PART 1: WRITE OUT YOUR HARDER BOUNDARIES

Create two columns in your journal as you see from above and write *"Harder Boundaries"* on the left and *"Softer Boundaries"* on the right.

To start writing down your harder boundaries, you can use the prompt below:

> I know that to be true to myself, I need _____ in my life
> for me to feel fulfilled and happy.

Take your time and write whatever comes to you down in the left column. This step is about getting clear about what you want, in your own private sanctum of truth. Feel free to refer back to the marriage wheel to gain further thought starters for the different areas that are important to you.

What Are Your Softer Boundaries?

Now that you have more clarity about your harder boundaries, it's time to see where you can be flexible. This is the time consider your partner's core needs and happiness, and the whole of your relationship.

Visualization: Awakening Generosity, Kindness,
and Care (for your softer boundaries)

Now allow yourself to continue or slip back into a relaxed state, in your body and mind. Find the voice of your core self that deeply wants your partner to be happy. Place your hand over heart and imagine the kindest thing your partner has done for you, what they have brought into your life. Feel the love inside of you and how much their happiness means to you. Whenever you feel ready, bring out your notebook or journal and prepare for the next step.

IDEA INTO ACTION PART 2: CREATE YOUR SOFTER BOUNDARIES

Bring back your journal page with the two columns. Now for each harder boundary you wrote, see what kinds of creative softer boundaries you can come up with to allow for give and take. You can bring these with you into step 3 as you talk compromise with your partner.

STEP 3: TALK ABOUT YOUR COMPATIBILITIES
AND DIFFERENCES SOULFULLY

Next step is for you and your partner to begin sharing what you've come up with. That is, how did you answer the questions regarding your compatibility and your differences? What are your core needs that form your harder boundaries? Be as specific as you can be, and share these with vulnerability and warmth, not aggression or defensiveness. *Make sure to explain why this core need is so important to you.* We presume all too often that our spouses live inside our heads. I hear this so many times from partners, "If you would have explained to me why you need this so much, I would have gladly been more supportive."

It's best to have a dialogue and do this exercise together when you are both in a neutral emotional state and your hearts are open. When your hearts are open, this will prime you best for step 4 as you brainstorm together to compromise with a spirit of generosity.

STEP 4: SEEK COMPROMISE TOGETHER, WITH GENEROSITY

Be prepared to be creative! Now that you've starting to talk about your harder boundaries, it's time to brainstorm about your softer boundaries together, *in the right spirit!* You can work as a team to sweeten your relationship with generosity, give and take, and a desire for *both* you and your partner to be happy. When compromise is approached with this intention, the spirit of unity shines through and will support you as a couple in often unexpected ways.

One Boat Mentality

Inspired by a metaphor from the ancient sages of Kabbalah, consider viewing the two of you as seafarers on a boat together.* Yes, two

---

* R. Michael Berg, ed., *The Zohar: Volume 17, by Rav Shimon bar Yochai with Sulam Commentary by Rav Yehuda Ashlag,* (Kabbalah Centre International, 2003), Naso paragraph 19.

separate mates, but sharing one boat. If you're tending to only your needs and desires at the expense of the other, then you're basically drilling a hole in your partner's side of the boat. Then you both go down. It's not easy to navigate this one boat mentality—where you see yourselves as interconnected—yet this is what it takes to fare the seas of long-lasting love. The whole boat can become a happy and healthy sanctuary when partners have a we-are-in-this-together motto, even if one of the rowers is not going in the exact direction or at the precise pace they had in mind.

Seeing your relationship as one boat means that when you are seeking compromise in a climate of agreement, you see the holiness in each other and what you share. You refrain from digs, pressuring, or manipulating, or holding your compromise over their head with resentment.

A FEW DOS AND DON'TS

Do the Generosity Math and Take Turns

Be on the lookout for the effort your partner has put in to make you happy and decide it's time to return the generosity. The math also includes assessing the importance of the need or desire to your mate. For example, my husband has events with his business group during the week, and I tend to be quite out of steam at the end of my day. Yet, I know *how very much this group means to him* and for me to be there with him. So, I put my nice dress on, freshen up my make-up, and off we go. Now if these meetings were weekly, that would be a different story. But these are special occasion events, and he gains so much fulfillment so it's a lot of bang for my generosity buck. Be careful about the negative side of this math game and try to stay focused on the good.

Do Think Outside the Box for Solutions

For example, take two cars if you each like to stay different lengths of time to something, hire more help if you can afford to do so and you can't find common ground domestically, and seek third-party expert advice to help you reconcile your differences, whether that's for parenting gridlock, dealing with in-laws, or financial tension.

Do Let Effort Count

When our partner has a different way of showing love or does something for us, but it didn't reach the sweet spot, or even close sometimes, we still need to approach this soulfully.

For the receiver. Even if your partner missed the mark, let's say it was on giving you a gift. The soulful, diplomatic way to approach this is to look beneath the outcome for the care and effort on the inside. Better to not make it a failure on their part. You can be honest that it's just not exactly your style but only when it's the right time.

For the giver. In this case, pay better attention next time. Or ask one of your partner's family members or friends for help with ideas. You can do something like this together to give you better cues.

Mini Case: Meet Stan and Becky

Stan: I created a slide show for your birthday party.

Becky: Can I see it first? I don't want it to be too long, which will make the important pictures have less view time.

Stan: Aren't you going to appreciate that I did this for you?

Try this instead:

Stan: I created a slide show for your birthday party.

Becky: Wow, that's amazing and so sweet. I appreciate it so much. Maybe I can take a look at it sometime before the party, just in case I'd like to narrow it down just a bit. You know, I'm kind of picky about these things. I can't believe all you put into this.

Do Grieve and Accept

Having a partner with differences that are meaningful to you is not always easy but a natural part of a relationship, of life. Let yourself grieve that and then move on to accepting, appreciating, and loving the partner you've been given.

Do Grow Your Care About Your Beloved's Happiness

While you should assert your needs and desires, ultimately, the goal in a relationship is not just about getting your needs met. That's unrealistic but also doesn't help you self-actualize into the loving, caring person you are capable of. Through the process of navigating your differences, set your sights on becoming more generous-hearted where the love you feel for your partner inspires you to care more and more deeply about their happiness. You can negotiate all you want, and even fight fair in the process, but nothing can replace the love the flows when you want what's best for your beloved.

Don't Let Issues Drift

Check in every now and again with your partner to see how they feel you two are we doing with the differences between you. You want to make sure to catch it before resentment builds up or too much distance.

Don't Take It Personally

While it can feel personal when your partner has different needs and desires than you, IT'S NOT PERSONAL. Especially when the differences are around your attachment style, neurology type, or approach to work-life balance, remind yourself that their way of doing things is not a reflection of your worth or lovability. Further, I see many couples where one or both have ADHD or other neurodivergencies. While there are great gifts in these differences, couples often need support to not take it personally and align together as a team.[*]

---

[*] Melissa Orlov, *The ADHD Effect on Marriage: Understand and Rebuild Your Relationship in Six Steps* (Specialty Press, Inc., 2010).

CHAPTER THIRTEEN

It's All About Growth, Baby

Everything depends on inner change; when this has taken place, then, and only then does the world change.

—Martin Buber

As we bring a close to Pillar 2, I say congratulations! We took a deep dive into your friction and how to use it for growth. These were not easy chapters to get through or even take a dip in. This pillar is the longest one by far, with the most intense issues to discuss and a steep learning curve for the communication skills that are essential to turn your conflict into closeness.

REFERENCE GUIDE

Please don't expect that after reading these Pillar 2 chapters *one time over*, you'll feel fully equipped to master the art of turning your conflict into growth. It's a lifelong project and practice. Even as these tools become more familiar, it will continually take great effort and patience to listen well and approach your conflict consciously and diplomatically. Slow and steady wins the race, as they say. And there are no small changes. Anything new that you can take forward into your relationship can create big shifts, especially when you are consistent.

YOUR GROWTH COMMITMENT

What we focus on expands. So, before we move into the next two pillars, *Priority* and *Purpose,* it's important to make a consciousness commitment to use your friction to grow, and to do so in concrete and actionable ways. When I meet with couples and individuals in my practice, they are there because they want change in their lives, a new and better life experience. As you have gathered by now, this better experience of life comes from committing to your own change, not anyone else's.

READINESS QUOTIENT

I invite you to PBR, *pause, breathe, and relax,* then ask yourself, *"How ready am I to commit to growth and change?"* There's no right or wrong here, but it's important to be honest with yourself, and your partner, about your readiness and commitment to grow—that is, your *readiness quotient.* How motivated are you to go out of your comfort zone, which can sometimes be scary, to put in the effort necessary to make change? You can't control someone else, but you have the free will to choose your own level of commitment to the process of growth. The discomfort of change is temporary but the magic force of forward motion is endless.

CHOOSE GROWTH FROM THE FRONT

The ancient sages* teach we are here to develop, to grow, so that we only desire to live what our soul wants, which is to love our life, draw closer to each other, and create goodness. This leaves us with only two choices in life, and they are not whether to grow or not grow. We have no free will on that. Let's remember the one choice we do have, which is the growth road we take—*from either the front or from the back.* Front meaning to grow proactively, willingly taking ourselves out of our comfort zone, committing to change and grow. Back meaning to grow by pain and suffering, from one wake-up call after another.

I hope that these chapters on friction and growth inspire you to change from the front, to look for the growth, before it sneaks up on

---

* Yehuda Ashlang, *The Wisdom of Truth: 12 Essays from the Holy Kabbalist Rav Yehuda Ashlang,* ed. Michael Berg (Kabbalah Centre Publishing, 2008).

you from behind, which will always arrive in a harsher way. I am not one to encourage living with fear, but there are some healthy fears. Complacency qualifies. Don't worry about the outcome in your relationship. If you lean strongly into your commitment to grow, then you can trust that it will be good, whatever happens.

IDEA INTO ACTION: JOURNALING YOUR TAKEAWAY AND YOUR GROWTH COMMITMENT

Writing helps to put words to our thoughts and feelings, at least for many people it does. Writing brings up more than we realize from inside of us, a deeper quality of inner awareness and insight than by merely thinking about something. So now you can pull out your journal or notebook and put into writing your own takeaways and your commitments for growth going forward. You can freely write or use the prompts below as thought starters if that's helpful. Let your first thoughts flow and stretch yourself to keep writing even if you think you're finished. Often, we discover our greatest insights as the layers unfold.

I learned that _____ and I commit to _____.

I realized about myself that _____ and I commit to _____.

I understand about my partner that _____ and I commit to _____.

Turn to Your Partner: Amend Your Couple's Conflict Constitution

Now is a good time to turn toward your partner and invite a dialogue about the commitments you want to make together during times of conflict. In line with your *Couple's Conflict Constitution* from chapter 8, work together to add the joint commitments for growth you want to make to each other and the sanctuary that is your relationship. Particularly, changes you want to agree to together that pertain to how you handle your conflict and your differences, and the way you want to approach the growth opportunities that your conflicts present.

Moving on to Pillar 3, Priority! Let's jump into how you can make your partner know and feel that they are the most important other person in your life.

PILLAR 3

Priority

Priority

We Make Our Mate the Most Important
Other Person in Our Lives.

E ach of the four pillars in this book start with a consciousness, that is, a foundational mindset toward your relationship that needs to then guide your words and actions. In Pillar 3, making your mate the most important other person in your life means you live consciously aware of how much you value your beloved, admire and treasure them, and how you make them your priority unlike anyone else in your life (outside your relationship with yourself, that's Pillar 1). If you are not treating your partner as a priority, it's an indication that you are not *thinking* of them as a priority. Maybe you never realized how important the element of *Priority* is for your relationship—and as you'll soon see, for your family as well. And maybe you once did, and like the case for most of humanity, you have become distracted and take the blessing of your partner for granted.

In this pillar, your relationship journey continues to move from the mindset of *This is who I am* (Pillar 1) to *This is how we grow* (Pillar 2), and now to *This is how much you mean to me* (Pillar 3) in your thoughts, words, and actions. Making your partner the most important other person in your life is a commitment to your partner, but also to the relationship itself. They go hand in hand. What we give energy to grows and expands. What we neglect, shrinks and dies. You cannot create a sanctuary out of your relationship if you don't treat your partner and your relationship with utmost value and respect. The priority pillar is so often neglected and underappreciated, particularly the negative impact when this is missing. I have seen it all too many times when enough priority is not present, it's like a silent killer—to the quality and endurance of your relationship.

UNSHAKEABLE ALLIANCE

When your partner is truly your priority, *and they feel and know it,* you tie yourselves together like in a true lover's knot. Two interlocking knots tied together such that when each partner pulls from their end, the knot grows ever stronger. Priority in your marriage allows your partner to *trust* you so deeply because no matter what, you've got their back and hold them as sacred, special, and an ever-present primary consideration. They feel secure in themselves and stable in the relationship by how you tell them and show them how important they are to you. When you feel so utterly special to someone, you know you can count on them—emotionally, physically, and spiritually. This doesn't mean you never leave their side or neglect your passions, even if honoring yourself conflicts with your partner's needs. However, with the strength of your lovers' knot, you trust your importance to one another is ironclad. Priority brings you to an unshakeable alliance and bank of goodwill that helps you prevent unnecessary conflict, weather even the worst arguments, and create a deep connection of two becoming one.

CHAPTER FOURTEEN

Love Is a Verb: Soulmating

*There are a hundred paths through the world that are easier
than loving. But, who wants easier?*

—Mary Oliver

Love must be seen as a verb, something you build not merely a feel-ing you expectantly hope for, or presume will last or get stronger on its own. This brings me back to Pillar 1: Responsibility. *We are each responsible for our happiness and well-being.* Similarly, to create a close soulmate experience, we need to reframe our expectation of a relation-ship and embrace our personal responsibility in creating it, giving to it. This means seeing our partner as someone to go toward in order to give and not a person to go toward in order to take. This is the active state of *"soulmating."* When someone is your priority, your thoughts, words, and actions toward them are filled with generosity.

THE F-WORD: EFFORT

We are naturally more inclined to consider how our partner and our relationship can serve and support us. The catch is that to become a true receiver, we need to become a true giver. Prioritizing our mate, and giving them love accordingly, feels so natural at the beginning. Eventually, the limerence fades and appreciation wanes. Then as the day to day ensues, our needs begin to clash all the while life's demands pile higher. This is the time to make friends with the *F-word*—that is, *effort*. Effort to appreciate, effort to be thoughtful, effort to open your heart, effort to address wedges, effort to be helpful, effort to make room on your calendar for not just what's urgent, but what's most important. On every level, in thought, word, and deed, effort is the only way you'll have a chance to consistently make your partner the priority needed to create a fulfilling, soulful marriage.

Effort must become a nonnegotiable expectation in your relationship. First of all, there are so many threats to long-lasting love that a passive, reactionary stance is simply a luxury we cannot afford. All the ways that we let our mates fall to a lower priority is one of the biggest enemies of long-lasting love. We are bombarded with constant intruders to our togetherness. It's important to keep in mind the idea that effort is your best friend.

GOING AGAINST YOUR NATURE CREATES MIRACLES

As we spoke about in the *growth* pillar, there is no fulfillment that is lasting when we have not invested effort and transformation. It's simply universal law and why we benefit greatly when we welcome effort instead of avoid it.

The force of life is ever present and shines endlessly, yet it needs a proper opening to flow in and through. We, with our effort going out of our comfort zone, create that opening. When you consider yourself an active cocreator—along with your partner and the Source of Life—together you form a three-way partnership in which love can flow endlessly. While making your partner a priority often means putting in great effort, it doesn't mean ignoring your relationship with yourself or your own well-being. It's not an either/or but a both/and. Effort includes seeking and tweaking the balance. There will be times for making your own needs a priority, and there will be times for grabbing the transformational opportunity to give and be generous when you feel tempted by your self-serving urges. It's the going against your nature that creates miracles, whether that's to show self-care when that's hard to do or set aside something of your own desire to lovingly be there for your partner. When it comes to making your mate a priority, there are so many competing voices and variables. This is why it's important to be on the lookout and be wary of those times you don't feel like making your mate a priority. You are likely being given a chance to go against your nature and make some magic.

EFFORT LEADS TO EFFORTLESSNESS

Yes, this chapter is about effort—and yet, there's a paradox here, just as it is for anything true and lasting. I invite you to open your mind to the idea that with greater effort you tap into the effortless. Once you make the shift and commit to investing in your partner as your priority, especially with the desire to give love and care, you begin to feel it and know it from the epicenter of your being. Then it's not as hard to think and act accordingly. When our relationships are fresh and new, we tend to have that effortless sense of priority, then we lose or forget it. These phases are normal and built into the universe. The essential ongoing phase of a soulful relationship must be that you choose *priority* amid life's opposing forces, which will ultimately bring you back to the beginning when it was effortless. But this time, it will be well-earned, so you get to keep it and nourish yourself from it.

The return to the priority, if you will, brings in a new momentum and a quantum energy that is hard to explain with if-then thinking. Rather than "I'll give more when I receive more," or "I'll make them a priority when I'm in the mood or when I'm not so busy and stressed," *step into being that partner now.* This doesn't mean staying in a toxic relationship or neglecting all of your other responsibilities. These are common clarifications I need to repeat. At the same time, I've seen again and again where a relationship that feels unsatisfying or even draining turns around when partners make simple yet profound shifts in their priorities.

COMMIT TO FIGHT FOR YOUR RELATIONSHIP

You can think of adding greater *priority* as fighting for your relationship. If you aren't going to fight for it, then who else will? Even when we start off with the right person, no relationship is immune to the need to continually prioritize one another and put in effort. Increasing priority can sometimes mean faking it. Don't worry if this feels un-·
realistic, unnatural, or seemingly unlikely to make a difference. Lean into being that partner who makes their mate a priority and let go of the outcome for now.

Case: Meet Andy and Diane

Andy and Diane were the love of each other's lives. Andy reached out for marriage counseling because he had had an affair and was desperate to save his marriage. He had become acutely stressed at work, wasn't dealing with his feelings openly, and felt neglected in his marriage because Diane traveled a lot for work and had less desire for sex than Andy. This wasn't meant to be personal, but it felt that way to Andy. Just as it certainly felt personal to Diane when Andy had a secret sexual relationship.

Effort for Andy meant addressing his feelings openly when he felt vulnerable to the attention of another woman. But this was so out of his comfort zone, growing up as the caretaker to everyone in his family. He was used to subjugating his needs and feelings, until they bleed out destructively. Andy needed this crash to break his patterns of self-neglect so he could grow his capacity to ask for what he needs, and in so doing, close the holes within himself that made him vulnerable to betraying the most important person in his life.

Of course, once the affair came out, Andy and Diane jumped into high gear, making their relationship and each other the top of the priority list. Neither wanted to lose what they had and fought together to heal their marriage—not only heal but change the dynamic going forward so prioritizing one another would remain a consistent way of life. The three boys grabbed dinner on their own while they came to therapy, something they would have never even considered. After each session, they made their own dinner date out of it. Diane now understood how important sexual communication was for Andy in order for him to feel like he was the most important person in her life. Diane worked on her perpetual worry about their boys, and reduced her travels, so she could have more bandwidth for connection with Andy. Andy stayed in therapy to keep learning how to put his feelings to words and practice going out of his comfort zone to express them.

In the pages that follow I will give you tools to bring *priority* into your relationship and explore all the ways you can ensure your partner knows and feels they are of utmost importance to you. The first step is to put yourself into a mindset of making your partner your priority and appreciating how important this is.

IDEA INTO ACTION: SOME JOURNALING QUESTIONS

- To make your beloved the most important other person in your life, what does effort look like for you?
- Where is it most difficult for you to make your partner a priority?
- Where you can you be more of a generous giver in your relationship, to be actively soulmating?

CHAPTER FIFTEEN

Order of Priority:
(Who Should Come First?)

Action expresses priorities.

—Mahatma Ghandi

The priority pillar is particularly personal to me, because it is something I learned from my husband. Years ago, when I shared my ideas for this book, he said, "This is all great! But there's a key element you're missing." I couldn't wait to hear. He continued, "Our relationship didn't become what it is today until I felt I was number one to you. Not just that I felt it, but I knew it, you truly *made me* number one. At the beginning, I felt how important and special I was to you. But once our daughter was born and then our son, I moved lower and lower on the list. You were so focused on each of them, and I trusted you as a parent so much that I thought this was the right thing to do. Once I felt you shift your energy back toward me, I felt better about myself. Until I became certain again of my importance to you, I hadn't realized how I was feeling bad about myself in our relationship. For me, your words made a big difference. Every time you'd say, "Honey you're my number one," I knew you meant them.

Day-to-day life invites a myriad of threats that can bring your relationship priority off balance. This chapter is about these third entity threats, starting with what I see as the most common—your children!

SHOULD KIDS COME FIRST?

When a new couple reaches out to me for counseling, time and time again, it quickly comes to light how their marital problems stem from this repeated proclamation: "Well, the kids have always come first." Now, here they sit on the counseling couch, sometimes mired in conflict or even broken from betrayal, starving for the love and friendship they once had. At least one of the partners typically confesses how putting the kids first still feels right, that they are simply bad parents unless their world revolves around their children.

Having children is a life dream for so many, and for obvious reasons. Yet there is no denying that these dependent beings instantly place the parents' relationship on the back burner—as they should. Adding the parenting friendship in your marriage wheel can put a strain on all the other seven friendships. Parenting becomes a true test of marriage and there is no way to prepare for such a disruption to the life you shared together beforehand. It's a tremendous blessing to become a parent and adds such a rich and deep experience to your relationship. Yet with the dramatic transition from duo to trio, many couples find it difficult to protect and restore their one-on-one bond. A few client comments come to mind. These are not meant to discourage you, but to highlight the healthy fear we must have of losing priority. One client told me, "As soon as we empty nested, my husband and I stopped fighting." Another, who is actually divorced, confessed, "If my husband and I never had kids, there is no doubt we would have stayed married."

With couples who have kids, one of the fastest ways to assess the priority given to the relationship comes when I ask them to rank in order the primary focus with these three key areas in their home: *Marriage, Kids, Self.* Guess what most say? If you have children, how would you do the ranking? Keep in mind that *Self* doesn't mean eating bonbons all day in between massages. *Self* means the responsibility we have to invest in our happiness and well-being, and to grow into who we want to be. Nonetheless, most people (especially moms) rank *kids* first, then *marriage*, then *self.*

I am always eager to address the who-should-come-first topic with couples because I see, day in and day out, how misguided so many good people are regarding their priorities in the family dynamic. In the earlier years of parenthood, when I fell hard into the "kids come first" mindset, my husband doubled down with me. Not only was my focus on the children apparent, I felt justified in making the children the centerpiece of our family. We both started to notice that our marriage bond was waning, and our kids were actually not thriving to the degree we wished for them.

Many neglect the marriage while raising kids, thinking, as I did, that they can rely on the love and priority they felt at the beginning. One client in a troubled marriage said to me recently, "I just thought that everything will be fine, it will be better someday, and we just need to get through these parenting years."

THE RIPPLE EFFECTS OF PRIORITIZING YOUR RELATIONSHIP

When our kids were in elementary school, my husband and I took a parenting with consciousness class that turned our priorities literally upside down. What we learned shocked us yet instantly resonated. The recommended order of priority went like this:

- Self
- Marriage
- Kids

The logic is: When we invest in our *Self*—that is, in our growth, happiness, and purpose—we fill ourselves with energy, which provides us with more to give to our relationship. In turn, as we invest in our marriage, keeping our friendship and connection strong, we fill the marriage sanctuary with loving energy that flows directly through us.

The closer and happier our relationship is, the more our children—who are a result of us—benefit from the unity we create. Happy parents make better parents.

I clearly underestimated the continual effort required to prioritize my husband so he would be certain of his importance. I was taking him for granted and staying in my comfort zone by directing my giving and responsibility to the kids. I had fallen into a mindset of expecting my beloved to be there when I needed him and counting on the strength of our original foundation to weather what I see now as partner and marriage neglect. It pains me to know Jeff was feeling bad about himself in our relationship for those years. Yes, it's natural and responsible that we need to spread our focus across all the important responsibilities we take on through life's stages. At the same time, we must remember who was there in the beginning and who will be there through it all. Our kids ultimately need to forge lives of their own. Similar to putting your oxygen mask on first before assisting someone else on a plane, our partner and the relationship cannot run out of oxygen, or everyone goes down. Heaven forbid.

At first pass, this order of priority might feel uncomfortable or sound neglectful of your children. Please be assured that, of course, children require and deserve a tremendous amount of love and care. At times, their needs will and should override any other priority. Nevertheless, when we take a look at the bigger picture—and the logic—this suggested priority holds its weight, both spiritually and scientifically.

ANCIENT WISDOM MEETS SCIENCE

This idea of prioritizing your marriage for the sake of your family goes back thousands of years. You as parents are intertwined with your children not just physically and practically, but metaphysically. As you grow your unity and love together as a couple, the benefit is quantum—your children depend on the energy they receive directly from the loving bond you create. You don't just feed them with meals and hugs, discipline and kindness. You feed them with loving energy you share with each other in your marriage.

Research* strongly suggests that children are happier and more secure when raised by parents whose love for each other is strong compared to those raised in a loveless or conflictual environment. Children can sense when there is discord between parents, and unfortunately, they tend to take responsibility for their parents' distress and unhappiness.

Relationship researcher John Gottman, PhD, has observed how the stronger the relationship, the greater the benefit to the children. Happier couples are also happier people. Anyone who is a parent can appreciate how much better we all show up for our kids when we are in a good place. I can't count how many times my husband and I would turn to each other and share our frustrations, glimmer with delight, or fall over in hysterics from some foible or ludicrous parenting moment or scenario. The more we prioritized our marriage, the calmer, stronger, lighter, and more empowering parents we became. Such is the healing and nurturing force that a close marriage brings to your family.

Some day-to-day parenting examples of making your beloved your priority:

- When conversing with your spouse, and your child comes in and interrupts, calmly put up your palm and keep your eyes on your partner and continue talking. You can also add a firm and loving statement like, "Right now, we are having a conversation. We will let you know when we're finished and then you can have our full attention." They will get used to waiting.
- Your partner wants to go on a trip, but it's hard for you to leave your kid(s). As long as, as a whole, you are also spending quality time with your children, take the trip.

---

* S. Gable, J. Belsky, and K. Crnic, "Marriage, Parenting, and Child Development: Progress and Prospects," *Journal of Family Psychology 5,* nos. 3–4 (1992): 276–94.

- When you walk into the house at the end of the day, greet, hug, and kiss your beloved before the kids. Don't worry, they won't feel slighted.
- You have a special event you want to go to together, but it falls on one of the nights your child has soccer (or dance, or math enrichment, whatever). Find a way to get them an alternative ride and go to the concert. It's okay to miss an event or two; there will be plenty more.
- Your relationship needs some attention, so your partner finds a special concert that reminds you of your early days. But you like to stay available in case your son needs a babysitter for your grandchild. Yes, babysit when called on, but make a commitment to your spouse. Don't neglect your relationship by going overboard to be there for your kids and grandkids.

CREATE A LEGACY OF PRIORITY

With both of our children now grown and married themselves, they frequently thank us for how we have modeled staying close and connected as a couple. They feel anything but neglected by the priority we placed on one another. Through all of their life stages, they see what it gives them to lean on our stability as a footing while they launch into the next chapters of their adult life. For our daughter who now has a child of her own, she regularly tells me how relieved she still is to know that she doesn't have to put herself, and her relationship, aside to become a mom. She and her wife both see how difficult it is to carve out time and energy for one another amid the relentless, 24/7 demands of a precious baby (on top of work, family, friends, and more). I watch before my eyes the lightness and joy in their whole bodies when they drop off our grandson and go on a date, or they take a little trip or keep their son in daycare just a little later in the afternoon so they can have time for themselves after work.

PRIORITY IMBALANCES FROM OUTSIDE PEOPLE AND ENDEAVORS

Triangles

To build an unshakeable alliance with your partner, you must become a proficient look-out guard for what in family systems theory is called triangulating. Triangles for a relationship are the endeavors or people you care about that become a threatening third entity in your relationship, *overriding your primary concern for your partner.* Triangles make a partner feel they aren't a top priority. Outside interests, endeavors, people, and passions can be very healthy for a relationship, as long as they are a friend to the marriage. That is, they bring you closer and don't interfere with your relationship with your partner. It's the divisive nature of these outside variables that can cause a triangle to form and directly threaten your partner as the most important other person in your life.

Spotting Triangles Is the First Step

Throughout the remaining pages of Pillar 3, you will find tools and strategies for keeping your priorities in balance by feeding and guarding the inner circle of your connection. To keep divisive triangles out, you first need to identify these pesky invaders. Again, awareness is the first step.

People or endeavors that can form a triangle and threaten your alliance—if you're not careful:

Kids	Emotional or sexual affair
Step-children/blended family	Friend or family member
In-laws	Boss or mentor
Work	House guest (could be adult child)
Addiction (substance, sex, phone, gambling, etc.)	Spiritual practice, hobby, or passion

Table 15.1 Potential Priority Blockers

Below is a visual of a triangle that causes division. You will see that an outside person or endeavor is blocking the direct connection between partners. The blockage could be on the side of Partner A or Partner B.

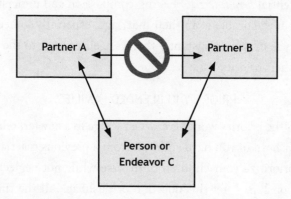

Communication Triangles

When partners feel stuck and don't know how to talk through their issues, they are at risk of a communication triangle. Most people need to talk things out, so if you can't open up to your spouse, you can find yourself reaching out to someone else. To seek support or guidance from someone else can be a good thing; you can get input on how best to approach your partner. A therapist or a wise friend you open up to is a great example of a positive triangle in your life, maybe about something you haven't talked to your partner about, but it's for the sake of healing your relationship and growing closer. Some communication triangles, however, are not only unhelpful, but they cause damage to relationship, keeping the complaining partner in a victim mindset and exacerbating the crooked view of their partner. Some communication triangles are also harmful for the person you're turning to. For example, when:

- one or both partners confide in a child as if they are the spouse
- someone regularly turns to a friend about marriage issues but without the intent of directly addressing and working on the issue with their partner

- parents stay too close to their adult children or demand it at the expense of the child's relationship with their partner
- a partner speaks to someone outside of the marriage, *who is a potential love interest*. Seeking compassion and understanding about the problems in their marriage, especially someone they're drawn to, instantly throws their partner to the bottom of their priority list.

PRIORITY IN BLENDED FAMILIES

How does the priority work here, when you're in a new(er) relationship and one or both of you have children from a previous marriage? How can you prioritize your children of divorce while not neglecting your new relationship? I get this question or pushback all the time, "Isn't this especially a case to put my kids first, to make sure they feel as safe and secure as possible? I feel so guilty that they have to deal with my relationship foibles."

Honor Your Children's Grief and Adjustment with Balance

Yes, with divorce and the blending of families, the kids will still be grieving the loss of their original family unit. You might be excited about a fresh start, but their deep sadness and anger can sometimes continue for years. And they are dealing with the discomfort of forming new relationships, new routines, and interruptions from alternating home bases. So, for this reality, your job is not to fix it for your kids or try and overcompensate. Supporting your child's grief and adjustment is a priority and you can help them in a balanced way. This can include:

- Making sure they have an open environment with you (and maybe a therapist) to express all of their feelings without judgement.
- Create special experiences that reinforce their original attachment with you, such as having one-on-one time without

your new spouse or their kids. Maybe you can keep certain rituals and sentimental traditions.

- Create new rituals and activities and involve them in how that might look.
- Have family meetings to discuss roles and dynamics, making sure the children feel included and valuable.
- Encourage their relationship with your ex-spouse.
- Be patient as they build relationships with their new family over time.

Supporting your children does not mean neglecting your new relationship. Putting the emotional needs of your new relationship on hold till either your kids are eighteen, or after, will never work. Not only is this neglect simply unrealistic and unreasonable to expect, but it's also not healthy for your new family unit. A new partner also needs consideration to feel like they belong with you and the family unit. Feeling like an outsider can be painful for both the adults and the children as you create a new community together.

Parents need to accept that the kids will be affected by your new romantic relationship, but neglecting your new relationship to try to compensate for their discomfort is not sustainable and doesn't allow your children to embrace the present reality and learn that they can go through an experience that is painful and still feel happy and part of something beautiful.

Your Relationship Must Be a Top Priority in Your Stepfamily

In a blended family, a strong and healthy marriage is just as much the foundation for the well-being of the children and the family unit as in your original family. Maybe even more so. Don't think this means you are choosing your partner over your kids. Making your marriage the top priority is about considering your partner's needs and feelings and should never be confused with depth of love. Please do remember that your love is what made this new family. And it's love that will keep it healthy and successful. Make your new couple relationship the rock of your family so you can build good things on top.

IDEA INTO ACTION: RELATIONSHIP PRIORITY ASSESSMENT T/F

Mark your answers to the following questions below with "true" or "false." Compare your score with the assessment scale below. Which questions surprised you or made you think about changes you want to make in your love and family life? What did you learn about the priority you're placing on your beloved and your bond—in your thoughts, words, actions, and schedule?

- I know very well what makes my partner feel number one in my life.
- Though it's okay to disagree about parenting, I don't openly disagree with my spouse in front of the kids.
- In my personal life, I spend more time interacting with my spouse than anyone else. We have somewhat regular conversations, check in with each other, laugh, and have fun.
- If I'm doing something special with my partner and someone else calls, I don't take the call. If the call seems time sensitive, I pause and check in with my partner first.
- When something significant happens in my life, my spouse is almost always the first person I want to share it with.
- My partner and I go out without the kids at least once a week and I feel good about that.
- I spend more time with my spouse than I do surfing my phone, playing video games, or watching Netflix.
- My children feel loved and a priority, but they also know they do not come before my spouse.
- I don't let my child play one parent against the other; we stay a united team in our parenting.

- I rarely change plans I've made with my spouse because the kids want something that interferes.
- My spouse and I take a vacation alone at least once a year and have a private date night at least once or twice a month.
- My spouse would definitely say that s/he feels cherished and appreciated by me.
- Our kids know that interrupting us is not a given. They have learned they'll often need to wait when my spouse and I are in the middle of a conversation.
- I make sure to keep our sexual and emotional connection a priority even amid the busyness of life.
- My spouse and I seek out and nourish our common interests and personal dreams that don't necessarily center around the kids.
- I never or rarely hear my partner complain that my drinking is an issue in our relationship, or any other activity I get involved in too excessively.
- I don't let my parents or other family members become a wedge between my spouse and I. We approach these relationships as a united team.
- I check in every now and then to be sure my partner is happy and feels I'm treating them as a priority in my life.

Your number of "true" responses could mean:

1-9 *Low priority range*—The priority and protection of your marriage is on the weak side.

10-14 *Mid-range priority*—Consider more effort, especially if your bond is in repair.

15-18 *Strong priority range*—You're clearly fighting for your relationship. Keep it up and consider sharing your trick with others.

CHAPTER SIXTEEN

Closing the Priority Gap: Eliminating Triangles

Good fences make good neighbors.

—Robert Frost

This chapter begins what will be the practical direction for the rest of Pillar 3—taking the idea of priority into a reality. I will now share some case studies of couples flung into counseling by way of a triangle they allowed to form, a breach of healthy boundaries—with in-laws, work, young children, and adult children. In each of these cases, partners identified their triangles that were threatening their relationship and eliminated them by creating new boundaries with great success. While these cases show a triangle that formed with serious potential to break up their marriage, even the triangles that have a mild impact on your relationship should be identified so you can close the gap. You will have a chance to go through steps to identify and eliminate your own triangles, then create a plan to make changes going forward: all with an eye toward protecting and building a soulful relationship filled with the fundamental knowing of your utmost priority in one another's lives.

SIX CASE STUDIES FOR ELIMINATING TRIANGLES

Case: Meet Noah and Evelyn: In-Law Triangle

At her wit's end, Evelyn blurted, "I told Noah we either come see you or a divorce lawyer. No in between." This was how our first session began. Noah had lost a sibling to suicide when he was a teenager, and he was the only child his parents had left. None of them had ever sought counseling to deal with the tragic loss. Noah's parents relied heavily on him to cope, and the trauma made them afraid of losing Noah. They moved where he moved, called frequently, and sought connection with him at every turn. Their close involvement knew no boundaries, even as an adult. Evelyn and Noah had two daughters and ran a successful business together, which made their private home time scarce and sacred. Evelyn was desperate for boundaries from the liberty Noah's parents took to come over unannounced, stay for as long as they wanted, and even undermine their approach to parenting. Mothers-in-law and daughters-in-law have an especially sensitive dynamic to navigate as it is, and in this case, because of their post-trauma response, Noah's parents were egregiously overstepping. Not only did this cause Evelyn terrible distress, but she felt that Noah cared more about his parents' well-being than hers. Noah divulged the tremendous loyalty, and also the burden, he felt toward his parents to take care of their needs. The divisive nature of Evelyn's in-laws in their family unit left Evelyn feeling isolated and alone. Here in Figure 16.1 you can see Evelyn's outsider position visually and the disconnect between them as a couple.

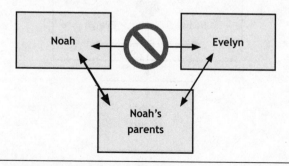

Figure 16.1   In-Law Triangle

Once Noah understood the damage to Evelyn's trust caused by his triangulating allegiance to his parents, he took matters into his own hands. He had thought the issue was between Evelyn and his parents and didn't appreciate his role in proactively prioritizing his wife and protecting the relationship. His parents' over-involvement and their enmeshed relationship wasn't bringing Noah happiness either, but he felt trapped in the pattern and caught between his parents and his wife.

Noah never doubted the importance of Evelyn in his life, so her unhappiness and the thought of her seriously contemplating divorce hit this strong and assertive man right where it counts. Evelyn's insistence that they seek help for their relationship allowed him to see that his priority in the marriage was out of balance. Within a matter of days, Noah sat down with his parents and laid down the parameters for the new normal of their dynamic. He assured them of his love and devotion to them, but laid out the decisions (not a discussion) he and Evelyn had made together for what will work for their family life going forward. He took the initiative, and Evelyn felt protected.

Once resolved, the shift in their relationship was dramatic, in the best way possible. Noah and Evelyn made each other their primary concern. Here's how their unified relationship looks today after closing the gap in their triangle:

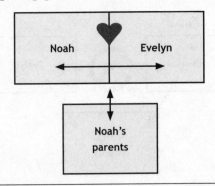

Figure 16.2 Closing the Gap

Case: Meet Karl and Eliana: Kid Triangle

Karl grew up in a pragmatic, stoic environment but was trying to change that with his children. Yet he still struggled showing warmth to his wife, starting with the greeting as he walked through the door. He grew up with no one greeting one another when coming home at the end of the day, or ever. You just went about your business. Acknowledging and warmly greeting one another was simply thought of as unnecessary. If you've said "I love you" once, then why have to say it again—this would be considered childish and weak. I asked Karl, "Do you greet your children when you come home and how so?" He reflected, "I give them each a hug hello. I want them to feel welcomed, something I never felt growing up." He was pleased with his progress.

I helped Karl remember why he came to counseling, because his wife was so emotionally starved and unhappy in the marriage. I asked him, "How do you greet Eliana?" He shrugged with what he thought was an obvious answer. "Well, I don't. The kids need this, but my wife, she's an adult. She already knows how I feel." This was my opening, and I could tell he was ready. Karl needed training in emotional connection 101. But like with the majority of partners I meet with, he needed training in priorities 101, that is, why and how to make his wife the most important other person in his life. And in a way that she will know it and feel it. It's about being an ongoing giver of love and generosity. His Idea Into Action after that session was to greet his wife warmly with an eye-to-eye hello, then a hug and a kiss—and before he greets any of the children. If any of the kids are in closer proximity to him than his wife, I prepared him to say, "Just a moment, _____ (insert name of child), I am going to first say hello and give Mommy a hug. Then it'll be our turn."

Case: Meet Alec and Anastasia: Stepchild and House Guest Triangle

Anastasia and Alec had been married for ten years, and they had two young children. Anastasia also had a son, Timothy, from a previous relationship who at this point was a young adult. Alec was the primary caregiver to their small children while Anastasia traveled a great deal for her work. Timothy had been living with his father until he recently moved in with them. Over time, Timothy's presence in the household came between them as a couple; Alec felt that Timothy had overstayed his welcome.

Timothy's mother, Anastasia, wasn't around enough to experience nor handle some of the challenges in the dynamic; the role of disciplinarian puts a stepparent in a very difficult position. Timothy had some struggles but wouldn't receive outside help. After several years, finally Alec put his foot down, saying, "Either he commits to get the help he needs and moves out . . . or I do." In the end, the boundary that Alec finally set was exactly what their relationship needed, and for Timothy too, who ultimately moved out and turned his life around. He now has a wife of his own and appreciates the strong family unit that Anastasia and Alec modeled and still provide him.

Case: Meet Frank and Amelia: Work Triangle

Frank and Amelia came to see me after Amelia rented an apartment for herself nearby. Still desiring connection to her husband, she chose to leave because of Frank's addiction to work. She tried to communicate how unhappy it made her, the way he allows work life to eat up so much of his time, focus, and energy. Even when together, he had one eye on the phone, claiming an urgent matter was on the dock. His sex drive was clearly affected as well, because he was would often claim he was too stressed to open up that part of himself, except for rare occasions. Disbanding their foursome family unit was the last thing Amelia wanted. However, she was willing to consider this worst-case scenario from the pain of perpetually not feeling important enough to Frank. She was emotionally and sexually starved.

Frank was stunned. He felt he was simply doing his best to navigate the corporate world, as well as parenting and household responsibilities that they shared. He couldn't see how out of balance he was. It took some time, but Frank began to understand the damaging impact that his priority imbalance was causing to Amelia and to the marriage. Little by little, he worked through his addiction to work, his fear of displeasing his bosses, and became more giving and present with Amelia. This shift saved their marriage.

Case: Meet Felicia and Benjy: Addiction Triangle

Married for twelve years, Felicia and Benjy both enjoy drinking and socializing, which was a fun and bonding part of their relationship from the beginning. Early on, Felicia noticed that Benjy got drunk quickly and then he would sometimes cross the line of good behavior. Initially, this wasn't a deal-breaker until Benjy began using poor judgment while drinking, especially when it came to driving and refusing to take an Uber. Though he never actually got hurt, nor caused an accident hurting another, she was constantly on edge worried that either could happen at any point. What was once a component of connection, alcohol use took a sharp turn and became a third entity divider. For Felicia, she couldn't get past that her husband's drinking was more important to him than his care for her. Such is the peril of addiction when it really takes hold. There was no going forward in the marriage unless Benjy took his sobriety more seriously. When he was about to lose everything, he finally acknowledged that he had lost control and needed help.

Case: Meet Amber and Henry: Friends and Family Triangle

Amber came back to counseling with a different partner this time. She brought Henry, who she said was her soulmate. She wanted to get ahead of their low boiling connection issues. During one of our sessions, Henry shared with her, "Amber, sometimes, I don't feel you admire me or put me first. You care so much about how your friends will view you, and me, that you'll correct me in front of them, and then pick on me during the car ride home over something so small. I know you love me, but it makes me feel in those moments like your friends are more important than me, and I am not someone you're proud to be with." Amber loves and admires Henry dearly so hearing that Henry felt like her friends were more important to her really hit her hard. Her parents were born in a country well known for a strong emphasis on reputation. Amber confessed her deep fear of being socially rejected. She realized she did the same micro-correcting with other partners, but with Henry, she didn't want to lose what they had.

Several weeks later, Henry shared a breakthrough from over the weekend. Henry said, "Amber, when you were so loving with me while with our friends, and even bragging about me, I felt like you and I were really together, that I was your priority. It felt really good." They were taking steps to close the gap.

CASE STUDIES TAKEAWAY: BRINGING BACK THE EIGHT FRIENDSHIPS AND THE MARRIAGE WHEEL

In each of these six case studies, you can see that a partner was showing other people or endeavors more concern than they showed their beloved. For Noah, he was living as if his parents were of more concern, which actually meant that in their marriage, through triangulation, their extended family or *community friendship* of the marriage turned from friend to enemy. This is an example of how *any of us can turn one of the eight friendships into an enemy of the marriage, so much so that it can wipe out all the other seven friendships.*

For Karl, he was learning how to warm up with his children and not with his wife. This made their *parenting friendship* rocky and their *emotional friendship* in greater jeopardy than it already was. For Anastasia, until she set boundaries with her son and heeded Alec's call for help with their "house guest," she was not prioritizing her husband's well-being and happiness. This added divisive bullets to their already strained domestic and parenting friendships due to a complicated scenario. The key to keeping the eight friendships strong in the marriage is the unity among partners within each friendship spoke.

With Frank, work was his top priority until the marriage almost broke. This work triangle he allowed to form turned their *emotional and sexual friendship* into an enemy of the marriage—until they eliminated the triangle and brought their marriage back into priority. Benjy's substance use had once been a friend of the marriage but eventually became its greatest enemy, putting their spiritual, emotional, sexual, and recreational friendships in serious jeopardy. To eliminate the triangle that was killing his marriage, he needed the humility and desperation to acknowledge that his drinking had become unmanageable. Finally, with Amber and Henry, though Amber really loved Henry, she was not making him feel number one when with her friends. She was creating a triangle born from her own insecurity. Fortunately, Amber's self-awareness and true adoration for Henry motivated her to be kinder and more accepting of him in social settings and face her self-love and self-worth issues directly.

THREE STEPS TO ELIMINATING TRIANGLES

My clients healed their priority gap by eliminating the triangles they allowed to form. Even if the triangles you've allowed to form don't create a crisis or a huge gap in your relationship, each and every one is worthy to identify and remove. It's a most important "I Spy" game to play. Here are the three steps to eliminating the triangles in your relationship:

1. Identify your triangles, through self-reflection and talking together.
2. Set agreed-upon new boundaries going forward, with the internal work necessary to address the issues causing the imbalance. You might need time to repair trust.
3. Go out of your way to express priority and loving-kindness to your partner, on a regular basis.

While the steps for eliminating triangles are simple and straight-forward, I want to prepare you that the process itself can be harder than it sounds. We have patterns in place and plenty of blind spots that leave our relationship vulnerable to outside forces that tempt our priorities to fly this way and that. Some outside priorities are harder to adjust than others, especially when we are feeling empty or resentful in our relation-ship. It's the "believe it before you see it" kind of mentality that you'll need to adopt to turn your relationship around. Once the injection of love and care that comes with making your beloved your top priority is set in motion, you can expect to see changes that can seem almost miraculous.

IDEA INTO ACTION STEP 1: IDENTIFY YOUR GAPS IN MAKING EACH OTHER TOP PRIORITY

This exercise will help you identify where a third entity is getting between you and your partner by drawing it out visually. You'll see the prompts for this below, but first, to help you do this exercise, you can reference the repurposed Table 16.1 with the common potential priority blockers as well as Figure 16.3, the marriage wheel:

How Might I Be Creating a Triangle?

Now using your journal, draw your own relationship as you see in the squares/arrows below. Then fill in any third entity that you're allowing (or might be) to form a barrier, whether that be mild or more serious.

Kids	Emotional or sexual affair
Step-children/blended family	Friend or family member
In-laws	Boss or mentor
Work	House guest (could be adult child)
Addiction (substance, sex, phone, gambling, etc.)	Spiritual practice, hobby, or passion

Table 16.1   Potential Priority Blockers

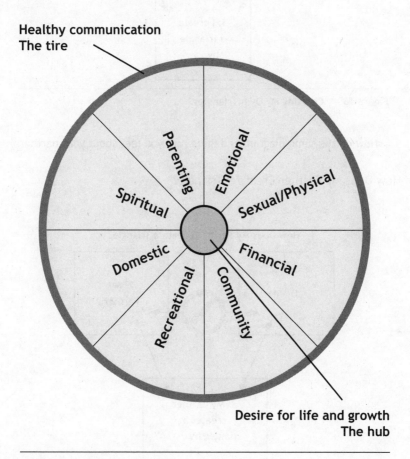

Figure 16.3   The Marriage Wheel

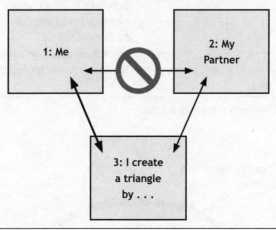

Figure 16.4   Charting My Own Triangles

Now do the same diagram and fill in how you feel about your partner.

How Does My Partner Create a Triangle?

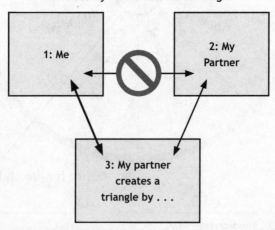

Figure 16.5   My Partner's Triangles

IDEA INTO ACTION STEP 2: CLOSING THE GAP

What's Working Well? What Do You Feel Proud Of?

When couples return for sessions, I first focus on having them share with one another what they appreciate, what they're proud of, and what they're generally happy about—individually and as a couple. Similarly, before moving into the work you need to do with your triangles, let's talk about what's already working well. Focusing on the positive first helps couples relax before we get to the harder conversations. Using your journal, draw the close and prioritized version of your relationship that you see below and complete the sentence in the lowest box by answering, "These are the ways I feel a priority to my spouse, and this is where I put my partner first . . .":

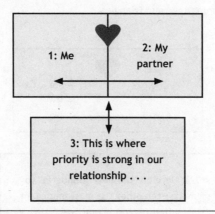

Figure 16.6   What's Working Well

MOVING FORWARD: STEPS I CAN TAKE TO
ELIMINATE A TRIANGLE I CAUSED

Creating Boundaries Together

Now, discuss *and negotiate* together what you each need to feel a priority. What you are willing to do for your partner so they feel number one and your request to help you feel the same? Brainstorm together about what boundaries, changes, and plans you can put in place to remove any triangle that is threatening your sense of priority.

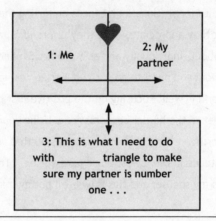

Figure 16.7   Eliminating Your Triangles

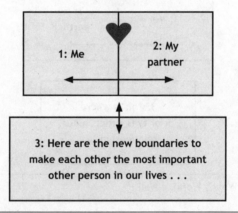

Figure 16.8   Creating Marriage Boundaries

CHAPTER SEVENTEEN

Cherish Is the Word

Happiness will never come to those who fail to appreciate what they already have.

—Buddhist saying

Now it's time for the fun stuff. Going out of your way to make sure your partner feels that they are the most special and loved person on the planet, to you. Prizing your beloved is fundamental to making your beloved never question they are a priority. Yes, you need to remove the barriers between you and resolve your conflicts with an eye toward growth, but that's not enough. You need to continually feed your partner with your love and admiration. This love stems from a core appreciation for their presence in your life and for who they are. So many couples I meet with, underneath it all, are missing that feeling of being prized and cherished; sometimes, they don't even feel liked anymore. They're lacking a deep friendship, which is the baseline ingredient for a happy marriage;* one that is filled with mutual respect and a simple desire to be near one another. This chapter will be all about appreciation, adoration, acts of loving-kindness, and good relationship habits to nurture your friendship and create an *environment of utter cherishment.*

---

* John M. Gottman, *The Seven Principles for Making Marriage Work: A Practical Guide from the Country's Foremost Relationship Expert* (Harmony, 2015), 21.

WHAT DOES IT MEAN TO BE CHERISHED?

Think of it as making your partner your king or queen. The implication is that you hold your partner in an elevated light, of awe, adoration, devotion, and respect. This is how you will receive the most from the relationship. You want to create an environment in which you mutually elevate each other because you can only enjoy the perks of royalty status when you're behaving well, which means treating your beloved as such. This doesn't mean your partner needs to be a perfect human being, but you see them through the eyes of their wholeness and perfection, you celebrate what's right about them. It's a choice you make not as a result of whether you feel they've earned it. Do not artificially hold them up in one breath and then knock them down in the next. The idea is to consistently nourish your partner, which I promise you will mean plenty of opportunity to go against your human nature.

There is an ancient teaching from the mystic and healer the Baal Shem Tov which explains that *God is our shadow.* Just like a shadow, whatever movement we make, the shadow moves the same. Treating your beloved with cherishment creates a spiritual connection of love and unity that casts a shadow of divine love onto you and the relationship. When "streams of light flow together," as the Baal Shem Tov said, "a single brighter light goes forth from their united being."[*]

HABITS FOR CONNECTION

So how do you grow cherishment practically? Good habits. Just like we all need healthy habits to stay personally balanced and connected, partners in a relationship depend on good habits too. When you nourish your relationship with your time and good energy, you feel closer and connected, which rolls out a red carpet of ease to cherish one another and enjoy each other's company. To stay on top of maintaining habits

---

[*] Meyer Levin, *The Golden Mountain* (Behrman House Publishers, Inc., 1932), 71.

you know make a difference, you can start with making a list by completing this sentence: "Something in our relationship is not right unless we are _____."

Here are some examples that might resonate with you. *Something is not right unless we are . . .*

- Having a date night together
- Making time for sex
- Seeing the good versus picking on the bad
- Carving out time to talk about our relationship
- Remembering to pause and fight fair
- Kissing and hugging good morning and good night
- Sending loving texts for no reason
- Telling each other what we appreciate
- Doing nice things for each other unrequested
- Going to bed at the same time
- Slowing down, being present, and really listening
- Being affectionate and snuggling
- Talking about our day without screens
- Laughing together
- Sharing at least one meal together
- Sharing our expectations for the day or weekend
- Being a team with entertaining and chores
- Going on a vacation once or twice a year
- Volunteering together or finding ways to give to others
- Going to church, temple, or study something spiritual together

Consistency Is Key

"Before enlightenment, chop wood, carry water. After enlightenment, chop wood, carry water."

This famous Zen Buddhist expression shows how the good habits that bring you where you want to go in life should never stop. It's easy to slack off after you have reached your destination (found your mate) or when you are not in a crisis. We get swept away with other priorities. Cherishing our partners means being diligent and proactive to maintain what brought you to come together. *No relationship is immune to a diminished connection, regardless of how strong your bond began.* We must never forget to "chop wood, carry water" consistently for the sake of your beloved. This requires appreciation.

The Most Important Habit Is Appreciation: There's More to It Than You Think

For any partner to feel cherished and adored, they need to know how much you appreciate them. As Fred Rogers said, "In appreciating our neighbor, we're participating in something truly sacred."[*] It's so easy to take our blessings for granted, but none as much as the gift of those closest to us. It's so backwards. We all need to offset what has been found as the negativity bias, that is, the tendency to notice the negative interactions and qualities over the positive.[†]

The ancient mystics of Kabbalah[‡] say that there are infinite blessings in the universe, and we are meant to experience these endlessly in our lives. So why don't we? How do we draw down endless blessings in our relationship?

What's the Secret?

Here we are back to the F-word. *Effort.* Appreciation is actually an active, rigorous endeavor to build a vessel for whatever blessing we

---

[*] Fred Rogers, "Commencement Address at Marquette University," YouTube, uploaded by MarquetteU in 2018, 2001, https://www.youtube.com/watch?v=qdcEGvk5764.
[†] Ezgi Sakman et al., "Negative Speaks Louder Than Positive: Negative Implicit Partner Evaluations Forecast Destructive Daily Interactions and Relationship Decline," *Journal of Social and Personal Relationships* 41, no. 6 (2024), 1415–38, https://doi.org/10.1177/02654075231224803.
[‡] Michael Berg, *The Way: Using the Wisdom of Kabbalah for Spiritual Transformation and Fulfillment* (JohnWiley & Sons, 2002).

wish to rest upon us. When you take your partner for granted, you are chipping away at the joy and connection you seek together. We get lazy, but this is simply a luxury we cannot afford. You can *say* you appreciate your partner, but how is this showing up in real time in your life together? You can't simultaneously feel appreciative and irritated or angry. Where is your appreciation in those moments when you forget something important for your partner?

Appreciation begins with your own consciousness being filled with gratitude and seeing your partner's goodness. When it comes to good relationship habits, place appreciation at the top of your list. PBR, pause, breathe, relax and spend *time and energy* really absorbing your partner as a gift in your life. You want to become *overwhelmed by gratitude*. This is what it takes to elevate your relationship to king or queen status. Go on detective missions, spying out what you appreciate, in actions, words, qualities, features, you name it—and let your spouse know. Tell them how you admire the way they handled something or how they did something even mundane and expected. Resist the urge to think it's phony to go over the top in noticing and expressing what you appreciate and admire. You need to be diligent, even obsessed, with searching for the small things, and big things, that you appreciate about your beloved.

DATE NIGHT AND GROWTH NIGHT

When couples begin seeing me, especially when they have really neglected the priority in their relationship, I recommend "Date Night and Growth Night." Starting with weekly and then adjusting as the relationship gets stronger. These don't need to be "nights" per se. Nonetheless, couples need to carve out time for play and laughter with no responsibility as well as time to have deeper, and if necessary, courageous conversations to grow their relationship.

Playful Bonding

Having fun together brings a lightness to a marriage. This is essential. We all want to be part of something when we look forward to it and can have some fun. Many couples report that when they are actively sexual, they can smooth over the rough edges—having fun together can also round out your relationship. Especially with kids and all the intense responsibilities that adulting brings, you need to enjoy time together like the free-spirited good ole days when you were dating or in the earlier years. *Show your commitment to making your marriage a priority with your schedule.* This will likely mean some kind of sacrifice elsewhere in your life. Choosing time together not just when it's convenient is priority in action.

I often ask couples, "What do you do for fun together?" When there's a long pause, which there often is, that's when I know we need to spend some time strengthening the *play* in their relationship. Like many couples I meet with, you may have to dig deep to even remember what you used to do that was fun together and explore what you consider fun at this stage of your life.

Laughter Bonding

When I meet with a couple, I love nothing more than to see laughter or some playful banter poking through. I find that partners who can joke about themselves and easily laugh together—even amid their relationship struggles—carry a fun-loving closeness and are more likely to find success in couples' therapy. Yes, relationships require effort, and some issues are not laughing matters. Yet in truly happy relationships, partners have fun together. They know how to temper tensions with some shared giggles—even laugh at themselves—and nurture their bond with friendship and lightheartedness.

When my mother was eighty-four, and she and my father had been married for sixty-six years, I asked her about the role of laughter in their marriage. Here's what she told me:

There is a commonality we share. It's through our history together that when we say things, or things happen, it just makes us both laugh so hard. I'm not sure why, but it tickles us when we both agree on something and then find out how wrong we were. We laugh at our fumbles, and sometimes we laugh at each other. When it's the two of us, our laughter is more intimate, like our own little secret.

Does your relationship lack fun and good humor? This is something you can change. You don't even need to come up with something new. What matters is the humorous spirit you create together along the everyday path of life. The truth is, most of what we laugh about are jokes and anecdotes, like my parents, parodying what we do every day. Being human offers plenty of room for the silly and quirky, the awkward and absurd—especially when we stop taking ourselves so seriously. When we laugh, it's contagious, and we make ourselves a most likable partner—like that friend you want to be around all the time.

Growth Night: Meaningful Meetups

Growth nights involve being present with one another to talk about your relationship, any needs or issues that need to be discussed, and also to deepen your relationship through vulnerable sharing. I can't emphasize enough how important these meetups are for keeping the lines of communication open to reduce conflict before it builds and to create emotional connection. When talking about your relationship, this should also include talking about what you appreciate about your partner, the effort you see them putting in, what you're proud of between you two, what's working well. I like to ask my husband, either on the fly or during a designated sit-down talk, "What can I do that will make you happier and feel more loved?" Growth nights don't need to be hard and heavy, though sometimes they might be.

Have these conversations while going for a walk, sipping coffee on the deck, at the kitchen table, or going for a drive. Find what setting works best for both of you, and *be mindful of the length of time*. Each partner has their own bandwidth for intense or emotional conversations.

Finding common ground is key or else one or both of you will dread these growth meetups, which makes them easier to avoid.

Seven Conversation Starters for Growth Nights

Encouraging a growth night is one of the ways I help empower couples to take what they are getting from our counseling sessions and weave it into their daily lives. Below are some of my favorite broad-based *conversation starters* I have developed to help prompt more meaningful, growing conversations. You can use these ideas and prompts if you are unsure where to start:

1. **Closeness Exercise**

   Each of you sit together with your journals. Make a list of what makes you feel closer to your partner, that is, what they do for you, say to you, how they treat others, their qualities, features, personality, and values. Also, you'll make a list of what makes you feel less close. This is the softest way I have found to give feedback, because it's ultimately about the desire to get closer.

   - I feel close to you when you _____ or that you

     _____.

   - I feel less close to you when you _____ or that you

     _____.

   Share your responses, taking turns. Use your active listening skills and make sure to check with your partners to see if your responses resonate with them.

2. **Highs and Lows**

   Share with each other the high points and low points of your day. Try to share your feelings and why it was important to you. Make sure to ask open-ended questions when your partner shares. Show that you believe in them and that you have their back. You can also add highs and lows for your relationship.

3. **Radical Appreciation: Seeing the Good**

Make a list of what you appreciate about your partner. Make it a long one. Nothing is too small or to be assumed they know. Share what you have written, and remember to make your appreciation a habit, a way of life as you *continually* look for what is good about your partner and share it with them.

4. **Feeling More Loved**

Imagine being asked, "What can I do to make you feel more loved and cherished?" or "What can I do to help you know and feel that you're my top priority?" Sometimes people don't even know how to answer, either because no one has asked or they haven't listened within.

5. **Dream-Scaping**

When couples share their dreams, it deepens the unity and capacity they have to support and nurture each other. You see one another not just for what they can get done, but for a deeper understanding of their inner landscape. No dream is too silly or unworthy of your partner's attention. It can be very vulnerable to share our dreams, so it's very important that you create an open environment. Next, find a desirable place where you can write. Put two hearts and the date in the center of a large notepad. Each takes turns drawing something that represents your dream or write a few words about it. They can be big dreams or little dreams, practical and impractical. Enjoy dreaming together.

6. **Sharing Your Biggest Fears**

Find an interrupted setting and time together and ask each other questions like:

- What keeps you up at night?
- What were you afraid of most as a child?
- What do you worry about the most in our relationship?
- What is your biggest fear in life?

- What are you afraid that people will think of you?
- What makes you a little bit nervous?
- What fear would you like to conquer?

If you don't know your partner's deepest fears, then you don't really know them. And you can't really love, accept, and cherish someone you don't really know. Therefore, knowing = loving and cherishing. Further, when we know our partner's fears, we know their comfort and discomfort zones better, which fine-tunes our capacity to show care and help them grow. Even those married for many years have much to find out about their partner.

7. **Buddy Reading**

You and your partner can use anything in this book as conversation starters, or any other book that speaks to you. Take turns picking a section you want to read to one another, or read on your own. Then share what you learned for how to have a better relationship or take the Ideas Into Action and work them through together. You can do the same with any book, not just one about relationships. Growth night types of activities are about deepening your relationship and they can be about any topic—your relationship and something else that inspires you or brings up thoughts or feelings you want to share.

Case: Meet Audrey and Jim

In their seventies, Audrey and Jim began counseling, an inspiring example that we can grow at every age. They spent years struggling to conceive and ultimately adopted their beloved son and daughter, one who was deaf. Audrey grew up caring for her sister with special needs, so she was accustomed to extending herself for others. She also subjugated her own needs. It took her all these years to tell Jim that she wanted more from him. Jim thinks the world of

Audrey but he's not naturally affectionate or attentive. One session, they walked in forlorn. Jim had forgotten their anniversary. She felt hurt and angry, and he utterly disappointed in himself. On the heels of this was a small incident that pushed Audrey to speak up more than she ever had. Each and every morning she kissed Jim on the way out for a walk. This particular morning, Jim had an early meeting and slipped out without a kiss. This was their most painful session but provided the breakthrough they needed. Audrey's pain overwhelmed Jim. I reassured him that we are all in training; he's not used to Audrey having needs so it'll be an adjustment for both of them. He initiated a fourteen-day appreciation challenge to cherish Audrey in his actions. He hasn't stopped since.

Your Favorite Person

We all want to feel that to our mate, we are the best person they know. It's so important to keep this adoration front and center with your partner. Even if they mess up, make a fool of themselves, have loads of imperfections, nonetheless, at the core, you just simply and unconditionally believe they are amazing—and they feel cherished for that. You are not trying to change them because you learn to accept them as they are, including their flaws. They are your favorite person, as they are, and they know it. This is what feeling cherished is like.

You might not naturally feel this level of regard for your partner right now—maybe it's due to resentment from hurts and disappointments, or your needs not being met. Maybe you're bored. Nonetheless, wherever you are in your relationship, start here. See how you can awaken this cherishing energy. Your thoughts and words declare reality. Don't make it dependent upon what you are getting in return. Look for the *yes* about your beloved, the elevation, connect with the good. Rest assured, awakening cherishment doesn't mean shoving important issues under the rug or expecting your partner to be responsible for your happiness. Issues must be addressed, and you need to remember that you are each responsible for your happiness and well-being. Nonetheless, we thrive in an environment of cherishment and whatever healing you need to do in your relationship and within yourself, this is best carried out surrounded by unconditional love and positive regard.

Intimacy-Destroying Outer Critic

We have talked about how forming a triangle with an outside some-one or something pokes holes in our relationship, but there are other ways we diminish the cherishing, loving environment. One of the most common is the outer critic, which I often see when one or both partners get caught up in what I call *micro-corrections*. More commonly known as nit-picking.

Gloria, the next-door neighbor to my counseling office, comes to mind. From our overlapping bathroom breaks overs the years, I got to know her a little bit—enough to know she was married for twenty-two years to her second husband. I asked her one day, "What did you learn from your first marriage ending, especially now that you are well into your second?" She answered instantaneously, *"I learned to not correct my husband all the time, to complain less, and speak to him more positively and kindly. I learned that he won't know how much I appreciate him if I criticize him all the time, which I regret to say is what I did in my first marriage."*

Most everyone is familiar with the inner critic syndrome and how it annihilates our self-esteem. The counterpart to the inner critic is the outer critic. According to author and therapist Pete Walker,* a way this can be understood is through the lens of childhood. The same tendency toward perfectionism that you might see toward oneself, rooted in un-worthiness, can be projected onto others. Similar to the mirror mindset, we want to look for how our perceptions of others are a reflection of some needed healing or change inside ourselves.

---

* Pete Walker, *Complex PTSD: From Surviving to Thriving* (Azure Coyote, 2013).

The unconscious role that our outer critic plays in projecting criticism onto others can also be an attempt to avoid the vulnerability that comes with close attachments. It's the *I'll-push-them-away-so-they-can't-hurt-me* protective mechanism. This displaced blaming can also lead to passive aggressiveness, such as distancing when hurt, withdrawing, backhanded compliments, defensiveness, and hurtful teasing.

We simply don't want to stay in environments where we don't feel good about ourselves. If we do stay there, it can mean that you don't yet believe in your own worthiness. It's a powerful arrival in life when we decide that the pain of staying the same is greater than the pain of changing.

Case: Meet Louise and Albert

Such was the case for Louise in her marriage to Albert. Not feeling cherished in the least bit, Louise stayed unhappily married for decades while they raised their two children. Completely concealed to Louise was her worth as a human being and exceptional candidacy to attract the kind of man she really wanted. She was drawn to Albert because he gave her the security of a family, and he was a safe bet to never leave her. Louise outgrew her overriding need for security around the same time she could no longer tolerate Albert's critical, blaming, and dismissive manner. So she ended the marriage, finally understanding she was worthy of a loving relationship.

You don't need to lose a relationship to learn the importance of actively showing appreciation and cherishment, but the important thing is to learn the lesson one way or another.

CHAPTER EIGHTEEN

Understanding Your Partner's Sweet Spot

*We cultivate love when we allow our most vulnerable and
powerful selves to be deeply seen and known.*

—Brené Brown

In order to fully love your partner, you need to know them—in
ever-growing ways. We are all like roses with protective petals that
need peeling back to open into our full beauty. You want to remember and search for the inner layers of your partner's rose, to make
sure you are touching them in a way that means the most. There are
two ways to unpeel the layers: (1) openly discussing expectations as
a couple and (2) understanding and searching for cues to hit your
partner's sweet spot.

STATING EXPECTATIONS IS GENEROUS

Expectations can sound like a bad word in relationships because if
you are too particular and demanding, your partner can feel pressured
and overwhelmed. However, if you don't have any expectations, it's a
set-up for disappointment and resentment. The truth is we tend to be
drawn and attracted to those who know what they want. Stating what

you want is vulnerable because you are exposing the underbelly of your needs and wants. It requires courage to be this authentic and risk that your wishes won't be honored. Approached in a balanced way, openly discussing what you want and desire is one of the biggest gifts you can give, to yourself and your partner.

Letting your partner know your needs, boundaries, and expectations actually brings connection and security. It's important to *be specific*. There's nothing more nerve-wracking than giving your partner what you think they want and missing the mark. You don't want so much guesswork in making your partner feel special. Partners prefer to know what you want so it's not so hard to hit your *sweet spot*. Your clarity will bring trust to your intimacy. If your partner doesn't get something right, they will find comfort in knowing that you will let them know so they can adjust.

Dismantle "They Should Know"

I often see in my clients an inner desire and belief that to be truly loved, their partner should just know what they need and want. "If I have to ask," they'll say, "this means she didn't care enough in the first place, and it won't feel real." I think this comes from the inner child we all have inside who wants to be seen and taken care of. We want to feel so secure and fully attuned to in the eyes and arms of another. The wise adult, on the other hand, has perspective. This part of us doesn't take it personally when our partner misses a cue, appreciating that we are all different, and aren't mind readers. While there is a place for the surprising or unsolicited thoughtful gestures—and we must become better and better at these—self-advocating actually feels good. We are ultimately responsible for our own happiness and well-being, which can also mean teaching our spouse what makes us feel special. It's on us to be as specific about our wants, considering what will help attain what we're seeking.

IDEA INTO ACTION #1: EXPRESSING YOUR EXPECTATIONS (DESIRES AND WANTS)

Using the eight friendships as a guide map, answer the question below regarding *your wants and expectations*, filling in each of the friendships as you travel around the marriage wheel. To tap into your honest needs and desires, fill these in as rapidly as possible. Write as many completions to the sentence as you can. Take two to three minutes to fill in at least six and up to ten responses.

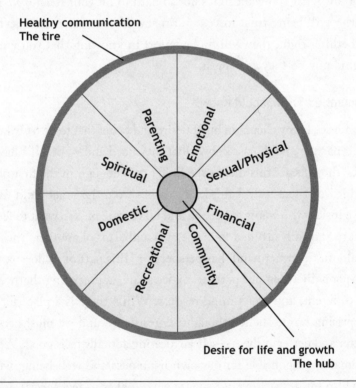

Figure 18.1   The Marriage Wheel

Here's an Example: Emotional Friendship

With our ____emotional_____ friendship, what I want and need in order to know I am the most important person in your life is:

- To have meaningful conversations about our dreams and fears, where we *both* open up and get a little deeper together.
- To talk about our day and share our ups and downs.
- To spend quality time together, that is not rushed and we both enjoy.
- To hear in words what you love, appreciate, and admire about me.
- For you to show curiosity and interest in me—my passions and experiences, feelings and insights.
- For you to turn to me as the first person you want to tell news to, the good and not so good.

Now it's your turn:

With our _____ friendship, what I want and need in order to know I am the most important person in your life is:

- _____
- _____
- _____
- _____
- _____

UNDERSTANDING AND SEARCHING FOR
YOUR PARTNER'S SWEET SPOTS

In addition to openly talking about your expectations, you strengthen your relationship by looking for love clues from your partner. Many of them you already you know, but there will always be more for you to discover. Love is a verb and a lifelong journey. Just when you think you know everything about your partner, they can always surprise you. You want to be on the hunt for aha moments, discovering new ways that will make your partner feel valued. Don't rely solely on what your partner has asked for. Opportunities for loving-kindness can be found in between the lines.

It's the Little Thoughtful Things

Sweet spots are unique to each couple, their individual personalities, and the personality that their relationship takes on. Sometimes, you'll notice cherishment coming through as big gestures or actions. More often, the cues of adoration are subtle and simple—but they say everything. The small everyday interactions alone can seem like the normal expectations of marriage, but over the years they add up to a lot of quiet thoughtfulness. They are what make a lifetime together sweet and happy. I took a little survey of my friends and family, who I perceive make their spouse and their marriage a priority. Here are some examples of "little things" they said their partner does that makes them feel valued and cherished.

- "The boasting things I catch my spouse telling others about me."
- "He always looks for me wherever we are—at events and everywhere."
- "He respects what I do and values my ideas and opinions."
- "He is physically affectionate, and I feel he has eyes only for me."
- "She anticipates a day that might be emotional for me and buys me little 'spot-on' gifts that only someone paying close attention could."
- "She reaches for my hand at night, and we wrap pinky fingers on walks."
- "The way we laugh together."
- "He asks my opinion on drafted letters in business or personal affairs."

- "She supported my decision to leave my job, even though it meant financial insecurity for a bit."
- "She winks at me across the room at any event."
- "He knows after forty-one years together I still need verbal reassurance from time to time."
- "She doesn't hesitate to tell others that we are soulmates, and she would marry me again, if she comes back to another life."
- "He always picks up the phone when I call, even if he's in a meeting."
- "He plays tennis with me on a Sunday morning when I know he would rather relax on the couch and watch sports."
- "I can't sleep when I'm not in the same bed as you."
- "I often find sweet little notes waiting for me in the morning with how special I am."
- "He brings me into conversations because he cares, and he respects what I have to say."
- "We work as a team."
- "He helps me take care of my elderly relatives without a single complaint."

IDEA INTO ACTION #2: UNDERSTANDING AND SEARCHING FOR CUES FOR YOUR PARTNER'S SWEET SPOT

Referring to the eight friendships as a guide map, complete the following sentence about *how you make your partner feel important*, filling in *each of the friendships* as you travel around the marriage wheel. To tap into your heart's knowing, fill these in as rapidly as possible. Write as many completions to the sentence as you can. Take two to three minutes to fill in at least six and up to ten responses.

Here's an Example: Recreational Friendship

With our _____recreational _____ friendship, I know I make my partner feel they are important to me when I . . .

- Plan a date for something fun together, maybe even a surprise.
- Experience an idea or something fun and I want to be sharing it with them (send a photo, can't wait to tell them about it, say, "I wish you were here with me.").
- Make sure I save energy for our quality time together, and not just give it to my work.
- Put my phone away and give them my attention when we have down time.
- Try not to be so serious all the time, instead be quick to laugh and joke around.
- Fill our calendar with dinner dates because we LOVE going out on Saturday nights.
- Plan special trips and make time on my calendar.

Now it's your turn:

With our _____ friendship, I know I make my partner feel they are important when I:

- _____
- _____
- _____
- _____
- _____

IDEA INTO ACTION #3: HOW ARE YOU CHERISHED ALREADY?

Below is the question I asked of my friends and one of my favorite questions to ask couples because they are typically so thankful for how it opens their eyes to the good *already happening* between them and makes them appreciate their partner more. I'd like you to fill in the blank to complete this question, with as many responses that come to mind over two to three minutes.

What does ____ *your partner* _____ *do, say, or decide over the years that makes you know and feel that you are the most important other person in their life? Other meaning besides their relationship with themselves.*

- _____
- _____
- _____
- _____
- _____

The ways to show love are endless, and the gateways and chambers of your beloved's heart never cease to unfold. So next are some other tips and tools to help you reach for the sweet spots of your beloved that maybe they're not telling you about or that you're missing.

THE ART OF NOTICING

Picking up on cues is an art, especially for the gestures that will hit your beloved's sweet spot. The *art of noticing* needs to be practiced and developed. Some people are more natural at this than others, picking up on nuances that will make someone feel warm, secure, and connected. Some know how to make you laugh just when you need it, find the gift that goes right to your soul, show affection that makes everything alright, say the perfect words to make you feel special, or anticipate what you need before you even do yourself. Please don't be put off by your own or your partner's shortcomings in this area of being emotionally attuned. *This art of noticing—it's a trainable skill!* And there are tools and tricks to help you. No matter your starting point, most everyone can become better at this. Your effort will matter the most. Because effort means you care.

Care Is Your First "Noticing" Tool

Care is the first tool because it's the fundamental ingredient to becoming better at noticing your partner's needs and wants, in a sustainable way. We prioritize what we care about. Care not just about what's in it for you (that will come back around, don't worry), but genuine care for your beloved's happiness and well-being. *For its own sake.* The spiritual logic goes like this: Caring takes you outside the limits of yourself as you become one with your partner's world. This oneness connects you to an infinite source giving you access to the endless light of wisdom. Then, you can better hear and see what's truly best for them. Here is the logic flowchart style:

C A R E → Outside of yourself → Oneness with your
partner → Oneness with Infinite Source → Endless Light
of Wisdom = Knowing Your Partner's Sweet Spot

Tangible Tools and Tips

Care is the foundation, but honestly, we all need concrete tools and tips to show up better for our partners. Try as we might, we still miss cues, especially amid the natural inclination to be self-focused. Here are some simple places to look and what to listen for when your partner doesn't verbally tell you what they want, or you feel stuck with how to do a better job. You'll want to use your five senses as much as you can. Watch their body language, listen to their words and what's in between them, notice their moods and reactions—depending on what you say or do, or in general, throughout your everyday life together. Here are ten thought-starter questions to prompt ideas for doing and saying those little things that go a long way:

• What makes your partner laugh, relaxed, and happy?

- How do you know in their face and body that you've hit the sweet spot?
- What does your partner look forward to that you can use as ideas for gestures of love?
- What kind of affection makes them melt into you?
- What do they say in passing about what matters to them or what they're experiencing?
- What do you do or forget to do that bothers them?
- What do they worry about that you can use as a clue to reassure or show comfort?
- What are their favorite rituals, habits, or hobbies?
- When do they want closeness and when do they need space?
- What do they do for others that maybe secretly they want you to do for them?

Another good resource to prompt understanding of your own and your partner's sweet spots can be found in Gary Chapman's classic book, *The Five Love Languages.** It describes the different ways people receive and express love including acts of service, words of affirmation, quality time, physical touch and sex, and receiving thoughtful gifts.

Life Cycle

Our sweet spots change over the life cycle. At some point, maybe you don't care about the toilet seat like you used to or that your partner just isn't a night owl like you. Some of your partner's wants and needs will stay constant, as will yours. Yet expect changes, depending on where you are in your relationship, your evolving parenting roles, what is important now versus what used to be important. This is part of knowing yourself and knowing your partner.

---

* Gary Chapman, *The 5 Love Languages: The Secret to Love That Lasts* (Northfield Publishing, 2010).

CHAPTER NINETEEN

Spiritual Lovemaking

During sex, a circuit is created in which you and your lover divinely intertwine with the Light Force.

—Karen Berg

You can't talk about sexual connection without emotional connection. When a couple is in sexual distress, sex itself is typically not the true problem. It's that partners are losing their connection. They likely don't have the rapport they once had or feel as relaxed, generous, or free with one another. Survey research by sex educators Barry and Emily McCarthy of American University in Washington, DC, found a curious differential in the role that sex plays in contributing to the happiness of partners.[*] They concluded that mates who were content in the marriage ascribed only 15 to 20 percent to a satisfying sex life. For partners who were unhappy together, they reported that 50 to 70 percent of the reason stemmed from issues with sex.

Brené Brown says, "In order for connection to happen, we have to allow ourselves to be seen, really seen."[†] This helps explain why emotional and sexual connection are so closely tied. The vulnerability that

---

[*] M. E. Metz, and B. W. McCarthy, *Enduring Desire: Your Guide to Lifelong Intimacy,* 1st ed. (Routledge, 2010).
[†] Brené Brown, "The Power of Vulnerability," YouTube, uploaded by TEDx Talks, 2010 (5:30), https://www.youtube.com/watch?v=X4Qm9cGRub0.

comes with being sexually intimate means feeling comfortable, letting go, being utterly transparent, and trusting someone else enough to let them in. Dr. John Gottman found in his research that both wives and husbands equally attributed that to "feel satisfied with the sex, romance, and passion in their marriage is, by 70 percent, the quality of the couple's friendship."*

Sexual upbringing and societal messages about pleasure and the body have caused so many partners to enter a relationship with an armor of shame. Not to mention the attachment fears lurking inside the sheets that cause many to see themselves perpetually at risk or broken. To shed inhibitions and reduce the anxiety of being vulnerable, at the very least, good sex partners must feel secure and close.

MAKING SEX IMPORTANT

Partners that sustain a good sexual connection are not only good friends who trust and admire each other, but they also prioritize sex as a special part of their relationship. It's a reflection of the priority they place on their beloved and the relationship. Regardless of the 24/7 demands of life, they slow down enough to engage in this unique and sensual endeavor in the scheme of all the responsibilities they have in life. They appreciate what sex can bring to their relationship—physically, emotionally, and spiritually.

Emily Nagoski, PhD, sex educator and researcher, found that when people were asked what they want to receive from sex with their partner, overwhelmingly the most common thing they want is *connection*.†

Following connection, partners want to share and receive pleasure, feel wanted, approved of and loved, and the freedom to be fully present in

---

* John M. Gottman and Nan Silver, *The Seven Principles for Making Marriage Work: A Practical Guide from the Country's Foremost Relationship Expert* (Harmony, 2015), 19.

† Emily Nagoski, *Come Together: The Science (and Art!) of Creating Lasting Sexual Connections* (Ballantine Books, 2024).

an experience that makes everything else in life seem smaller and more manageable. When I meet with couples who are struggling with desire discrepancy, I rarely hear any partner say that it's actually the physical sex they want. It's the myriad needs and desires they find fulfilling surrounding have a close sexual experience.

SEX AS SPIRITUAL LOVEMAKING

The trusting emotional connection, filled with mutual love and appreciation, is also a building block for couples to bring lovemaking to a spiritual experience. According to the mystics of Kabbalah, the deeper meaning of sex is to bind two souls together. We have the capacity for more than simply being two intertwined bodies. For this kind of unification—letting someone's energy into your own soul and the giving of yours to them—you better be darn sure to know them well and trust them emotionally. More than merely our own desire for approval, freedom, warmth, or closeness (while all of these are certainly amazing byproducts), the spiritual goal of sex is to connect to something bigger than yourself. In doing so, you can draw down the infinite energy of love and support from the higher realms—for you, your relationship, and the entire world. Spiritual sex has a higher purpose and gives loving partners the sweet taste of creating goodness together beyond themselves.

MANTRIC SEX: SPIRITUAL LOVEMAKING
STARTS WITHIN THE MIND

For a deeper, spiritual connection through lovemaking, your thoughts leading up to and during sex will make all the difference. If your goal is to create oneness, your mind must be *one with the experience,* that is, you will need to be as present in the moment as possible. Distracted sex and selfish sex do not lead to spiritual sex. They can actually lead to empty sex. This doesn't mean you need to be a master of mind control or that you should not fully embrace the pleasure you receive during sex. Pleasure is not only healthy and natural but a valuable way to connect with your beloved and the divine. *It's about intention—doing your best to be present, focused on giving love to your beloved, and joining your souls together.*

emotional connection + sexual connection + soulful thoughts = spiritual lovemaking.

I call this *mantric sex,* that is, choosing higher level thoughts that bring your soul into the lovemaking experience. Here are some example mantras to consider using or customizing to bring divine energy into your love making:

- I am giving love to my partner, and I want them to feel my love surrounding them.
- I am fully present with my beloved, in my heart and soul.
- Together we are becoming divinely intertwined.
- I appreciate the gift of my beloved and my Source for bringing us together.
- With every kiss, we are spiritually connecting our souls.
- I am giving as much as I can to support the journey of my beloved's soul.
- I feel my beloved's soul joining together with mine.
- Together we are creating energy of love to bring benefit to the world.

Don't judge yourself for having thoughts about something else, even negative thoughts, or that your mind pulls you into thinking of yourself. Simply use a mantra to gently bring you higher and deeper into the joining of souls, into the most positive, loving thought that you can. It's also natural to focus on one's performance or on reaching the orgasm. Try to focus on the outpouring of love that comes with the pleasure.

COMMON SEXUAL BARRIERS TO NAVIGATE

Emotional Intimacy Twist: Body to Mind Versus Mind to Body

When it comes to emotional connection, while there are exceptions, I find that men generally operate more "body to mind." That is, the physical experience of sex tends to help men open up emotionally, softening them into their vulnerable, emotional side. Biologically, the oxytocin release from an orgasm tends to awaken the desire to cuddle, protect, even help out more around the house. Women, on the other hand, tend to be "mind to body." They generally seek the emotional and intellectual connection first. Feeling close, heard, loved, and respected can be considered foreplay to even begin feeling sexy and ready for intimacy.

With same sex or binary couples, I find this same dynamic often playing out, depending on the level of masculine or feminine energy they identify with or embody. This mind-to-body/body-to-mind dynamic doesn't mean that emotional connection is only a womanly trait. I have seen many men in my practice who longed for a more emotional connection. Further, sex doesn't just open up certain folks to their emotional side. The main idea is that you and your partner need to work on this dance of arousal that can often come with a twist.

Getting Over the Wall

One tool I love to share with couples comes with understanding that the "mind to body" partner who seeks emotional connection first often has a wall that needs to come down. Once it's down, I never hear anyone regret that they were intimate. So if you're the one who needs more warm up time, you can talk with your partner about the wall and discuss what helps you climb over. Maybe you want to be flirted with or teased, or to communicate and open up first or, perhaps, you need time away from the duties of life and go out on a date. To help yourself get over the wall, remember that your wall is just a part of you, not all of you. You have other parts of you that know that once you approach and climb over the barrier, you'll enjoy the experience and the close, connected feeling.

Don't Resolve Conflict Under the Sheets

A word of caution about trying to resolve emotional disconnection under the sheets, whether from a fresh argument or the place of resentment. Working through conflict ahead of time, with dignity and respect, primes you for a more spiritual lovemaking experience. The sex as an attempt to compensate for unresolved friction can create the opposite: negative energy that can actually divide rather than join you. Yes, sex can awaken a closer emotional connection, but not to be used as a substitute for doing the work necessary to keep your lines of communication open and loving. Arguing and having differences is not only expected but healthy. However, when you are actively angry or reactive, you're not in a mental or emotional space of love and appreciation.

Navigating Desire Discrepancy

Having mismatched libidos, where one partner is consistently in the mood more than the other, is common. Research[*] shows that up to 80 percent of couples experience desire discrepancy on a regular basis, that means at least once a month and up to five to seven times a week. The biggest problem isn't the difference in desire, it's the meaning partners ascribe to the mismatch and their expectation. When we expect that our partner should share our same desire, this causes the most damage to the relationship. Mostly because each partner in the dynamic can feel undervalued for who they are and what they need.

There are so many reasons why one partner might be the higher-desire partner and the other the lower-desire. The reasons range from

[*] L. C. Day, A. Muise, S. Joel, and E. A. Impett, "To Do It or Not to Do It? How Communally Motivated People Navigate Sexual Interdependence Dilemmas," *Personality and Social Psychology Bulletin* 41, no. 6 (2015): 6.

physical (e.g., fatigue, medication, pain with intercourse) to hormonal (e.g., pregnancy or menopause) to psychological (e.g., stress, body image issues, trauma, or porn abuse) or relational (e.g., lack of trust, respect, resentment, conflict, or poor communication). The discrepancy can put the higher-desire partner in the exhausted and unwanted pursuing position and the lower-desire mate on edge, feeling devalued and smothered.

This isn't a problem that needs fixing and doesn't mean you are sexually incompatible. Fundamental and perpetual differences are common in the best of relationships. But you'll need to work together to adapt around your desire difference. Lest your emotional, sexual, and spiritual connection might all be compromised. See the suggestions below for *creating lasting sexual connection* that can also help with navigating your mixed libidos.

Kids and Sex

Most parents feel their sex life could use help after having children. This is normal. Common blockers include exhaustion, feeling over-touched, hormones, changes in the body, mismatched libido, body image issues, and overscheduling. It's wonderful how child-centered our society has become in many ways, but couples need boundaries because the kids are the result of the bond between them. Remember, the order of priority that is best for everyone in your home is: Self. Relationship. Kids.

HOW TO CREATE LASTING SEXUAL CONNECTION

Talk about Sex

Couples who talk about sex have been shown to feel more satisfied with this intimate part of their relationship. So much so, that only 9 percent of couples who can't comfortably talk about sex report feeling satisfied. It's actually even more intimate and vulnerable to talk about it than to let your bodies do the talking. Communicating—in between sexual encounters and also during—helps you bring everything about you together in the experience, which is what spiritual lovemaking is about.

If you have a desire discrepancy, talking about this can help clear the air and alleviate judgment and rejection. Some couples have sex less because they've never talked about what they would enjoy more and therefore the experience is not as great as it could be in their eyes.

It's important to talk with your partner about what you want from a sex life together, and your desired frequency. From there, each of you must be willing to compromise. **Think about sex in your marriage as the two of you on one boat together:** "It's not all about me, but all about we."

Schedule Sex

Most people throw their arms up over this idea, but scheduling sex can help you make sure you are keeping your sexual connection a priority. Scheduling can also help eliminate the psychological pressure and the confusion of the higher-desire partner about whether to initiate. The higher-desire partner can relax knowing that sexual connection won't be indefinitely postponed. The lower-desire partner can have a break from resist mode where touch doesn't always mean a sexual inuendo. Scheduling can help you set aside real-life demands and create the right environment for physical intimacy.

Intentional Sex Vacations

Some restraint can help couples appreciate and feel more excited about sex, especially those who have a desire discrepancy. Some couples create a two-week sexual break each month while a woman is on and completing her cycle. In those two weeks with sex off-limits, the innate desire for one another can be rekindled. Intentional sex vacations are not in the spirit of being punitive or withholding but for the purpose of building other parts of the relationship as feeders to better, more passionate sex together. When we have access to what we desire with no limits, it's easier to take our blessings for granted. Research has shown that a little break can go a long way.

Expand and Take Responsibility for Your Own Sexuality

We are each responsible for our own happiness and well-being, and this includes our experience as sexual and sensual beings. This can include working on the barriers you have around yourself as a sultry person, whether that be from unfortunate societal or religious messages or how you feel about your body. Taking responsibility for your own sexuality means being mindful of the context that cues you to feel ready for sex. In the book *Come as You Are*, Emily Nagoski noted that 25 percent of men and 85 percent of women do not experience spontaneous desire.[*] So don't expect or wait around for random desire. Instead, keep track of what direct stimuli tends to set you in the mood, and the context. Maybe it's a bath, going on a date, treating each other with extra loving-kindness, or talking about sex together.

Be Careful with Pornography

Sex should be fun. However, it's important to differentiate between the fun from impersonal sex versus personal. I have seen in my practice what pornography can do to the addictive brain and how relationships can be ruined from their potential for lifelong intimacy. It's a societal issue and not something anyone should feel shame about. But it's important to be informed about the common negative side effects for meaningful and long-lasting sexual connection.[†]

---

[*] Emily Nagoski, *Come as You Are* (Simon & Schuster, 2015).
[†] Fight the New Drug, n.d., "10 Negative Effects of Porn on Your Brain, Body, Relationships, and Society," accessed October 16, 2024, https://fightthenewdrug.org/10-reasons-why-porn-is-unhealthy-for-consumers-and-society/.

Feed Your Life Force

Connect to the creativity of your unique individuality. This can help awaken more sexual desire. Some couples whose lives, and sense of selves, overlap to such a degree they become enmeshed into one. Enmeshment is not the same idea as two unique souls joining into one. Not enough individuality, or a lack of new growth and change, actually diminishes the circuitry of energy. The more we awaken what gets us turned on and inspired about life as an individual, the more spiritual energy we bring to the sexual connection.

Awaken Generosity

Sexual generosity is at the heart of spiritual lovemaking. When we care about someone, we naturally want to be generous with them. When a couple's sex life together is in distress, I try to look for how generous they feel and act toward one another on a regular basis. Are they cuddling? Do they give each other compliments? When was the last surprise romantic gift? Do they say "I love you" every day and kiss every night before bed? Do they go out on dates? Reciprocal emotional generosity leads to sexual generosity. Sometimes we are not being generous with ourselves, and then we feel bitter about what we're not receiving. Make sure you have a generous heart with yourself too, which will lead to a generous heart and body in your bed.

SEX ACROSS THE LIFE CYCLE

I'll always remember when my husband, Jeff, and I had this older couple over for dinner early in our marriage. While we were just getting started with our child-rearing years, they had completed theirs. The wife, Cindy, announced, "Our sex is better now than it has ever been. We are so comfortable with each other. We can say or ask for anything and we don't have the distractions of the kids and the stress of just getting started with our lives." I looked at my husband and we both gave each other a smile-wink that implied, "See what we have to look forward to!"

These bold and passionate friends of ours are not alone. While some stages are harder on our sex life (e.g., child-rearing), aging can bring transitions that create opportunities to reinvent and expand sexuality and intimacy. Even amid the physical changes that force couples to be creative, many couples enjoy coming into their own as sexual partners. It's the gift that a life together can bring. Each couple is unique here, for sure. Some couples decide this part of their shared experience is not as important anymore. The key is being open to change and finding what works for both of you.

Case: Meet Rory and Joanne: I Don't Feel Cherished

Rory and Joanne came to see me the first time because Joanne discovered that Rory had been having impersonal sex with people he met online. The couple loved each other, and this was clear from the get-go. The problem Rory was experiencing was that he didn't feel cherished by Joanne. His predominant love language was touch and sex, but for Joanne, this was nice but not nearly as important. Joanne knew that their desires were mismatched, but what she didn't understand was that without Rory seeing that she desired him, he just didn't feel important to her. Rory needed to learn to be more open with how deeply he was hurting and not take Joanne's lower-desire baseline personally. For Joanne, a highly introverted women, she learned to talk more openly with Rory about what she needs in order to feel sexy and in the mood. They had never talked about their sex life together, which proved to be an almost lethal element in their relationship. They still have unmatched desire levels but have found their compatibility groove by keeping the lines of communication open, both ways.

Case: Meet Barbara and Tony: She's Too Pure to Be Sexy

Barbara and Tony came to see me after decades of marriage and they had a son and daughter together. They hadn't had sex in years. It started when they had to live apart for three years due to Tony's job. Barbara was beside herself. She was still very attracted to him and didn't understand what changed. There wasn't anything they didn't know about each other, except they both were in the dark, in denial, about how damaging Tony's porn use was for his own sexuality, his mental health, and their marriage. Most couples I meet with who have porn as a culprit for their sexual demise don't bring it up, either out of embarrassment or they have no idea that this habit/addiction is even part of the problem. I started to learn more about the trouble Tony was having. He shared with me, "Barbara is the most amazing woman I have ever known, but since we lived apart and I started using porn more and more, I can't get aroused any other way." Turns out that Tony had been using porn and masturbation for escape here and there most of his life, but the addiction progressed when he lived out of town and as they were raising their family together. Tony kept comparing how Barbara looked and acted to the women in his porn videos and could only feel turned on by the impersonal and exaggerated erotica from these women who were not meant to be true intimate sexual partners. The quick-fix dopamine surge his brain had grown addicted to robbed him, and his wife, of the emotional intimacy they once shared.

Case: Meet Ellen and Jack: Rounding Out the Edges

Ellen and Jack were empty nesters and had not had sex in several months because something had shifted in Ellen's body. She was having trouble with pain and reaching orgasm. She was afraid that in this new phase of life something had changed and so she avoided finding out whether this was a one-off or something long term they'd need to deal with. Ellen was open about this with Jack in their counseling sessions, and while Jack understood and didn't pressure Ellen, they both knew they would need to get back in the bed together and give it another go. In the meantime, during the months when they were not having sex together, there was something missing. They were less playful, more irritable, and focused on the grind of tasks versus simply enjoying being near one another. I suggested that when the time felt right, and to not let too much time pass, that they should allocate the time, patience, and energy to experiment and discover. Knowing they were a spiritual couple, I reminded them about the idea of giving generously to one another—regardless of the outcome. With no pressure, but I suggested that they talk openly throughout the experience and to really lean into the deep friendship they shared.

The night finally arrived when Ellen and Jack made it over the hump and took their time to have an experimental sexual experience, fully prepared for whatever may unfold. With some new adjustments that talking openly helped them navigate, they were able to have a shared and satisfying sexual connection again. The main thing they reported is how much lighter their overall connection felt, with greater laughter, playfulness, and generosity. Ellen said, "I didn't realize how different our relationship is when we are making the time for sex, until we had this break. Sex adds a whole dimension to the rest of our life together, it's rounded the edges and makes everything else seem more fun and go smoother."

Here we can see that Ellen and Jack's emotional and spiritual connection, and their deep trust in one another, helped them navigate a sexual challenge into another good sexual experience. It worked in the other direction too—sharing sex together deepened their emotional connection and softened the edges all around.

IDEA INTO ACTION: SPICY GAME OF TWENTY QUESTIONS

Pick a time for you and your partner to ask each other the questions below. Don't worry if it feels vulnerable and initially awkward. Remember that going out of your comfort zone is the way to build for yourself a sanctuary that can be filled with blessings. You might use these as foreplay to wake up that tingly, giddy feeling together.

- How and what did you learn about sex growing up?
- What helps you feel most comfortable telling me what you want?
- Where do you like to be touched and what makes you feel uncomfortable to be touched?
- To reach orgasm, can you tell me and show me what you like me to do?
- Think about all the times we've had sex. What are some of your favorites? What made those times special?
- How often would you like to have sex?
- What is your ultimate fantasy of our lovemaking?
- What have you learned about your body lately, that maybe has changed?
- In what context do you feel the sexiest? What turns you on and what turns you off?
- Have you had any past experiences that have negatively impacted you that you think I should know about?
- What's your favorite way to kiss that makes you feel like we are joining souls?
- What's your favorite part of my body?
- What can I do that makes you feel sexy throughout the day?
- What helps you get over the wall of resistance and ready to be intimate with me?
- What's your favorite part of foreplay?

- Are there any times you feel shame for having pleasure or hesitant to ask for what you want that will please you?
- What's your favorite way for me to let you know I want to have sex with you?
- What's your favorite thing about our sex life?
- How can we make our sexual connection more spiritual together?

PILLAR 4

Purpose

Purpose

We Make the World Better Through Our Bond.

As you enter into Pillar 4, you can think about your relationship moving through the pillars like this:

Pillar 1: *This is who I am.*
Pillar 2: *This is how we help each other grow.*
Pillar 3: *This is how much you mean to me.*
Pillar 4: *This is who we are for the world.*

Pillar 4 is the elevating pillar that adds endurance and tenderness to your relationship through a bigger picture purpose together. A purpose that is two-fold: (1) evolving to learn real love and generosity and (2) sharing with the world through your bond. Purpose elevates your relationship to a soulmate relationship as you grow your capacity to go beyond the self through giving to others. This is the essence of a spiritual relationship. You can think about Pillars 1, 2, and 3 as a three-legged stool that gives your connection stability and balance. Pillar 4 brings in the Divine as your third partner, giving your relationship the kind of strength that goes on endlessly—not just the relationship itself, but the love and closeness. With a higher purpose for being together, you take your relationship beyond the physical realm. This is where the magic happens.

PURPOSE IS SIMPLE AND POTENT

You'll see there are only two chapters in Pillar 4. Please don't mistake this to mean this element is of lesser importance to your relationship. Quite the contrary. If you want to find the most impactful things in life, look for the unnoticed and uncomplicated. Our ego complicates things. Spiritual truths, however, are simple. So too is the healing power of *Purpose* in your relationship.

Or to make as a circle:

As you enter into Pillar 4, you can think about your relationship moving through the pillars like you see below:

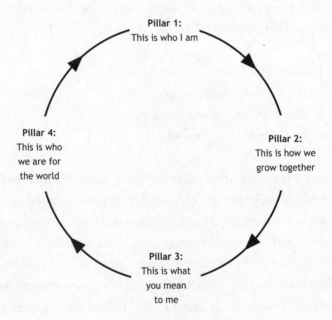

Pillar 1:
This is who I am

Pillar 2:
This is how we
grow together

Pillar 3:
This is what
you mean
to me

Pillar 4:
This is who
we are for
the world

You are never done. You can see your relationship is an ever-evolving creative process. As you move through the pillars, your relationship with yourself, with one another and with the world continually grows and changes.

CHAPTER TWENTY

The Ultimate Fulfillment

*The meaning of life is to find your gift. The purpose of life is to
give it away.*

—Pablo Picasso

Pillar 4 is *not* what most couples come in complaining about. Purpose is typically not even on their radar, because unfortunately this best kept secret is the least talked about ingredient for a happy and fulfilling lifetime together. I came to bring purpose into my work with couples when my husband and I discovered this ourselves. We began volunteering together and found our stride. Serving food in shelters, creating clothing bazaars for the under-resourced, opening our home for spiritual events, donating with intention, and even taking volunteer vacations. Sharing these experiences gave our relationship a greater sense of purpose, which deepened our fulfillment and our bond. A light bulb went off. I knew I needed to weave this element into my sessions. Just as it helped us, I began watching couples speed up their healing and grow visibly closer. I knew *purpose* had to be Pillar 4. Now I can't imagine my or any relationship without it. This book itself is an expression of this secret ingredient in motion.

FINISHING STRONG

Pillar 4 brings in the ultimate strength and fulfillment to your marriage, the kind with no end and clarity of purpose. Connecting to something bigger together keeps the flame going strong because your relationship becomes imbued with a third partner—a partner with "connections." To eternity, that is. Purpose makes your relationship like baked bread, fresh and warm out of the oven, perpetually.

My husband is in the retail clothing business and he often says, "The back of the store should be just as exciting as the front of the store." I joke and say, "Yes, Honey, just like our marriage." But I'm not joking at all. Through a commitment to your marriage, and especially a strong Pillar 4, this is how you keep the front and the back of your marriage perpetually exciting, fresh and strong.

CREATING A SOULMATE RELATIONSHIP

A relationship based on chemistry alone and need-satisfaction consists of what you receive from your partner and what they receive from you. It's a single-line, finite relationship that ends with the two of you. A relationship with purpose creates an unending circle that continuously expands. Choosing to become a positive force together, directing your desire together for the sake of the world, taps you into a higher state of mind. Here, you begin to see an expanded vision of yourself, and of your relationship. Nothing is overwhelming or beyond your ability, because you are connecting with forces bigger than yourself. Resisting the urge to receive, just for yourself alone, and going out of your way for others encircles you and your relationship and opens the channels of abundance. Even a little bit goes a long way.

Soulmating

Many people say they are looking for their soulmate, or wish they had found theirs rather than their current mate. Try viewing it differently: it's not about "having your soulmate" (though who you pick matters), it's about embracing the gradual growth process that a soulful marriage requires of us. Remember we talked about soulmating, that love is a verb, not a passive state or lucky experience. Again, it's less important whether you're with "the one." What matters most is to be with someone you're drawn to and enjoy, *and* who has enough maturity and insight that you see yourself being able to grow together. You don't find your soulmate; you become a soulmate and create a soulmate kind of relationship. You do this together by way of purpose—inside your relationship and outside.

Inside Your Relationship: The First Three Pillars

Purpose is embedded in each of the first three pillars of your relationship, particularly as you strengthen them. You are living with purpose together when you continually invest in your own happiness and well-being, seize the growth opportunities embedded in your friction, and make sure without question that your partner is and feels of utmost importance to you. You can think of purpose inside your relationship like a contract each of your souls have decided to sign, that together, you will help each other become all that you can be, to experience love like you are meant to—for yourselves and the world. This means being able to show each other what needs fixing, so you can gradually move from *what's in it for me* to *how can I give,* not as a chore, but from tasting the fulfillment of giving.

A soulmate relationship should stretch you, push your buttons, and inspire you, because how else can you see the issues you need to overcome and manifest the changes that matter most? Leading with love and cherishment, your partner becomes your clearest mirror to help you become who you're meant to become. The joy is in the transformation process itself. To harness purpose inside your relationship, you must take full responsibility for yourself. In Hindu culture, each person has a karmic connection with certain souls. You keep finding each other to help you lead a life with higher purpose. My husband and I learned this same idea through Kabbalah which has helped us turn more fervently toward our relationship and lean into times of conflict—with certainty that we are exactly where we need to be. Purpose inside our relationship awakens a deep sense of meaning and urgency to make the most of our time together. We feel more serious about our union, and yet lighter, more playful at the same time.

When couples come in with a challenge, I typically say, *"Try not to rush through this. Your friction has a higher purpose. There's an opportunity here for each of you and the relationship. Slow down, be kind, and patient as you embrace the lessons and growth trying to benefit you through the process."* The key is to do everything you can to embrace the difficulty, and at the same time, make the environment as lighthearted and kind as possible. We are here to grow but not to suffer or beat up on ourselves or each other. We grow better when we feel loved and cherished, and when we are having some fun.

Outside Your Relationship: Open to the World

Purpose in a soulmate relationship also means that together you extend yourself to share goodness with the world. Your love forms the foundation of what you have to give, whether it be your time, treasure, or talents. This means viewing what you have and who you are as not existing just for yourself alone. We need to be reminded of this paradox again and again: you actually receive more this way. As Chinese philosopher Lao-tzu said, "The wise man does not lay up his treasures. The more he gives to others, the more he has for his own." A giving purpose can mean sharing a passion or can come through supporting each other's individual endeavors. While giving to family and close community is vital and has purpose (more about that in the next chapter), it's through being *open to the world* versus closed that adds a secret sauce to your relationship. *Open to the world* means going outside of your smaller collective to give.

This more expansive purpose means seeing *yourself as part of the whole world, not as a separate reality.* The law of divine oneness is where religions across the world, modern science, and the laws of nature come together in agreement. All living beings are interconnected as a physical manifestation of the same source energy. It's human nature to think narrowly and underestimate how utterly unified and dependent we each are on the larger collective. This is why we need help to break out of the matrix of separateness.

Unity Mantra

Mantras have a powerful purpose to elevate our consciousness. There is a reason why yogis have brought in mantras at the end of their practice for thousands of years. It takes so much practice to really change the thoughts we believe in, especially about our unity. I use a unity mantra to help my clients (and myself) begin thinking and living more *open to the world*. Simply reading this to yourself a few times can become a powerful meditation.

> I am not a separate entity.
> I only exist because I am part of the whole.
> I choose to live with this understanding every single day,
> which opens the channel of abundance that is meant for me.

Reframing Receiving

The purpose pillar is really about sharing. Your purpose outside your relationship is part of a larger transformation process as you gradually reframe your understanding of how it works to truly receive joy and fulfillment. When you share with an open heart, appreciating your interconnectedness with all that is, was, and ever will be, you open the gates of abundance to receive. "In this way, it's self interest in the highest sense," says Michael Berg in his book *The Secret*.[*] Receiving the ultimate abundance must come with skin in the game. Again, you

---

[*] Michael Berg, *The Secret: Unlocking the Source of Joy and Fulfillment* (Kabbalah Publishing, 2004), 52.

need the F-word—Effort! It's not just a cliché, to give is to receive. It's science, it's spiritual, and it's practical.

There is a part of us all that will always be receivers. That's not only okay, it is our purpose. To receive all that life and love have to offer. The key is to learn how to be smarter about our receiving, which means gradually transforming ourselves into givers, and in so doing it's a win-win for everyone. Especially your enduring bond.

RESEARCH AGREES WITH PILLAR 4

Kindness Is Chemical

Studies[*] have shown that volunteering with your partner facilitates feelings of closeness and trust because of the "love hormone" oxytocin that's released. And have you heard of helper's high? It's the dopamine euphoria—likened to the waves of good-feeling during sex—that has been shown to be released in our brain when doing acts of kindness. Doing for others has also been shown to release serotonin, which helps us regulate our mood. These feel-good effects of volunteering can make you feel closer to your partner, even if you don't engage in these together. Yet when you share a giving experience together, working as a team driven by generosity and kindness, the positive chemical flow is exponential.

Selflessness Is Sexy

In another study,[†] men and women appeared more attractive in the eyes of others, particularly as potential long-term partners, when they displayed helping behaviors. Altruism was deemed as sexy, especially for long-term love.

---

[*] Allen Lucks and Peggy Payne, *The Healing Power of Doing Good* (Fawcett Columbine, 1991; repr., iUniverse.com, 2001).
[†] David Moore et al., "Selflessness Is Sexy: Reported Helping Behaviour Increases Desirability of Men and Women as Long-Term Sexual Partners," *BMC Evolutionary Biology* 13 (2013): Article 182.

Seeing the Best in Each Other

When you do something for the sake of others, together with your partner, you allow each other to see and connect with the best part of you, your generous side. Sometimes partners see a side of one another that they've never seen before. This generous side is your soul and when your two generous sides touch, something sweet and wonderful happens.

Finding a Common Purpose

When you bring your minds together for a common goal, or even in supporting one another's altruistic passions, you bring in a sense of unity to your relationship. Couples report that through sharing outside of their relationship, they feel a closeness because they are building on their shared core values. This reminds me of a story about Joel, a man my husband and I met while traveling. He told us about the nonprofit work he and his wife have been up to. Sixteen years ago, they saw an opportunity to help low-income folks receive proper medical care. They followed their calling, and the project has been hugely successful. What Joel didn't expect was the positive impact on his marriage. He said, "It got us through stuff, having a mission together. The common values and open communication we shared on the project carried over into some areas of rough patch." One downside he said from working so closely: they do butt heads more. This is not surprising and common for couples who work together, even when purpose driven. In these scenarios, it's especially important to keep all four pillars balanced and strong.

WHICH COMES FIRST: PURPOSE INSIDE OR OUTSIDE YOUR RELATIONSHIP?

You can't completely bypass the inside purpose of growing your relationship (Pillars 1–3) and skip to exclusively sharing outside with the world. You need the foundation of love within your relationship, the contagious spirit of generosity that you share together, to take with you as you make an impact. Just like putting your airflow mask on first before helping someone else, you want to make sure to continually strengthen your relationship or it will catch up with you. Some couples end up in a gray divorce (that is, calling it quits after twenty or thirty years of marriage) even with an outside mission together, because the innards of their bond grew fatally weak. Purpose can heal a relationship to some degree but without really creating and enjoying your unity together, without that deep friendship and spirit of growing together, an outside purpose can only buy you time. Once you have lost that close connection, just between the two of you, then all the sharing with the world won't be able to make up for the pillars of your relationship that have no strength to hold you.

That being said, I am now going to share an anomaly—the complete opposite. I have seen couples whose first three pillars were suffering but who turned their relationship around with purpose. A sense of shared meaning along with witnessing their partners show tenderness toward others helped them begin closing the gap. Their sense of purpose gave strength to all of their pillars, but they were also putting energy directly into their marriage. My point here is that they weren't waiting until everything was perfect before facing out to the world together. Pillar 4 works both ways, as a culmination and as a healing remedy. But no matter how you slice it, all four pillars are essential.

PURPOSE OVER THE LIFE CYCLE

When you are younger and trying to get your feet off the ground, and/or immersed in raising a family, it's hard to think about anything beyond your four walls. Purpose will be even less likely on your radar as a key factor for relationship success. I've been there and am reminded of this regularly when I meet with couples who are in the thick of these earlier adult life stages. The purpose pillar, and to some degree the priority pillar, tend to be more mature elements. Once reaching later life stages, you'll find more openings for thinking outside of your own life and your family. You'll actually need to because oftentimes, there's a void in purpose once the children are grown. Further, it's not uncommon for people to begin soul-searching as they reach later stages in life and the yearning for purpose becomes more likely to poke through.

Beware of "Later" Syndrome

However! A strong word of caution regarding this notion of "*Later, when I have more time.*" We see this reactive tendency in us humans all over the place. "Later, when I have _____, that's when I'll _____." For example, *when* I get this or that, *then* I'll think bigger about the world or about myself, that's *when* I'll give of my money, my talent, or my time. When my partner gives me what I need, then I'll be loving and kind. When I am happier, then I'll give more. This is where I sincerely hope to inspire change in your heart and mind.

The truth is you don't need to wait. You really can't afford to. The insertion of purpose early on, when you're in distress or at any point in your relationship, has the power to add a dimension that no other element can. Spirituality often goes beyond physical logic. The logic of this world supports *when-then* thinking. Higher, purpose-driven logic says that so I *can* receive what I'm truly desiring, I trust that I'll receive more as I let go and start giving—even just a little and especially when it makes no sense. Your life and your relationship will actually make more sense when you make room for the light of generosity to enter.

Case: Audrey and Jim

Audrey and Jim are the more mature couple I spoke about in Pillar 3, who grew closer through thoughtful gestures of cherishment, sometimes as simple as a warm kiss goodbye. They didn't want to stop there, so we kept meeting to deepen their connection. Jim's way of operating often made him admittedly preoccupied and hard for Audrey to reach, sometimes feeling as if they weren't even in the same room together. So, I asked them, "When do you feel most like you're connected, that is, in the same room?" Altruistic by nature, they both agreed, "It's when we are doing things for others. When one of our kids or grandkids need something, or a neighbor or someone in the deaf community [their son was born deaf], we come together like bread and butter." They've always admired the good-heartedness in each other; I could see that was unwavering. I encouraged them to take whatever sharing they are doing already and see how they could expand it, maybe find new outlets they feel passionate about to have greater purpose together. As the months passed, Audrey and Jim began to serve as mentors for at-risk youth; they had a soft spot for children, especially from the struggle they had to start a family. Before I knew it, they were skipping into sessions with pictures of their "children," stories of their accomplishments and progress in life. They couldn't help but get involved with the mentoring organization itself, finding new and better ways to reach and support the children and their communities. They were proud of each other and excited to share beautiful, openhearted experiences. Another vacation on the beach (which they still enjoy) could not have created this level of togetherness from their shared experience of giving.

IDEA INTO ACTION: REFLECTIVE JOURNALING

- Growing up, this is what I saw my parents do or not do when it came to giving, both inside and outside of their relationship . . .
- What I previously thought about purpose in my life and relationship was that . . .
- After reading this chapter, here are some simple steps I can take to explore bringing purpose into my life and my relationship . . .

Now, ask your partner these same questions above and talk about it together. Then, get ready to become more concrete and practical with your purpose together in next chapter.

CHAPTER TWENTY-ONE

What Purpose Looks Like Practically

*Never doubt that a small group of thoughtful committed
citizens can change the world; indeed, it's the only thing that
ever has.*

—Margaret Mead

This chapter is about how you take purpose from an idea to a reality—day to day, moment to moment, in big and small ways all through your lifetime together.

THE SPIRIT OF GENEROSITY

Making the world better through your bond is all about awakening the spirit of generosity in your heart. This is the essence of who you are and what allows for the most joyful rapport in your relationship. The generous spirit you bring to giving, regardless of the actions or even the outcome, strengthens not only your relationship but makes the world a better and happier place. Even something as simple as one person paying for the coffee of a stranger behind them, you can see how this uplifts the whole line. Love and kindness are inspiring to watch and contagious to be around. You don't even need to be in close proximity to make a difference. We are quantumly connected. Awakening generosity in your own heart heals something within you, and because we are all connected, heals others too.

Let's now talk about the specific ways you can make the world better through the loving energy you generate (1) as a couple, (2) in your family and closer community, and (3) as you open yourself to the world. Keep in mind that while you are making a difference in others' lives, on a deeper level, you are actually not doing anyone a favor. You are helping yourself as you help others. Truly, everyone wins.

Your Love Energy as a Couple

The first contribution you and your partner can make to the world is through the energy of your love. Just like how you can feel it walking into a room when there's tension between people, you can also feel when love and generosity are in the air. The environment around us has such a profound impact on how we feel and behave. So, when you invest in your first three pillars, the momentum of your positive energy tips the scales toward goodness. Examples of investing in your relationship, directly and indirectly, are strewn through the whole book. I've highlighted some below, because there are so many positive and purpose-filled actions that are all too often misunderstood as tangential.

Within you:

- Taking care of your body and your mind
- Living true to yourself and loving who you are
- Addressing your fears and insecurities
- Doing what makes you authentically happy and fulfilled
- Working on your character, your habits, and becoming a better version of yourself

Between you:

- Pausing to stay calm when you're upset
- Listening better and cherishing your partner

- Embracing your friction and being open to the lesson
- Repairing broken trust
- Making time for fun, for pillow talk, and meaningful conversations
- Owning your mistakes and shortcomings, resisting the blame game
- Guarding your relationship from third entities that may weaken your bond
- Making your spouse feel special
- Being sure to make your partner a top priority
- Keeping a work-life balance, making time to play and dream together
- Deepening your emotional friendship
- Keeping your sexual connection healthy and intentional
- Appreciating the gift of your partner and seeing their goodness

Love in Your Family

When couples talk about purpose in their relationship, raising a family together is hands down the first (and typically the only) thing that comes to mind. This is because of the obvious value of investing in your children and family unit. Our world desperately needs parents who find purpose in attuning to their children. Every child needs good enough parenting, raised with a healthy balance of warmth and boundaries, to grow into an adult who feels good about themselves, values kindness, and feels a responsibility to do their part. This is no easy or casual task.

Here's the caveat. Raising your children is not the whole purpose story. Most couples stop there, but your children are extensions of yourselves. This is typically a sensitive subject with my clients, so I try and break the news as gently as I can. We can't move closer to the ultimate fulfillment meant for us unless we reach out beyond our orbit.

Altruistic Love

If you want the kind of unending love we are talking about here, then you need purpose that definitely includes your children or smaller collective, but also stretches beyond that. This could mean giving to people you may never meet or to people or causes you may never receive anything back from. Altruistic love goes straight to the soul, bypassing our ego's unsatiable quest for instant gratification and self-centric satisfaction. Please don't think this farther-reaching altruism negates the value of showing up for and prioritizing your family and friends. Something vital will be missing if you don't. It's just that while your couple love and family love are good for the world, they don't allow you to capitalize fully on the tool that purpose gives to you and your marriage.

FINDING YOUR PURPOSE—INDIVIDUALLY AND TOGETHER

You will have your individual purpose and your joint purpose. Sometimes your individual callings will directly overlap, sometimes indirectly, or maybe not at all. The first place to start is exploring within to know what passions, needs, or pains in the world speak to you. Then there's identifying the unique talents and gifts you have to offer—your generous heart being your greatest resource. From there, you and your partner can explore intersecting purposes, which typically come with some meeting in the middle.

While it's important to pause and reflect for what feels authentic for you, please don't fall into the delay trap of feeling that you need to identify "*the purpose*" before you get started. As you dip your toe in the water, you'll get feedback from the Universe with every step. We often find our purpose by way of our own pain. Maybe you went through a difficult health challenge or a loss and this moves you to help alleviate the same pain in others? One client of mine, inspired from her own abusive upbringing, has become a long-term mentor to two teenage boys who have a rough home life. Another scenario that drives purpose is appreciation for what you've received. For example, if you feel so blessed by being able to have a healthy home and a good education, you might feel a desire to help in a school that is empowering at-risk students. Maybe it was time in nature as a child, or with animals, that made such a difference in your life, and you want to help those who don't have access. You don't need a reason from your past to feel moved to help a person, a family, or the environment in need. If you feel the calling, just run with it.

You and your partner can explore your individual passions together by talking about what stirs your heart. You'll see some prompting questions in the Idea Into Action at the end of the chapter. It's vital to live true to yourself when it comes to purpose, which will help you come from a place authenticity and strength when you join forces. Even if your partner is not directly involved in the volunteer work you choose, the two of you can still consider this part of being a purpose-driven couple. We draw energy from each other and to the extent that you support each other in your individual callings plays a vital role in having purpose as a couple.

Some couples have trouble finding something they are both equally passionate about. This is where compromise comes in. See where you can find the most overlapping interests. If it starts to get complicated, pause, keep it simple, and just pick anything for the sake of others.

BONDING THROUGH SHARING

Be on the Lookout, Together

Whether you bring a meal for someone who is ill, network for a friend who needs a job, or take an hour out of your Sunday to visit elderly who don't get visitors, the idea is to be on the lookout for how you can give. I recently asked my husband what he's learned about us becoming more sharing as a couple over the years. He said, "We're closest when we're doing something sharing together. When I see a couple who is in a really rough spot, I think the best thing they can do is find an act of sharing they can participate in together." He went on, "I like when you move something over to me where you think I can have a greater effect. And when I feel that you could really help someone in a situation, I'll move it over to you. The tag-teaming we do makes me feel like we are more together as one unit."

I hear many couples report that some of their favorite marriage moments are when they hear from someone else, or find out from their partner, about a small extra mile action their beloved did. The warmth inside can sound like, *"I'm so lucky to be married to someone with such a big heart."* A deep respect and awe awaken when you see the person you love going out of their way for others. Some even consider this foreplay. Creating unity with others through loving-kindness enhances the unity between you and your mate.

One Step at a Time

There is no small action, and it's important to just get started. Bigger, more long-term impact giving is also important to build toward. But I want to make sure that you don't feel overwhelmed and then give up the whole idea. Slow and steady wins the race and with time, the more you make sharing as part of your life and relationship, the more you get used to it, get high from it, and lose the taste for thinking of just yourself. Like Audrey and Jim, who became involved with mentoring children, before they knew it, they were making a difference in the entire mentoring program. They inspired other people in their life to do the same, because as it turns out, the more you give, the more people you bring into the circle of your sharing.

Meaning-Making

Many couples who devote a great deal of their energy to sharing have gone through something painful or traumatic together and find purpose and healing through helping others. Finding meaning is now considered the sixth stage of grief and is a powerful way to move from suffering toward healing. I've seen this firsthand with partners who have lost a child, gone through a life-threatening health challenge, are in recovery for addiction, or have survived a marriage crisis and want to give back. One such couple is Veronica and Jonathon who channeled their grief into something for good.

Case: Meet Veronica and Jonathon

Veronica and Jonathon's lives turned upside down when they discovered their young son, Matt, had a life-threatening illness. He was a twin, so they also carried the burden of helping Matt's twin sister navigate this. I started to see them midway through their son's five-year journey. They were smart enough to realize that their whole family was relying on them to stay strong as a couple. The illness was taking a toll on their marriage, and they wanted some help to communicate better and have some sort of relationship outside of being the parents of a child patient. When their son passed, they leaned on the bond they forged through their shared grief and received support from a local grief group. But as the months passed, they felt an emptiness not only in their lives but also in their relationship. When I asked what brings them solace or any kind of comfort, it was the fundraising for a cure and volunteering they were doing to help other parents going through the same traumatic ordeal. With that in mind, I suggested they expand this purpose-filled work together while at the same time making sure they nurture all the other facets of their relationship and their lives. They turned their grief into growth and found meaning through their traumatic loss. Sharing a common cause helped them find each other again.

TEN WAYS TO CREATE PURPOSE IN ACTION

Below are a wide range of practical ways to bring purpose into your relationship as you make the world better through your bond:

- **Volunteer together,** one-time projects or recurring longer term roles. Go beyond complaining and get your hands dirty. Dig in, maybe in the very area that you are finding so unfair or tragic. Maybe somewhere else. But do something that adds light. You can direct that energy you are generating wherever you want it to go.

- **Show up for others,** individually or together. For example, bring a meal to someone who is sick, fly in for your friend's mother's funeral, take that phone call for someone in need, visit your lonely friend, write a card, go to a house of mourning, Facetime with your aunt who has Alzheimer's.

- **Give hospitality.** This is one of the highest spiritual actions, when you go out of your way to welcome people into your home, serve them plentifully, and escort them out happier than they came. The ancient sages teach that we are covering our guests with the divine feminine when we are hospitable, allowing the felt presence of the Source of Life to go with them on their way.

- **Plan a volunteer vacation.** Build intimacy and a sense of togetherness through a shared giving adventure. Lounging on a beach is not necessarily the answer all the time. Voluntourism, as it can be called, is not for everyone and not for every trip you take. But couples find these volunteer trips bring them closer and help them change in authentic ways that last.

- **Back one other,** in your professional and charitable endeavors. Don't underestimate the energy you bring and the shared purpose you create when you support something meaningful or altruistic that your partner is involved in. My husband says again and again how much he appreciates my support. It gives him energy. I feel the same from him. Backing your partner happens when you take an interest, serve as a sounding board, accommodate schedules, give input, say affirming and admiring words, share in their triumphs and struggles, show up at events. Everything we do to uplift our mate has purpose.

- **Attend spiritual services.** Finding or attending a spiritual place you love can remind you what matters and who you really are, replacing the human tendency for anxiety and selfishness with a sense of peace and gratitude. Find a house of spiritual practice that you can be a part of together that awakens the urgency to care more about the world and all living things in it.

- **Pray together.** Prayer can mean different things to different people. I'm using the word prayer as some form of *intentional thought* which can range from awe and appreciation, seeking guidance, desire to become one, asking for what we need—including forgiveness, patience, compassion, or certainty. When couples share even a brief intention-setting or meditation practice, an inspiring thought or teaching, a favorite prayer this can help partners align with each other and with the Divine. You can put your heads and hearts together to meditate to bring light to the darkness of our ailing world. Even meditating together on the word "*loving-kindness*" can awaken the visceral experience of love and strengthen your desire to give.

- **Be intentional in your sexual connection.** Sex should be about pleasure. At the same time, there is so much more potential for lovers to be intentional in their lovemaking to spread unity—between them and for the world. This higher intention in a long-term sexual relationship connects the couple to the circle of endlessly growing fulfillment versus the finite line of physicality. When you meditate on sending your love, energy, and unity out to the world, your sexuality has meaning and purpose beyond just the two of you. This connects your bond to the endless perpetuity and makes whatever you share even more whole and fulfilling.

- **Pay it forward.** That is, take each blessing and privilege you have and view them as on loan. Ask yourselves, how can we use what we've been given to create goodness with others? For example,
  - *Your home*—as we spoke about with hospitality, use your home to bring people in, to make them feel warm and welcome, to enrich others with spiritual opportunities, artful experiences, good food, joyful times, and/or charity events.
  - *Your car*—use it for charity work. In addition to driving yourselves, your kids, and whomever else you support, find ways to use your car to help strangers. Fill it with clothes for donating to charity, offer to drive someone needing extra support for an appointment, drive to areas where homeless dwell, and hand out sandwiches.
  - *Your money*—tithe and give to charity. Discuss together how you want to use what you manifest financially to share a portion with the world. What are the causes or organizations that touch your soul and/or feed you spiritually? Replenish those places and your remaining money will be filled with that light of purpose and sharing.
  - *Your love*—be humble about you two finding one another and know it was never meant to be just the two of you. Go out of your way to give loving-kindness, which is the best way to appreciate the love you've been given. Your love will grow as you consistently stay on the lookout for how your love can be a source of goodness to others.
- **Create a Life and Relationship Legacy.** Living each of the four pillars is a powerful way to create a legacy. You become

role models to other couples, your children, your community, and the world when you build a strong, loving, fun, and meaningful relationship, starting with yourself. Living as a purpose-driven couple is especially valuable to pass on. This shows others the great gains and joy from going outside of yourself. Your choices in life create a legacy, but to create a positive one means paving a path of what goodness and taking responsibility looks like. Actions speak louder than words or opinions. Here are just a few examples of teaching (not just preaching) in order to pass on an inspiring legacy:

- Build a close family that balances empathy and feelings with good boundaries that teach cause and effect: a family that welcomes others in and does good for the world.
- Create rituals and good memories doing wholesome, respectful, fun, and compassionate activities.
- Model what marriage and commitment look like, such as embracing the tough times and using them to grow. I am open with my clients about the rougher times in my marriage, and open with our children, because I want to model the normative and essential process of growth in a relationship.
- Show healthy ways to deal with conflict. It's okay to fight and it's a good sign of growth potential. Model addressing conflict with respect and human dignity and an eye toward closeness and transformation. Repair is vital for others to learn from.
- Show tolerance for others who are different or difficult, while at the same time having limits and a backbone with conviction about what you feel is right. These could be with family members, friends, public figures, or world events.
- Model doing for the world outside the home and inside the home.

○ Be hospitable and generous-hearted, tolerant of people's quirks and differences.

○ Live a work-life balance. Work hard, grow hard, play hard, relax hard.

○ Be humble and appreciative, admit and make amends for your shortcomings and mistakes.

IDEA INTO ACTION

• **Be on the lookout.**

Our egos make it easy to overlook helping opportunities right under our noses. We need to put in effort, to search and be on the lookout for where we can serve. I remember when I first understood how important sharing and a sense of purpose was for our relationship. It was 2005, just before Hurricane Katrina hit the Golf Coast. It wasn't in our own town, so it would have been easy for us to send money (which would have been valuable) and just feel bad for them. We took it as a sign that we should get more involved. We formed a committee and brought a displaced woman with her five children to St. Louis and helped this family navigate a devastating time in their lives. It was from this experience that other opportunities opened up. When you look out for ways to make a difference, you also open the gates for where you are needed most.

• **Brainstorm with your beloved and take some steps.**

Ask one another what areas of and people in the world really awaken compassion and a desire to support and help. What touches your heart strings? Then get creative together and see what might overlap, and what you can support in one another's individual callings. Every small action is a big one, and consider this an experiment and opportunity to build your muscle for giving. Then you can network, see what you learn, and allow yourself to be guided where your unique contributions are needed.

- **Reflect and journal these questions:**
  - How do you feel when you do something good for others?
  - What do you notice happens together when you are involved in something for the sake of helping?
    - Notice your body sensations, how you feel toward your beloved, and the quality of your thoughts and feelings.
    - Do you feel any closer?
    - How does sharing with others affect your appreciation?
    - Do you feel more awe and respect toward your mate?
    - What happens to the issues you're dealing with in your relationship that are troublesome?
    - What kind of feelings do you have about yourself, your life, and the person you're married to?
    - How does having a common purpose together, impact your connection, your sense of feeling one and close?

Acknowledgments

I have put my heart and soul into writing this book, but all that I have created and expressed is not mine. I have had extraordinary teachers, especially Life itself. I want to thank you all.

Starting with my doctoral training at the University of Missouri–St. Louis, studying approaches from theorists like Carl Rogers, Irv Yalom, Viktor Frankl, and Carl Jung felt like coming home. They taught such dignity for the essence and potential of a human being, it was intoxicating. Therapy is a craft you hone over the years, and I learned from some of the masters. They insisted on self-as-instrument, which began the hard work and rewarding journey of examining myself.

Now for my teachers at the Kabbalah Centre, going back through the deep and rich lineage that the Rav and Karen opened for all, and up to today with our dear friends and mentors, Monica and Michael Berg—thank you for holding the flame. I would absolutely never be able to help myself, my marriage, or my clients as deeply without the privilege of weaving in these timeless teachings. It's the secret ingredient. I am in awe of the privilege to have found my spiritual home. Thank you for your loyal friendship.

I wish to thank the couples I've had the honor to work with, especially for trusting me to enter their most intimate chambers. They are the reason I keep doing what I do and why this book calling refused to relent. They have delighted, enriched, amazed, and touched me deeply. Through our sessions, they have taught me the ins and outs of loving and heartbreak, resilience and healing, and deep connectedness.

All my gratitude goes to those who were part of the divine synchrony of making this book come to be. To William Green for making this entire thing possible by your willingness to be helpful and channeling the all-time perfect editor for me: Laurie Harting.

How to thank you, Laurie? If we were to ever wonder if there are forces bigger than us, the way we found each other and how this book came to publication should surely seal the deal. Who knew that the dots connecting us from across a country and a continent would come full circle to discovering that you basically grew up in my backyard? Thank you for every time you turned what felt complicated into something simple, made the lofty more relatable, and weighed in from your own marriage experience. Most especially I thank you for your generous spirit and extra-mile commitment to helping bring this book to reality.

I sincerely appreciate everyone at Morehouse Publishing for first and foremost giving me the opportunity to share my life's work. And for all the fine-tuning, bringing the book to fruition, and helping it reach a wider audience. I can honestly say I couldn't have done this without you.

Now onto my family, my greatest blessing:

I must first thank who this whole book is lovingly dedicated to, my husband, Jeff. Your love and support of me, and commitment to us, is unwavering. I have no doubt that your believing in me, relentlessly, is the reason I am able to express the god spark in me in whatever way I have been able to thus far. I thank you for being my absolute greatest teacher of real love. This book is our third baby, but this one we pushed out together. Thank you for your patience with not only a therapist as a wife but also a writer.

To my children, Andrea and Jeremy, you are stellar human beings. You naturally cheer me on and get excited about what I am doing, especially this book. I can tell it's genuine and this touches me deeply. Thank you for taking me to new chambers of love in my heart that I never even dreamed existed, with every stage of your life. Now you have added more love to our family with your wives, Katie and Carly, and our shooting star grandchild, Leo, who has completely stolen my heart for good.

I wish to thank those who were there from the beginning, who I owe everything to: my parents, Moishe and Eileen. I knew from a young age that I had a responsibility to pay back to the world the favor of having you as my parents, so loving, patient, and solicitous. You have showed me the purest unconditional love and modeled a marriage that was lasting, always growing, and filled with laughter and friendship. Dad, you'll have to read this book from the upper worlds now. Thank you for always being proud of me but never pressuring me one iota. I promise I'll get some rest.

In my own humble way, I want to finish by acknowledging the Source of all that is, for all I have been given, and infinitely more. None of this is me or mine and I pray to remember this well. I wish to fasten myself to the Creator by loving life (all of it) and growing closer to the person I am capable of becoming. I wish this for us all.

Four Pillars Relationship Assessment and Marriage Action Plan

RELATIONSHIP PILLARS ASSESSMENT

Please enter the number that best expresses how true each statement is about your relationship with yourself and your partner, using the scale: 0 = not true at all, 1 = somewhat true, 2 = true, 3 = very true.

After you've completed the assessment, you can read about the meaning of your scores below. Ideally, you can invite your partner to also complete the assessment. Then you can discuss what steps you want to take to grow forward.

Pillar 1: *We are each responsible for our own happiness and well-being.*

Pillar 1	How true is this statement?	0-3
Self-awareness	I know what makes me happy and fulfilled.	
	I am curious about myself. I take the time to self-reflect.	
	In general, I know myself well.	
	I know my core beliefs and values and try to live in line with them.	
	I know myself well: my passions, dreams, strengths, quirks, fears, addictions and bad habits.	
	I understand how my moods and behavior impact my partner.	
	I make sure I'm living authentically, being true to myself.	

Pillar 1	How true is this statement?	0-3
Self-love	I believe I am worthy of love and good things.	
	I check my thoughts and self-talk, making sure I'm kind with myself.	
	I appreciate who I am and the gifts I've been given.	
	I give myself patience and grace to learn from my mistakes.	
	I accept myself and my feelings without judging myself.	
	I work at not falling into perfectionism.	
	I try to live in the present and accept myself right where I am.	
Self-care	I make taking care of myself a priority, in mind, body, and spirit.	
	I make sure to talk about things that bother me.	
	I am good about caring for my physical health, nutrition and sleep.	
	I carve out time to be with friends and people that energize me.	
	I keep up with passions and hobbies that make me balanced/happy.	
	I nourish the deeper, spiritual part of me.	
	I set appropriate limits in my personal and work relationships.	
	I seek and accept help from others.	
Self-development	Maybe not right away, but when something doesn't go my way, I consider how I can use the challenge to grow and change.	
	I find it important to learn from my mistakes and experiences.	
	I reflect on what areas of my life need to be improved.	
	Others see me as someone who prioritizes my personal growth.	

Pillar 1	How true is this statement?	0-3
	As I work on myself, I remember that I am already good and whole.	
	I know the difference between developing myself and perfectionism.	
	I accept feedback on strengths and weaknesses and my impact on others.	
	I reflect on my what matters most so I can live up to my values.	
Total		

Pillar 2: *We use our friction to help us grow, individually and together.*

Please enter the number that best expresses how true each statement is about your relationship with yourself and your partner, using the scale: 0 = not true at all, 1 = somewhat true, 2 = true, 3 = very true.

Pillar 2	How true is this statement?	0-3
Communication	I address issues as they come up in our relationship. I generally don't avoid conflict.	
	I can put my feelings to words with my partner.	
	I say more positive, appreciative words than saying what's wrong.	
	I know my strengths and weaknesses as a communicator.	
	I genuinely want to know my partner's thoughts and feelings, and I ask open-ended questions to draw these out.	
	I know the best time and way to approach my partner when I need to say something that might be hard to hear.	
	I make sure my partner feels heard and validated.	

Pillar 2	How true is this statement?	0-3
Growth	I look for where we can grow closer when we have conflict.	
	I look at myself in the mirror and not just blame my partner.	
	I am open to feedback, let my partner influence me and my growth.	
	I try to work on being more giving.	
	I am open to going out of my comfort zone.	
	I have an interest in my partner's growth.	
	I know my hot buttons and my areas of growth.	
Friendships	My partner and I have a close physical and sexual connection.	
	I feel emotionally connected and have a strong rapport with my partner.	
	We get along well when it comes to parenting our kids.	
	We make sure to be playful and have fun times just as a couple.	
	We are on the same page with our finances.	
	Our relationship with family and friends works well for us.	
	I feel spiritually connected to my partner. We live similar values.	
	We share chores and household responsibilities in a harmonious way.	
Conflict	I have tools to calm myself when I get upset with my partner.	
	I own my part in the conflict we experience.	
	I feel good about how we handle our arguments. We have good tools and find solutions and compromise in the end.	
	When we argue, I feel that I am heard and understood.	
	I make sure to give my partner time to share their side so I understand them.	

Pillar 2	How true is this statement?	0-3
	If we have wounds in our relationship, we know what they are and we work to repair them.	
	We put in effort to find compromise when it comes to our differences.	
	I go out of my way to honor my partner's needs and preferences.	
Total		

Pillar 3: *We make our mate the most important other person in our lives.*

Please enter the number that best expresses how true each statement is about your relationship with yourself and your partner, using the scale: 0 = not true at all, 1 = somewhat true, 2 = true, 3 = very true.

Pillar 3	How true is this statement?	0-3
Cherish	My partner knows they are the most important person in my life.	
	I go out of my way to do extra things to make my mate feel loved.	
	I know what makes my partner feel number one in my life.	
	I feel cherished and a priority to my spouse.	
	I tell and show my partner that I appreciate them regularly.	
	I care deeply about my partner's happiness, their dreams and desires.	
	I know my mate really appreciates me and I can feel it.	
	My partner is the first person I want to share my news with.	
Protect	We communicate about barriers that might come between us (like work, kids, in laws, drinking, etc.).	

Pillar 3	How true is this statement?	0-3

We resolve whatever is getting in the way of our priority.

My partner and I have fun and laugh together a lot.

We have a date night regularly.

We have good habits as a couple to make sure we stay connected.

We make time to talk and see where we need to grow our relationship.

(If you don't have kids, answer 3, very true to each)

Kids

I make sure we regularly spend some time together, *without the kids.*

We don't openly disagree about parenting in front of the kids.

My partner and I take an adult vacation without the kids.

We don't let our kids play one of us against the other. They know we are a united team.

Our kids feel loved and special but also know that my spouse and I don't let anything or anyone come between us.

My partner and I seek out passions and interests that don't necessarily involve the kids.

Total

Pillar 4: *We make the world better through our bond.*

Please enter the number that best expresses how true each statement is about your relationship with yourself and your partner, using the scale: 0 = not true at all, 1 = somewhat true, 2 = true, 3 = very true.

Pillar 4	How true is this statement?	0-3
Purpose	We share common goals that bring us closer.	
	Doing something together for the world is important to me.	
	I try to become the best partner I can be.	
	We support each other with our individual passions and purpose.	
	A sense of shared purpose is a strong part of our relationship.	
	We view the impact of our relationship beyond our family unit, our smaller collective.	
	I find meaning in giving to (or raising) my family.	
	I see our relationship as a way to connect with the Divine.	
	We put purpose into action with our time, talent and financial resources.	
	Growing more generous-hearted is an active goal of mine.	
	I believe that the more we give to others, the deeper our relationship grows.	
	We spend time brainstorming about how we can make a difference together.	
	We love opening our home and making guests feel loved and welcome.	
	We spend some of our extra time volunteering.	
	We go the extra mile when someone needs a hand, a meal or some comfort.	
Total		

HOW TO TURN YOUR ASSESSMENT INTO ACTION

To get an idea of which pillars are stronger and which need attention:

- Add up your score for each pillar and consider where you fall in the range below.
- Look for individual statements or group of statements within each pillar that stand out because you ranked them as a 0 (not true at all) or 1 (somewhat true).

Pillar 1: Responsibility

Your relationship with yourself can be seen on a continuum. See below for an overall way to look at your score.

61–90: You have a strong sense of self-awareness, self-love, self-care, and self-development. Keep up the good work, and if you're in the lower end of this range, consider what else you can add.

31–60: You have definitely invested in yourself to some degree, but the priority on your own happiness and well-being needs some definite attention.

0–30: You need and deserve to focus more on yourself than you have managed to do so thus far. This would be a good place to start. Taking time to learn more about yourself, loving and caring for yourself, where you want to grow—these will be the biggest gift for yourself and for your relationship.

Pillar 2: Growth

Your growth pillar can be seen on a continuum but here's an overall way to look at your score.

61–90: You have a positive mindset about conflict and growth, productive listening and communication skills, a strong marriage wheel, and know how to navigate your differences and heal your wounds in a healthy way. Keep up the good work, and if you're in the lower end of this range, consider investing in learning more about turning your conflict into growth.

31–60: You have some degree of strength with your growth mindset and approach to conflict, your marriage wheel, and the way you navigate your differences and repair from wounds. You could be at risk for creating disconnection if you're not giving more attention and becoming more proficient in these communication and conflict skills.

0–30: Your relationship needs some attention to strengthen this pillar. Consider the tools in this book and seek a marriage counselor to support growth or to help you assess where you stand in your relationship. Your effort can really turn things around.

Pillar 3: Priority

Your priority pillar can be seen on a continuum but here's an overall way to look at your score.

41–60: You have a strong sense of priority and cherishment in your relationship. You protect your relationship well and make sure your partner is loved and appreciated. Use these questions to take your priority to the next level and keep up what you're doing.

21–40: Your sense of priority is approaching the weaker side. Just know that working on this area will bring you a better more fulfilling connection.

0–20: Your relationship needs some attention to strengthen this pillar. Consider the tools in this book and seek a marriage counselor to support growth or to help you assess where you stand in your relationship. Your effort can really turn things around.

Pillar 4: Purpose

Your priority pillar can be seen on a continuum, but here's an overall way to look at your score.

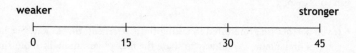

31–45: You have a strong sense of purpose in your relationship. A spirit of generosity and a shared vision of yourselves as making a difference in the world is integral to your relationship. Use these questions to take your purpose to the next level and keep up what you're doing.

16–30: Your sense of priority is approaching the weaker side. Just know that working on this area will bring you a better more fulfilling connection.

0–15: Your relationship needs some attention to strengthen this pillar. Consider the suggestions in chapters 21 for some simple ideas to begin bringing the power of purpose into your relationship.

OVERALL RELATIONSHIP SCORE (TOTAL FOUR PILLARS)

weaker   stronger

0   95   190   285

Now you can add up each of your pillars for a total relationship score at this point in time. Allow yourself to appreciate what you already have together and try not to feel discouraged about your score if it's lower than you hoped; a soulful relationship is a process. Consider focusing on how much stronger your relationship can become. Here are some simple steps to create a marriage action plan to improve your bond:

With your partner:

- Ask your partner to take this assessment. If they are willing, then . . .
- Come together after you've both completed it to discuss the strengths and weaknesses of your relationship pillars. Make sure to keep blame out and curiosity in the conversation. Keep it light to help prevent defensiveness.
- Read the sections in the book that address your weaker pillars and discuss.
- Pick one or two actions you each can commit to in order to begin enhancing your connection.
- Revisit after a couple weeks and see how it's going. Maybe you can alter or add something else. Make these check ins as part of your growth night a couple times a month. More frequently if your relationship problems are more urgent. Consider discussing with your marriage counselor.

On your own:

- If you partner isn't interested in taking the assessment, that's okay. See how you can find a more casual way to share the four pillars and talk about them.
- Ask your partner what they think are the strengths of the relationship and what are the areas that need improvement.
- Regardless of their participation, you always have agency to work on being the best partner and person you can be. This can help your relationship a great deal and also give you clarity if you're unsure whether you should keep investing in the relationship you have.

DOUBTS ABOUT YOUR RELATIONSHIP?

If you're having doubts about the future of your relationship, especially from taking this assessment, you can find some guidance in the next addendum to help you gain clarity if fighting for your relationship makes sense and feels right at this time.

Should I Stay or Should I Go?

I f you're reading a relationship book, I suspect that some level of doubt about your relationship may have crossed your mind. This is normal. I'm an advocate of long-term relationships because I believe they offer a path to live your best life—and to become the best version of yourself in the process. However, not every relationship should be saved and not every partner deems it's worth what it will take to try and improve things. I see too many partners hold on to a relationship that detracts instead of enhancing all the other areas of their life, including the version of themselves they'd like to be. While a right or wrong decision does not exist when it comes to ending a relationship, here are some guidelines I want to offer you for gaining clarity on "what's right for you."

The following is a checklist with some honest questions—seven about yourself, seven about your partner/relationship. Keep in mind that I find with my clients that the underlying question for making a clear and peaceful decision is, "Have I done everything I can to try and make this work?"

CHECKLIST 1: QUESTIONS ABOUT YOURSELF

Clarity is earned and will come through turning your attention inward. You can start by asking yourself the following questions and better yet, journal your answers with your first thoughts that come to mind:

- **Have I put in effort—and in the right way?**
  For a certain period, regardless of what I was receiving back from my partner, have I:
  - Showed up in the relationship that reflects my best self?
  - Been the kind of partner, friend, and person I know I should be?
  - Explored what I need to change and where I need to grow? For example:
    - My self-confidence and honoring myself
    - Working on anger or trust issues, and childhood wounds
    - Opening up
    - Taking things less seriously
    - More giving, understanding, and kind
    - Showing appreciation and patience
    - Setting good boundaries without guilt

- **Have I done my research on relationships?**
  The very purpose of this book is to fill a gap for this checklist item. Most of us grasp that we need to read, study, and learn in school, and for our professional lives. We overlook this when it comes to relationships. Relationships require education and skills you can and need to build. There's a method to navigating the times you don't feel connected or have friction. It's a practice with tools and tips. Without gaining knowledge, and practicing again and again, it's like trying to do your relationship double blindfolded, baffled by how hard it is.

- **Are my expectations balanced?**
  Am I expecting too little, settling for less, and glossing over important red flags? On the other hand, am I expecting perfection? Am I overlooking the good and what I'm blessed to receive in my relationship? Am I putting too much emphasis on my partner making me happy and fulfilled, unrealistically?

- **How independent and fulfilled am I?**
  When dependent on someone, it's hard to make a clear decision about love. Because it's about need. To what extent am I independent—emotionally, financially, spiritually, and for my needs overall? The more independent you are, along with putting effort into a relationship from a place of fulfillment, the more clarity you will gain.

- **Do I know my purpose and goals?**
  Knowing your values and exploring your unique direction in life, as best you can, serves as a compass for your own direction, personally and in our relationships.

- **Am I clear on my relationship boundaries and criteria for me to be happy?**
  Gaining clarity of what works for you and what won't work for you is a good start to seeing if your partner crosses the line with any of your deal breakers. I suggest to my confused clients to make a list. What works for me, what doesn't work for me? What do I need to feel fulfilled in this relationship? What can I let go of and accept? If you don't know where you stand, then it's harder to live an authentic life and make choices accordingly.

- **Have I tried counseling?**
  We all have blind spots, and areas of growth and learning, that we can't see on our own. Seeking help can help you work through problems that from your vantage seem hopeless and irreconcilable. A trusted professional can highlight the issues in your uncertainty and help you gain clarity. If you're on the brink of divorce, or your partner is, there's also a targeted approach called *discernment counseling* to help you decide whether to end a relationship or invest in trying to heal.

CHECKLIST 2: QUESTIONS ABOUT YOUR PARTNER AND RELATIONSHIP

Now you can take an honest look at how you feel about your partner and the relationship. To help you gain clarity, you can ask yourself:

- **Are they worth the investment?**
  All relationships take effort, some more than others. Maybe it sounds
  harsh, but if someone in your life doesn't feel worth the effort to you, then
  you might want to reconsider how much you invest. Maybe you're just
  comfortable and worry about what others will think. That's human but not
  a recommended reason to stay. If you are willing to put in effort, value your
  partner, and see their willingness to grow and change, then this could mean
  the relationship is worth it.
- **Does my relationship enhance or diminish the other important areas of
  my life?**
  We have many important aspects in our lives, like our self-care, mental health,
  friends, career, family relationships, hobbies, purpose, spirituality, and sense
  of community. Do you feel supported and encouraged in these areas by your
  partner? Do you feel brightened or dimmed by the relationship overall?
- **Is my partner someone I trust, who I feel safe with to be my real self?**
  Love can grow endlessly but only when we are in an emotional climate that
  feels deeply comfortable, when we can be vulnerable, authentic, and let our
  guard down. Is my partner someone who I can talk about anything with and
  know that they want harmony and closeness?
- **Do I like what I see now?**
  It's not recommended to move forward in a relationship thinking you can
  change someone. Once you are in a long-term relationship, sure, things
  you don't like are going to surface. Maybe even big things. We each
  need to decide to what extent we can accept and love the other person
  unconditionally, as they are. You want to influence one another, yes. This
  means gradually over the years to help each other grow. However, if you are
  staying with the mindset of needing to change your partner, that might lead
  to an endless loop of frustration.
- **Do our values or spirituality align?**
  For long-term fulfillment, being aligned in the way you view life and
  challenges, along with your values and the way you live by them, make a
  significant difference in how deeply you can connect and grow together. You
  don't need to be perfectly aligned, but it's an important question to think
  about.
- **Is this someone with whom I can grow, who also has a desire to grow, and
  who I feel can help me become a better version of myself?**
  Does your partner welcome change and feedback, even if initially defensive?
  Are they open to counseling and to learning about how to be a better
  person? Can they admit when they are wrong or have made a mistake?
  If you're with someone who is not open to growing and sees the issues as
  yours and yours alone, that is hard to work with. The capacity for insight,
  accountability and the desire and willingness to grow, these are key for
  finding happiness in a long-term relationship.
- **Does my partner seem ready for a mature relationship?**
  To what degree is my partner happy within, ready to give, secure, and
  trustworthy? Can you count on them? We can give all we have to a

relationship, but when we are taking the lone soldier approach, this can prove unproductive and futile. You also want to consider whether your partner depends too much on you for happiness or security—and if so, are they working on healing that? Not that any of us need to be a finished product of mental health and wholeness, but a person's sense of emotional and spiritual maturity, and security in their attachments, can make a significant impact on sustaining a balanced and healthy bond.

NEXT STEPS TOWARD GREATER CLARITY

• Look at your journal or simply reflect on how many of the *seven-item checklist about yourself* brought you to say or write, "Yes, I've tried that or done this." Which ones seemed unfinished where you said or wrote, "Now maybe I tried a little but not as much as I could, or maybe I haven't tried at all." From there you can see where you can put more effort into investing in order to help you turn things around or gain more clarity about whether to leave.

• Now take a look at what you thought or wrote for the *seven-item checklist about your partner and relationship*. With brave honesty, what did you discover? Where do you see that you haven't put in effort, where is their potential and how many red flags did you count?

WRAPPING IT UP

These questions are not here so you will find an answer that exists somewhere out there, but they are here to help the clarity that lives within you reveal itself, and when the time is right. If you are unclear, then you know what, that's totally okay. Clarity is a process. Lean into the growth. *Making growth your compass is the only way to never be in the wrong place.* The best thing you can do is to embrace the present moment and simply keep working on it, meaning working on being your best self and watch what happens when you bring that self and put in effort with your partner.

I do wish for you that if you are in a relationship that has a lot of red flags and you have given your effort over a substantial period, please don't overlook the quality of your life experience for the sake of a relationship that doesn't hold much promise. Maybe it's comfortable and known, and the illusion of it getting better is feeding something inside of you, but you deserve real happiness and a relationship that fulfills you. If I had a penny for each client who finally left a relationship and discovered (eventually) a whole new beautiful world and life, I would have a full jar.

To help my clients find their own answers, or when they want to make changes that are hard to make, I often suggest that they ask themselves, "If my dearest friend were in an intimate relationship like I'm in, what would I want for them? What would I say?" If you are sitting in the seat of uncertainty in your relationship, know that you are not the first, the last, or the only. As difficult as this place in your life may be, try and remember the universal and wise axiom, *"The greatest light is truly found within the greatest darkness."*

Further Readings

Books and lectures that have inspired me over the years that have influenced my approach with the four pillars. Starting with Pillar 1 and traveling through the pillars:

PILLAR 1: RESPONSIBILITY: WE ARE EACH RESPONSIBLE FOR OUR HAPPINESS AND WELL-BEING.

Self-Awareness, Authenticity

Ashlag, Yehuda. *The Wisdom of Truth: 12 Essays by the Holy Kabbalist Rav Yehuda Ashlag.* Edited by Michael Berg. Kabbalah Centre Publishing, 2008.

Berg, Monica. *Rethink Love: 3 Steps to Being the One, Attracting the One, and Becoming One.* Kabbalah Centre Publishing, 2020.

Branden, Nathaniel. *How to Raise Your Self-Esteem.* Random House Publishing Group, 1988.

Brown, Brené. *The Gifts of Imperfection: Let Go of Who You Think You're Supposed to Be and Embrace Who You Are.* Hazelden Publishing, 2010.

Emerson, Ralph Waldo. *Self-Reliance.* 1841.

From the Teachings of Rav Berg. *The Power of Kabbalah: Thirteen Principles to Overcome Challenges and Achieve Fulfillment.* Kabbalah Centre Publishing, 2018.

Kahneman, Daniel. *Thinking, Fast and Slow.* Farrar, Straus and Giroux, 2011.

Ware, Bronnie. *Top Five Regrets of the Dying: A Life.Transformed by the Dearly Departing.* Hay House, 2019.

Yalom, Irvin D. *Existential Psychotherapy.* Basic Books, 1980.

Self-Love and Self-Care

Berg, Michael. *The Way: Using the Wisdom of Kabbalah for Spiritual Transformation and Fulfillment.* Wiley, 2001.

Brown, Brené. *I Thought It Was Just Me: Women Reclaiming Power and Courage in a Culture of Shame.* Gotham, 2007.

Dana, Deb. *Anchored: How to Befriend Your Nervous System Using Polyvagal Theory.* Sounds True. 2021.

Holden, Robert. *Be Happy! Release the Power of Happiness in YOU.* Haye House, 2010.

Neff, Kristin. *Self-Compassion: Stop Beating Yourself Up and Leave Insecurity Behind.* New York: William Morrow, 2011.

Remen, Rachel Naomi. *My Grandfather's Blessings: Stories of Strength, Refuge, and Belonging.* Riverhead Books, 2000.

Self-Development

Berg, Michael. *Becoming Like God: Kabbalah and Our Ultimate Destiny.* Kabbalah Publishing, 2004.

Clear, James. *Atomic Habits: An Easy & Proven Way to Build Good Habits & Break Bad Ones.* Avery, 2018.

Gottlieb, Lori. *Maybe You Should Talk to Someone: A Therapist, HER Therapist, and Our Lives.* Harper, 2019.

Stutz, Phil, and Barry Michels. *The Tools: 5 Tools to Help You Find Courage, Creativity, and Willpower—and Inspire You to Live Life in Forward Motion.* Random House Publishing, 2013.

PILLAR 2: GROWTH: WE USE OUR FRICTION TO HELP US GROW, INDIVIDUALLY AND TOGETHER.

Barry, Cliff. "Clean Talk." Shadow Work. 2024. https://shadowwork.com/clean -talk/.

Brown, Brené. *Atlas of the Heart: Mapping Meaningful Connection and the Language of Human Experience.* Random House, 2022.

Buber, Martin. *I and Thou.* Scribner, 1958.

Gottman, John, and Nan Silver. *The Seven Principles for Making Marriage Work: A Practical Guide from the Country's Foremost Relationship Expert.* Harmony, 2015.

Hendrix, Harville. *Getting the Love You Want: A Guide for Couples.* Henry Holt & Co., 2007.

Rodsky, Eve. *Fair Play: A Game-Changing Solution for When You Have Too Much to Do (and More Life to Live),* Penguin Publishing Group, 2021.

Rogers, C. R., and R. E. Farson. *Active listening.* Industrial Relations Center of the University of Chicago, 1957.

Rosenberg, M. B. *Nonviolent Communication: A Language of Life.* 2nd ed. Puddle Dancer Press, 2003.

Tatkin, Stan. *Wired for Love: How Understanding Your Partner's Brain and Attachment Style Can Help You Defuse Conflict and Build a Secure Relationship.* 2nd ed. New Harbinger, 2024

PILLAR 3: PRIORITY: WE MAKE OUR MATE THE MOST IMPORTANT OTHER PERSON IN OUR LIVES.

Chapman, G. D. *The 5 Love Languages: The Secret to Love That Lasts.* Northfield Publishing, 2010.

Metz, M. E., and B. W. McCarthy. *Enduring Desire: Your Guide to Lifelong Intimacy.* 1st ed. Routledge, 2010.

Nagoski, Emily. *Come Together: The Science (and Art!) of Creating Lasting Sexual Connections.* Ballantine Books, 2024.

PILLAR 4: PURPOSE: WE MAKE THE WORLD
BETTER THROUGH OUR BOND.

Berg, Michael. *The Secret: Unlocking the Source of Joy and Fulfillment.* Kabbalah
    Publishing, 2004.

Frankl, Viktor. *Man's Search for Meaning: An Introduction to Logotherapy.* Beacon
    Press, 1962.

Lucks, Allen, and Peggy Payne. *The Healing Power of Doing Good.* Fawcett
    Columbine, 1991; repr., iUniverse.com, 2001.

Yusim, Anna. Fulfilled: *How the Science of Spirituality Can Help You Live a Happier,
    More Meaningful Life.* Grand Central Life & Style, 2017

About the Author

DR. RACHEL GLIK is a licensed professional counselor with thirty-plus years as a couples, individual, and family psychotherapist in private practice. Since 2014, she has appeared regularly on Fox 2 in St. Louis as a relationship and mental health expert. She has been studying Kabbalah since 2004 and was honored to begin teaching with the Kabbalah Centre in 2011. She is a featured author for *Mind Body Green* and a subject expert for CNBC's *Make It, Town and Country,* and Scripps News. She creates workshops for organizations such as Young Presidents' Organization, OneVillage, and the University of Missouri. She is the author of two books of poetry, *Where the River Runs Wild* and *Come with Me.* She lives with her husband in St. Louis, along with her children, grandchild, and large extended family. Learn more at drrachelglik.com or by following @drrachelglik on Instagram.